GOD'S LITTLE
DEVOTIONAL
JOURNAL

FOR
Mothers

RACINE, WI

God's Little Devotional Journal for Mothers
ISBN: 979-8-88898-061-3 - *Paperback*
ISBN: 979-8-88898-062-0 - *Hardcover*
Copyright © 2023 by Honor Books, Racine, WI

Introduction

K eeping a journal is a valuable and time-hon-
ored tradition—one that has been practiced
by kings and queens and philosophers for centuries
and one that has gained renewed popularity in recent
times.

Psychologists support the therapeutic benefit of
writing down our thoughts. Teachers encourage jour-
naling as a proven method of improving communication
skills. Business leaders suggest using a journal for setting and keeping goals. But one of the greatest benefits
of writing regularly in a journal is spiritual growth.

In the opening words of his first journal entry on
September 3, 1822, Eugene Delacroix—a nineteenth-
century French artist—writes: "I am carrying out my
plan, so long formulated, of keeping a journal. What I
most keenly wish is not to forget that I am writing for
myself alone. Thus I shall always tell the truth, I hope,
and thus I shall improve myself."

God's Little Devotional Journal for Mothers has
been designed with the specific needs and interests
of mothers in mind. This beautifully crafted 365-day
journal includes an inspirational story, plenty of room
to record your thoughts, as well as a scripture and
inspirational quote to take with you through your day.
At the end of the year, you will be amazed at how
much you've grown spiritually. Read and write with
an open heart, and let God speak to you.

A Mother's Legacy

Her children arise up, and call her blessed; her husband also, and he praiseth her.

PROVERBS 31:28

MY THOUGHTS:

_____
_____
_____
_____
_____
_____
_____
_____
_____
_____
_____
_____
_____
_____
_____
_____
_____

WHAT KIND OF LEGACY DO I WANT TO LEAVE FOR MY CHILDREN?

After the famous food distributor Henry J. Heinz died, his will was found to contain this confession: "I desire to set forth at the very beginning of this will, as the most important item in it, a confession of my faith in Jesus Christ as my Savior. I also desire to bear witness to the fact that throughout my life, in which there were unusual joys and sorrows, I have been wonderfully sustained by my faith in God through Jesus Christ. This legacy was left me by my consecrated mother, a woman of strong faith, and to it I attribute any success I have attained."

Heinz is not the only famous American to credit his mother for his success, of course. Consider these words of another American hero, Thomas Edison: "I did not have my mother long, but she cast over me an influence which has lasted all my life. The good effects of her early training I can never lose. If it had not been for her appreciation and her faith in me at a critical time in my experience, I should never likely have become an inventor. I was always a careless boy, and with a mother of different mental caliber, I should have turned out badly. But her firmness, her sweetness, her goodness were potent powers to keep me in the right path. My mother was the making of me."

Just Like You'd Talk to a Friend

"I say unto you, What things soever ye desire, when ye pray, believe that ye receive them, and ye shall have them."

MARK 11:24

A minister and his wife were once met at a train station by a woman who had been assigned to drive them to their hotel. As they approached the center of town, the traffic was very heavy. "You can let us off at the nearest corner," the minister suggested, certain she would never find a parking space close to their hotel.

"No trouble," she said. Then she began to pray, "God, we really need a parking space. If one is nearby, please lead me to it." She drove around the block a couple of times, then just as they turned the corner, a car pulled out of a parking space right in front of their hotel. She said sincerely, "Thanks, God. I really appreciate this!"

The minister's wife asked the woman if she always asked God for such favors. She answered, "Oh, yes. I chatter to God all the time. I can't help it. He seems to be so close that I talk to Him just the way I'd talk to my best friend."[1]

God delights in meeting our small needs as well as our big ones, just as we delight in meeting the needs of our children. Prayer and answers to prayer build our relationship with God. And a deep personal relationship, marked by ongoing, free-flowing communication, is what God desires to have with each of us.

MY THOUGHTS:

_____
_____
_____
_____
_____
_____
_____
_____
_____
_____
_____
_____
_____
_____
_____
_____
_____
_____
_____

WHAT WOULD I SAY TO GOD IF I WERE TO TALK TO HIM AS THOUGH HE WERE MY FRIEND?

Traveling on My Knees

I sought for a man among them, that should make up the hedge, and stand in the gap before me for the land . . . but I found none.

EZEKIEL 22:30

MY THOUGHTS:

_____
_____
_____
_____
_____
_____
_____
_____
_____
_____
_____
_____
_____
_____
_____

FOR WHOM OR FOR WHAT DO I FEEL GOD IS LEADING ME TO INTERCEDE?

Sandra Goodwin's poem, "Traveling On My Knees" reminds us that prayer is the generator for God's power at work in our world. Because He desires to release His will in the world through our prayers, less is accomplished in God's kingdom when we fail to pray.

> Last night I took a journey to a land across the seas;
> I did not go by boat or plane, I traveled on my knees.
> I saw so many people there in deepest depths of sin.
> But Jesus told me I should go, that there were souls to win.
> But I said, "Jesus, I cannot go and work with such as these."
> He answered quickly, "Yes, you can by traveling on your knees."
> He said, "You pray; I'll meet the need; you call, and I will hear;
> be concerned about lost souls, of those both far and near."
> And so I tried it, knelt in prayer, gave up some hours of ease;
> I felt the Lord right by my side while traveling on my knees.
> As I prayed on I saw souls saved and twisted bodies healed, and saw God's worker's strength renewed while laboring on the fields.
> I said, "Yes, Lord, I have a job, my desire Thy will to please; I can go and heed Thy call by traveling on my knees."[2]

Love and Prayer

Pray in the Spirit on all occasions with all kinds of prayers and requests.

EPHESIANS 6:18 NIV

In *Who Is for Life?* Mother Teresa writes about the link between love and prayer—both of which must find daily expression:

Let us pray for each other so that we grow in tender love, that we allow God to love us, and that we allow God to love others through us . . .

I will never forget that I once met a man in the street who looked very lonely and miserable. So I walked right up to him, and I shook his hand. My hands were always very warm; and he looked up, gave me a beautiful smile, and he said, "Oh, it has been such a long, long time since I felt the warmth of a human hand!" How very wonderful and very beautiful that our simple actions can show love in that way.

And let us remember to bring that kind of love into our family. We can do this through prayer; for where there is prayer, there is love. And where there is love, there is the complete oneness that Jesus was talking about when He said, "Be one, as the Father and I are one. And love one another as I love you. As the Father has loved me, I have loved you."[3]

When you pray for your family and friends—and even your enemies—you are expressing love. When you express love to those same people through your actions, you are living out your prayers in your way of life.

MY THOUGHTS:

_____
_____
_____
_____
_____
_____
_____
_____
_____
_____
_____
_____
_____
_____
_____
_____
_____
_____

HOW SHOULD I PRAY FOR EACH OF MY CHILDREN TODAY?

Dearer with Age

Despise not thy mother when she is old.
PROVERBS 23:22

MY THOUGHTS:

_____
_____
_____
_____
_____
_____
_____
_____
_____
_____
_____
_____
_____
_____
_____
_____
_____

*HOW CAN I INVEST
IN THE FUTURE OF
MY CHILDREN?*

The first memory that John H. Johnson has of his mother is of gripping her hand as they ran from the rampaging waters of a broken Mississippi River levee.

The family lost everything, but "Miss Ger" was not one to quit. A field worker and later a domestic, she had known little but backbreaking work in her life. She had a dream, however, that her son would one day live in a city and become "somebody." She saved her money until she could move her family to Chicago. There, John graduated from high school with honors. When John had an idea for a magazine, it was his mother who came to his aid, allowing her new furniture to be used as collateral for a start-up loan. After *Negro Digest* became a success, John was able to do what he had dreamed about for years: he "retired" his mother, putting her on his personal payroll.

For fifty-nine years, John saw or talked to his mother almost every day Even when he found himself in other nations, he called his mother daily—once, from atop a telephone pole in Haiti. He continued to draw upon her spiritual and physical toughness until she died. John went on to publish *Ebony* and *Jet* magazines, and his company owns three radio stations. He says, "Not a day passes that I don't feed off the bread of her spirit."

True Freedom

We are troubled on every side, yet not distressed; we are perplexed, but not in despair . . . We look not at the things which are seen, but at the things which are not seen: for the things which are seen are temporal; but the things which are not seen are eternal.

2 CORINTHIANS 4:8,18

Victor Frankl was a psychiatrist and a Jew. While imprisoned in the death camps of Nazi Germany, he suffered unthinkable imprisoned torture and innumerable indignities. His parents, brother, and wife all died in the camp or were sent to the gas chamber. Frankl never knew from one moment to the next if his path would lead to the ovens or if he would be among the "saved" who were forced to shovel the ashes of the ill-fated.

One day, alone and naked in a small room, Frankl became aware of what he later called "the last of the human freedoms"—the control over his inner environment and his basic identity. He could decide within himself how all of this was going to affect him. Through a series of mental, emotional, and moral disciplines—largely using memory and imagination—he exercised this freedom, and it grew.

Eventually, he felt he had more freedom than his captors. They might have had the liberty to make choices in their external environment, but he had more freedom, more internal power. He became an inspiration to the prisoners around him and even to some of his guards. He helped others find meaning in their suffering and dignity in their prison existence.[4]

MY THOUGHTS:

DO I EVER FEEL IMPRISONED BY MY RESPONSIBILITIES OR THE CIRCUMSTANCES OF MY LIFE? HOW CAN I EXERCISE MY INNER FREEDOM?

Enjoy the Ride

january 7

Trust in the Lord with all thine heart; and lean not unto thine own understanding.

PROVERBS 3:5

MY THOUGHTS:

_____
_____
_____
_____
_____
_____
_____
_____
_____
_____
_____
_____
_____
_____
_____
_____
_____
_____

IN WHAT AREAS DO I
NEED TO LET GO
AND TRUST GOD?

James Hewett has written the following:

When I recognized this Higher Power, it seemed as though life was rather like a bike ride, but it was a tandem bike . . . God was in the back helping me pedal: I don't know just when it was that He suggested we change places, but life has not been the same since . . . When He took the lead, it was all I could do to hang on! He knew delightful paths, up mountains and through rocky places—and at breakneck speeds.

I worried and was anxious and asked, "Where are you taking me?" He laughed and didn't answer, and I started to learn trust. I forgot my boring life and entered into adventure. When I'd say, "I'm scared," He'd lean back and touch my hand. He took me to people with gifts . . . of healing, acceptance, and joy They gave me their gifts to take on my journey, our journey, God's and mine. And we were off again. He said, "Give the gifts away; they're extra baggage, too much weight." So I did, to the people we met, and I found that in giving I received . . .

At first I did not trust Him to be in control of my life. I thought He'd wreck it, but He knows bike secrets— knows how to make it lean to take sharp corners, dodge large rocks, and speed through scary passages . . . I'm beginning to enjoy the view and the cool breeze on my face with my delightful, constant Companion."[5]

He Knows the Hidden Man of the Heart

We do not have a high priest who is unable to sympathize with our weaknesses, but we have one who in every respect has been tested as we are, yet without sin.

HEBREWS 4:15 NRSV

On a trip to Israel, a tourist was amazed to hear a young Jewish man recite his family lineage back fourteen generations. She compassion reflected upon her own family tree and realized that she could only trace her own lineage back five generations. She concluded, "God is the only One who knows my beginning from my ending."

Ultimately, that is true for each person. No one fully knows what another has experienced early in life or what genetic influences may be present in someone's life because of the behavior of his or her parents and other ancestors. A part of each person will always remain a mystery, known to God alone.

*Don't find fault with the man who limps
Or stumbles along life's road,
Unless you have worn the shoes he wears,
Or struggled beneath his load.
There may be tacks in his shoes that hurt,
Though hidden away from your view,
The burdens he bears, if placed on your back
Might cause you to stumble, too.
Don't be too hard on the man who errs,
Or pelt him with wood or stone,
Unless you are sure—yea, double sure,
That you have no fault of your own.*[6]

MY THOUGHTS:

_____

HOW CAN I SHOW TRUE COMPASSION TO THOSE I MEET TODAY?

Contentment

Godliness with contentment is great gain. For we brought nothing into this world, and it is certain we can carry nothing out. And having food and raiment let us be therewith content.

1 TIMOTHY 6:6-8

MY THOUGHTS:

_____
_____
_____
_____
_____
_____
_____
_____
_____
_____
_____
_____
_____
_____
_____
_____
_____
_____

WHAT BLESSINGS HAVE I TAKEN FOR GRANTED AND HOW CAN I LEARN TO APPRECIATE THEM MORE?

In *The Fisherman and His Wife*, Lucy Crane tells the story of a fisherman who catches a large fish who is really an enchanted prince. The fisherman lets the prince go free and returns home empty-handed. His wife persuades him to return to the sea and ask the enchanted prince to grant him a wish in return for sparing his life.

He does so, asking (at his wife's request) that their small hut be turned into a cottage. By the time he returns home, her wish has been granted. His wife soon tires of the cottage, however, and sends her husband back to ask the fish for a large stone castle. Again, her wish is granted.

After the wife has tired of her castle, she asks to become queen, then to have a palace, to be made an empress, and finally to be made ruler over the sun and moon. At this, the enchanted prince tells the fisherman to return home where he will find his wife back in their old hut.[7]

We can waste an amazing amount of time, energy, and resources wishing for possessions, relationships, and achievements. When we do this, we fail to enjoy God's immediate gifts. God desires that we savor each moment of every day. It is only when we see God in the now moments of our lives that we can truly recognize His work in our future.

Love Confronts and Disciplines

Those whom I love, I reprove and discipline; therefore be zealous and repent.

REVELATION 3:19 NASB

Richard Exley, in *Life's Bottom Line*, writes:

Several weeks ago I was agonizing over a situation in which I had to discipline a man. Though I felt I had done the right thing, and in the right way, I still grieved for him. As I was wrestling with my feelings in prayer, I sensed the Lord speaking to me and I wrote: "My son, power is a dangerous thing, and it must always be mitigated with My eternal love. I will cause you to feel the pain of My discipline even when it is toward another. You will feel every sting of the lash in your own flesh. You must, or in your zealousness you would go too far. You will grieve, even as Samuel grieved for Saul. Yet I will also make you feel the awful pain of their sin, for if you do not feel that terrible pain, you will draw back from administering the discipline of the Lord."

Confrontation is invariably necessary. A relationship seldom achieves its full potential without it; but it is almost always doomed to failure unless it grows out of a deep trust built on honest communication . . . It is extremely important to take great care to create a safe place of affirmation and acceptance, where a person can be assured, again and again, of our love. Even then, confrontation will be risky and should be undertaken only after we have carefully prepared our hearts before the Lord.[8]

MY THOUGHTS:

HOW DO I FEEL ABOUT CONFRONTING ANOTHER PERSON?

Laughter Works Wonders

A happy heart is good medicine and a cheerful mind works healing, but a broken spirit dries up the bones.

PROVERBS 17:22 AMP

MY THOUGHTS:

_____
_____
_____
_____
_____
_____
_____
_____
_____
_____
_____
_____
_____
_____
_____
_____

WHAT CAN I DO TO BRING MORE LAUGHER INTO OUR HOME?

Scientists have studied the effect laughter has on human beings and have found, among other things, that laughter has a profound, instantaneous effect on virtually every important organ in the human body.

Laughter reduces health-sapping tension. It simultaneously relaxes the tissues and exercises the organs. It causes the release of both dopamine and serotonin in the brain—natural substances that contribute to a general feeling of well-being.

Similarly, the great preacher Charles H. Spurgeon once emphasized to a preaching class the importance of making facial expressions that harmonized with one's sermon.

"When you speak of Heaven," he said, "let your face light up, let it be irradiated with a heavenly gleam, let your eyes shine with reflected glory. But when you speak of hell—well, then your ordinary face will do."[9]

While we may think it contrived to "force" a facial expression, such as a smile, or to force a laugh, scientists have found that even forced laughter has a beneficial effect, both mentally and physically.

Keep an Open Mind

I warn everyone among you not to estimate and think of himself more highly than he ought [not to have an exaggerated opinion of his own importance].

ROMANS 12:3 AMP

For more than one hundred years, the Swiss set the standard for excellence in watchmaking. In 1968, they held 65 percent of the world market and an estimated 80 percent of the profits. Ten years later, their market share was less than 10 percent. Over the next three years, more than half of the sixty-five thousand watchmakers in Switzerland became unemployed.

Today, the world leader in watchmaking is Japan. In 1968, the Japanese had virtually no share of the watch market. Then, they began to manufacture totally electronic, quartz-movement watches. Far more accurate than mechanical watches, they could run for years on one small battery.

Who invented the quartz-movement watch? The Swiss! Swiss researchers presented the quartz watch to Swiss watchmakers in 1967, but they rejected it, saying it would never work. The watchmakers rejected the idea so soundly that the researchers didn't even protect their idea with a patent. When they later presented their invention at an international watch convention, representatives from Seiko and Texas Instruments jumped on it immediately.

Every invention can be improved upon. Creative ideas, or witty inventions, come from God, and His creativity is infinite!

MY THOUGHTS:

_____

_____

_____

_____

_____

_____

_____

_____

_____

_____

_____

_____

_____

_____

_____

HOW OPEN-MINDED AM I TOWARD NEW IDEAS?

Calm in the Midst of the Storm

I have set the Lord always before me: because he is at my right hand, I shall not be moved.

PSALM 16:8

MY THOUGHTS:

_____
_____
_____
_____
_____
_____
_____
_____
_____
_____
_____
_____
_____
_____
_____

HOW CAN I
DEVELOP MY TRUST
AND THE TRUST OF
MY CHILDREN IN
GOD'S
UNSHAKEABLE
CHARACTER?

Several years ago on a flight out of Orlando, the pilot recognized that something was amiss the minute the plane took off. He quickly turned back to the Orlando airport and warned the passengers to prepare for a crash landing because the hydraulic system had failed.

The passengers were stunned and visibly frightened. Many began to cry, and some even wailed or screamed. Almost everyone lost their composure in one way or another, but one woman continued to talk in a calm, normal voice. She stared into the face of her four-year-old daughter, who was listening to her intently.

She said, "I love you so much. Do you know I love you more than anything?"

"Yes, Mommy."

The mother continued, "And remember, no matter what happens, that I love you always. And that you are a good girl. Sometimes things happen that are not your fault. You are still a good girl, and my love will always be with you."

Then the mother laid over her daughter, strapped the seat belt over both of them, and prepared to crash. The mother's love and character had given her courage. Miraculously, the landing gear held, and the plane landed safely.[1]

Character is built layer upon layer, not in one big act. "Having what it takes" for tomorrow will be a direct result of "doing what is right" today.

Getting the Upper Hand Over Negative Emotions

A gentle answer will calm a person's anger, but an unkind answer will cause more anger.

PROVERBS 15:1 NCV

In the early 1950s, President Truman appointed Newbold Morris to investigate allegations of crime and mismanagement in high levels of government. Just a few months later, Morris was himself in the witness chair in the Senate hearing room, answering a barrage of questions from a Senate subcommittee about the sale of some ships by his own New York company.

The investigation was intense, and the subcommittee's questions were becoming increasingly accusatory and fierce. Morris's face first recorded pain, then surprise, and then anger. Amidst a flurry of angry murmurs in the room, he rose and reached into his coat, producing a sheet of white paper. Then he shouted: "Wait a minute. I have a note here from my wife. It says, 'Keep your shirt on!'"

Everyone in the room burst into laughter, and the angry situation was temporarily diffused.[12]

Anger that is allowed to rage on eventually plays out in one of two ways: abuse—which may take the form of physical blows or emotional wounds—or estrangement. Both abuse and estrangement are painful situations, and reconciliation can be very difficult. The healing process is often a long one. Choose, instead, to lighten the moment and to channel the intense feelings of anger into positive, productive expenditures of energy.

MY THOUGHTS:

_____
_____
_____
_____
_____
_____
_____
_____
_____
_____
_____
_____
_____
_____
_____
_____
_____
_____
_____

WHAT STEPS CAN I TAKE TO TURN THE TIDE OF NEGATIVE EMOTIONS IN MY HOME?

21

Seeds of Good Character

Teach a child to choose the right path, and when he is older he will remain upon it.

PROVERBS 22:6 TLB

MY THOUGHTS:

_____
_____
_____
_____
_____
_____
_____
_____
_____
_____
_____
_____
_____
_____
_____
_____

WHAT SEEDS CAN I
PLANT TODAY THAT
WILL HELP MY
CHILDREN DEVELOP
GODLY CHARACTER?

Through the years, one of the most popular comic strips about family life was that of "Momma," by Mel Lazarus. Momma was always trying to straighten out her three grown children. Of major concern to her was the proper courtship and marriage of her daughter, Mary Lou.

In one strip, Mary Lou is shown on the front porch saying good night to her boyfriend. He is whispering sweet nothings into her ear. Momma is trying to eavesdrop from the window but can't quite hear what's going on.

Once Mary Lou is inside the house, Momma asks, "Mary Lou, what did he whisper to you?"

Mary Lou answers, "Ah, just 'love stuff,' Momma."

Momma then says, "Decent 'love stuff' can be spoken freely, out loud . . . Decent 'love stuff' can be shouted from rooftops." In the final frame of the comic strip, Momma's voice crescendos to a climax: "DECENT 'LOVE STUFF' CAN BE EMBROIDERED ON SAMPLERS!"

God Loves a Cheerful Giver

God loves (He takes pleasure in, prizes above other things, and is unwilling to abandon or to do without) a cheerful (joyous, "prompt to do it") giver [whose heart is in his giving].

2 CORINTHIANS 9:7 AMP

Hyrum Smith has written, "When I was eight years old, living in the Hawaiian Islands, it appeared that Christmas was going to be pretty lean for our household. My parents . . . gathered us together . . . to explain to my siblings and me (there were seven of us) that there was not a great deal of money for Christmas. Each of us would have to select one gift that we really wanted, and that one gift would likely be the only one we would receive." Smith loved apples, so he asked for a bushel of them.

His parents were astonished, but on Christmas morning they managed to present to him "the most wonderful bushel of apples I have ever seen." It was only years later that Smith realized that since apples don't grow in Hawaii, they had to be shipped in. He had asked for a very expensive present!

He recalls, "As soon as the rest of my family had opened their presents, I grabbed my bushel of apples and went out into the neighborhood to find all my friends. Within a few hours, I had given all of my apples away . . . I remember how wonderful it was to share my apples with all my friends . . . The fact that they were gone before sundown was not a problem for me." Out of that experience, Smith later came to an understanding of what he calls, "the abundance mentality."[13]

The more cheerfully we give to others, the more abundantly we receive.

MY THOUGHTS:

_____
_____
_____
_____
_____
_____
_____
_____
_____
_____
_____
_____
_____
_____
_____
_____
_____
_____

WHAT ARE SOME PRACTICAL WAYS THAT I CAN BE AN EXAMPLE OF A CHEERFUL GIVER TO MY CHILDREN?

Somebody's Mother

Treat the older women as you would your mother . . . with all purity.
1 TIMOTHY 5:2 NLT

MY THOUGHTS:

_____
_____
_____
_____
_____
_____
_____
_____
_____
_____
_____
_____
_____
_____
_____
_____
_____

WHAT STEPS CAN I TAKE TO INSTILL IN MY CHILDREN THE PROPER RESPECT FOR OTHERS?

Mary Dow Brine's "Somebody's Mother"—here abbreviated—is a classic worthy to be memorized:

She stood at the crossing and waited long,
Alone, uncared for, amid the throng.
Past the woman so old and gray
Hastened the children on their way.
No one offered a helping hand to her—
So meek, so timid, afraid to stir
Lest the carriage wheels or the horses' feet
Should crowd her down in the slippery street.
He paused beside her and whispered low,
"I'll help you cross, if you wish to go."
Her aged hand on his strong young arm
She placed, and so, without hurt or harm,
He guided the trembling feet along,
Proud that his own were firm and strong.
Then back again to his friends he went,
His young heart happy and well content.
"She's somebody's mother, boys, you know.
For all she's aged and poor and slow.
And I hope some fellow will lend a hand
To help my mother, you understand,
If ever she's poor and old and gray,
When her own dear boy is far away."

This boy's parents taught him to be not only kind, appreciative, and pleasant to his own family and friends but to even see a stranger as someone special.

Stay Out of Trouble

I would have you learn this great fact: that a life of doing right is the wisest life there is. If you live that kind of life, you'll not limp or stumble as you run.

PROVERBS 4:11-12 TLB

One day, three rough-looking fellows on huge motorcycles pulled up to a highway cafe. Inside, they found only a waitress, the cook, and one truck driver—a little guy trouble on perched on a stool at the counter. The driver was quietly eating his lunch.

The motorcyclists, angry because they felt a trucker had cut them off several miles back, decided to take out their revenge on this innocent man. They grabbed his food away from him and mocked him, laughing in his face and calling him bad names. The truck driver said nothing. He simply got up, paid for his food, and walked out.

One of the three men, unhappy that they hadn't succeeded in provoking the little man into a fistfight, said to the waitress, "He sure wasn't much of a man, was he?"

The waitress replied, "I guess not." Then looking out the window, she added, "I guess he's not much of a truck driver either. He just ran over three motorcycles on his way out of the parking lot."[14]

The majority of the problems we have in life are actually of our own making—through things we have or have not said or done. Now is always a good time to ask God for the wisdom to make choices that will keep us out of trouble in the future.

MY THOUGHTS:

IN WHAT WAYS DO I BRING TROUBLE ON MYSELF?

Paying the Price

I count all things but loss for the excellency of the knowledge of Christ Jesus my Lord: for whom I have suffered the loss of all things, and do count them but dung, that I may win Christ.

PHILIPPIANS 3:8

MY THOUGHTS:

_____
_____
_____
_____
_____
_____
_____
_____
_____
_____
_____
_____
_____
_____
_____
_____

WHAT ARE SOME OF THE THINGS OUR FAMILY CAN SACRIFICE FOR THE GOOD OF OTHERS AND THE GOSPEL?

Sadhu Sundar Singh was born into an Indian family of high caste. When he became a Christian and told his parents of his decision to follow Christ, they said, "You have broken caste. You cannot live here any longer." They immediately banished him from their home.

It was the wet season, and the rain was coming down hard as he left his home, clad in only his insubstantial Indian robes. He sat under a nearby tree all night, soaked to the skin. He said that he felt so radiantly happy, however, that he forgot any physical discomfort. He had the freedom to travel throughout the region, telling the Gospel story.

He became known as the apostle of India. Once, he went into Tibet, where he was arrested, put into a pit, and branded with irons. He bore those scars the rest of his life. While speaking in England, he said, "I am going back to do what I have done. I am quite aware of the cost." Some time after his return, he disappeared and appears to have suffered a martyr's death.[15]

Singh moved from "high caste" in India into a "servant's caste" for the Gospel. His position in Christ was not only marked by the privilege of eternal life, but by the responsibility to serve others and share Christ's love.

Prayer Makes a Difference

Confess your sins to each other and pray for each other so God can heal you. When a believing person prays, great things happen.

JAMES 5:16 NCV

In an upscale neighborhood of Chicago, a young married woman—popular, intelligent, wealthy—found herself overwhelmed by the headlines she read every day. Finally, she went to a neighbor and said, "Mary, you can laugh if you like or say no if you want, but would you consider meeting with me once a month, just the two of us, to pray for the world?"

Her friend was startled but answered her seriously, "Let's make it once a week." And so these two women met together for weekly prayer. As the months went by, they invited others to join them, and before long, they had a fully functioning prayer group.

One day one of the women asked, "I wonder if I might share something personal?" She told the group about certain marital difficulties she was having. Other women expressed similar problems, and that day, the group did what it could to help its own members. Their prayer focused on their own needs. It quickly became evident to these young women that they could not hope to reform the world unless they began with themselves. They invited their husbands to join the group and help them to combat the immorality that was the cause of so many of their personal problems. The results were so far-reaching that the entire community was changed![16]

MY THOUGHTS:

_____
_____
_____
_____
_____
_____
_____
_____
_____
_____
_____
_____
_____
_____
_____
_____
_____
_____

WITH WHOM COULD I BECOME A PRAYER PARTNER? HOW WOULD I APPROACH THAT PERSON?

A Little Produces a Lot

january 21

Bring the whole tithe into the storehouse . . . and see if I will not throw open the floodgates of heaven and pour out so much blessing that you will not have room enough for it.

MALACHI 3:10 NIV

MY THOUGHTS:

_____
_____
_____
_____
_____
_____
_____
_____
_____
_____
_____
_____
_____
_____
_____
_____

WHAT ARE SOME CREATIVE WAYS OUR FAMILY CAN GIVE TO GOD'S WORK?

A priest in a rural area asked one of his parishioners to serve as the parish's financial chairperson. The man, who managed the largest grain elevator in the area, agreed based on two conditions: no report would be due for a year, and no one would ask any questions about the finances during the year. Although the second request seemed unorthodox and would involve a great deal of trust, the priest and other key parishioners agreed. They valued the man's expertise and wisdom.

At the end of the year, the man made his report. He had paid off the church debt of $200,000. He had redecorated the church, given $1,000 toward missions, and had $5,000 in the bank.

"How did you do all this?" the priest asked, having some understanding of what the weekly offerings had been. The congregation, the vast majority of whom were grain farmers, were equally shocked.

The man answered quietly, "Well, you people all bring your grain to my elevator. As you did business with me, I simply withheld 10 percent and gave it to the church. You never missed it. But it sure added up."[17]

When we are generous toward God's work, we will usually find that what remains is more than sufficient to meet our own needs.

Be Prepared

A sensible man watches for problems ahead and prepares to meet them. The simpleton never looks and suffers the consequences.

PROVERBS 27:12 TLB

One day in a very busy factory, an intricate piece of machinery broke down. The company's best machinists were called in to diagnose the problem, but they couldn't come up with a solution.

Finally, they suggested a specialist be brought in. The master mechanic arrived, looked the apparatus over thoroughly, and then asked for the smallest hammer they had on hand. He then pecked on a critical area of the machine with the hammer and said, "Now turn on the power. It ought to work." His small peck apparently released a mechanism that had jammed, and sure enough, the machine worked.

Later, when the specialist sent a bill for $100, the managers were astounded! One hundred dollars was an exorbitant fee for one small peck! They asked him to send them an itemized statement. He complied but didn't reduce his fee. His statement read:

$1 for pecking
$99 for knowing where to peck.[18]

A similar story is told about a young medical student who asked an experienced surgeon how long it would take to learn how to perform an appendectomy. The surgeon replied, "Three hours." Then he added, "And three years to learn what to do if anything goes wrong."

MY THOUGHTS:

WHAT PRACTICAL STEPS CAN I TAKE TO PREPARE MY CHILDREN FOR THE FUTURE?

january 23

Your Life is a Witness

Your very lives are a letter that anyone can read by just looking at you. Christ himself wrote it—not with ink, but with God's living Spirit; not chiseled into stone, but carved into human lives.

2 CORINTHIANS 3:3 MSG

MY THOUGHTS:

_____
_____
_____
_____
_____
_____
_____
_____
_____
_____
_____
_____
_____
_____
_____
_____

WHAT PRACTICAL STEPS CAN I TAKE TO MAKE MY LIFE A TESTIMONY THAT GOD IS ALIVE?

Gordon Liddy, a White House aide during the Nixon administration, was a student of the German philosopher Nietzsche. Nietzsche taught that one's will was of supreme importance not God's. A man with a will of iron, Liddy saw no need for God.

After serving a four-year prison term for his part in the Watergate scandal, Liddy renewed his friendship with some former FBI colleagues who asked him to join their Bible study. He agreed, with one caveat: "Please do not try to convert me." Of course, things didn't work out as Liddy had anticipated. He had been willing to read the Bible as a historical document, but his friends' attitudes toward the Bible made him take a closer look.

He began to think about God. *If God is infinite and we're finite, he thought, how can we ever understand Him?* Liddy reasoned, *God will have to communicate with me.* Then he realized that the Bible is God's communication. Still, he argued, *We can never be worthy of God.* And again, he was hit by a thunderbolt: *God sent His Son to make us worthy* (by virtue of His crucifixion and resurrection) *and to keep the dialogue going between God and humanity.* Liddy suddenly perceived a need for God, and he accepted Christ.[19]

If You Can't Say Anything Nice . . .

When she speaks, her words are wise, and kindness is the rule for everything she says.

PROVERBS 31:26 TLB

In *Lessons from Mom*, Joan Aho Ryankind writes the following about loyalty in friendship:

We went to one of the local shopping malls recently where Mom ran into two women who live in her development . . . They greeted her effusively. It was a brief exchange, during which she introduced me, and they were on their way. "What phony baloney," she said excitedly when they were well ahead of us. Since her remark came from no-where, I asked her what she meant.

With obvious disdain, she explained that she had sat under the canopy at her pool on several occasions with these two women and one of their friends, Sylvia. One day, she said, she sat nearby and heard the three of them talking about the wedding reception of Sylvia's daughter the week before. They raved about the food, the flowers, the elegant country club location, the beautiful bride . . . Mom said Sylvia was obviously beaming with pride.

"Well, then Sylvia left, and you should have heard them," Mom said . . . "I couldn't believe friends could be that two-faced. They ripped her apart, talking about how cheap she was, her homely son-in-law, the music they couldn't dance to. It was awful. And they call themselves friends," she clucked. "Who needs friends like that?"[20]

MY THOUGHTS:

_____
_____
_____
_____
_____
_____
_____
_____
_____
_____
_____
_____
_____
_____
_____
_____
_____
_____

WHAT KIND OF FRIEND AM I? HOW CAN I BECOME A BETTER FRIEND?

Don't Be Afraid of the Truth

If you profit from constructive criticism, you will be elected to the wise men's hall of fame. But to reject criticism is to harm yourself and your own best interests.

PROVERBS 15:31-32 TLB

MY THOUGHTS:

_____
_____
_____
_____
_____
_____
_____
_____
_____
_____
_____
_____
_____
_____
_____
_____

HOW CAN I BECOME MORE COURAGEOUS IN SPEAKING AND SEEKING THE TRUTH?

The story is told of two Christian men who once had a "falling out." One heard a rumor that the other was speaking against so he went to him and said, "Will you be kind enough to tell my faults to my face, that I may profit by your Christian candor and try to get rid of them?"

The other man replied, "Yes, I will."

They then went aside from the crowd, and the first man said, "Before you begin telling what you find wrong in me, will you kneel with me and pray, that my eyes may be opened to see my faults as you cite them? You lead in prayer."

The second man prayed that God would open the eyes of his friend, and when he was finished, the first man said, "Now, please proceed with your complaints."

The second man said, "After praying over it, it looks so little that it is not worth talking about. The truth is I have been serving the devil myself and have need that you pray for me and forgive me the wrong I have done you."[21]

Two things are admirable: to speak the truth to another person with love and to seek the truth from one who will be honest with you. In speaking the truth to others, you often hear the very truth you need to hear from your own lips. In seeking the truth, you often gain a friend.

Actions Speak Louder than Words

The tree is known and recognized and judged by its fruit.
MATTHEW 12:33 AMP

A minister was scheduled to speak at an all-day conference. He failed to set his alarm, however, and he overslept. In his haste to make up for lost time, he cut himself while contradict shaving. Then he discovered his shirt was not ironed, and he scorched it because the iron was too hot. To make matters worse, as he ran out to his car, he noticed that he had a flat tire.

Disgusted and distraught by the time he finished changing the tire, he was an hour behind schedule. Nevertheless, the minister felt encouraged when he was finally "under way." He figured that if he hurried, he might be only a few minutes late for the first session. He raced through town, failing to notice a stop sign along the way. As he rushed through it, he caught a glimpse of a policeman, who as expected, stopped him.

Jumping out of his car, the agitated minister said sharply, "Go ahead and give me a ticket. Everything else has gone wrong today."

The policeman quietly responded, "I used to have days like that before I became a Christian."[22]

As a Christian witness, how you behave in your everyday lifestyle is much more important than what you have to say about your Christianity.

MY THOUGHTS:

IN WHAT AREAS DO MY ACTIONS CONTRADICT WHAT I BELIEVE? HOW CAN I CHANGE THAT?

The Mark of a Professional

january 27

To win the contest you must deny yourselves many things that would keep you from doing your best.

1 CORINTHIANS 9:25 TLB

MY THOUGHTS:

_____
_____
_____
_____
_____
_____
_____
_____
_____
_____
_____
_____
_____
_____
_____
_____
_____

IN WHAT WAYS CAN I BE MORE "PROFESSIONAL" WHEN IT COMES TO PARENTING?

A husband and wife rose early one Sunday morning. They had breakfast, and then the wife retired to the bedroom to dress for church. As the time was approaching when they needed to leave for the morning service, she noticed that her husband hadn't made any move toward getting dressed. She asked, "Why aren't you getting dressed for church?"

He replied, "Cause I don't want to go."

She asked, "Do you have any good reasons?"

He said, "Yes, I have three good reasons."

"And they are?" she asked.

"First, the congregation is cold. Second, no one likes me. And third, I just don't want to go this morning."

The wife replied with wisdom, "Well, honey, I have three reasons why you should go."

"Convince me," he said.

"First, the congregation is warm. Second, there are a few people there who like you. And third, you're the pastor. So get dressed!"[23]

Nobody likes doing what is right and good all the time. We each have moments when we would rather give a halfhearted effort or yield to temptation. The mark of professionalism, however, is in facing down what you don't want to do and doing it anyway.

Allowing God and Others to Help

Cease striving and know that I am God.
PSALM 46:10 NASB

Someone once studied the inaugural speeches of United States presidents. Special focus was placed upon presidents who had been reelected to a second term. One of the purposes of the study was to determine how many times the word "I" appeared.

Washington's first inaugural address contained 1,300 words and 20 'Ts." His change second inaugural speech was much shorter.

Lincoln's first inaugural speech had 3,588 words with 43 Ts." His second had only 588 words and a solitary "I."

In the Bible, Romans 7 is a chapter filled with struggle, conflict, and failure. It contains thirty-two Ts" and sixteen "me's" and "my's"—48 personal pronouns in all. In chapter 8, which tells of victory, triumph, and peace, "I" and "me" are hardly mentioned.[24]

One of the great lessons to be learned in life is that we are not the prime motivator or catalyst of the success we experience in life. While we may be the engineer of our own failures more often than we care to admit, we rarely reach the heights of success on our own. We usually have the help of others in reaching the top—regardless of our field or endeavor—and ultimately, we are enabled by God. We accomplish only what He enables us to do.

MY THOUGHTS:

IN WHAT WAYS DO I STRIVE TOO HARD TO RUN MY FAMILY'S UNIVERSE? HOW CAN I CHANGE THAT?

Keeping Priorities in Line

Be very careful, then, how you live—not as unwise but as wise, making the most of every opportunity.

EPHESIANS 5:15-16 NIV

MY THOUGHTS:

_____
_____
_____
_____
_____
_____
_____
_____
_____
_____
_____
_____
_____
_____
_____
_____

HOW AM I DOING WHEN IT COMES TO SPENDING TIME WITH MY CHILDREN? IN WHAT AREAS COULD I IMPROVE?

In *From Bad Beginnings to Happy Endings*, Ed Young writes:

Several years ago I was invited to the White House to meet with a few key religious leaders and the President of the United States. Now that was a pretty good offer, wasn't it? It was the first invitation from a president this old country boy from Mississippi had ever received. I'd been out of town during the first part of the week, and between flights I called home to check in. When I did, I learned that my son Ben's basketball game originally scheduled for midweek had been rescheduled for the end of the week—and I'd missed one game already!

The question was one of simple priority: "What's the most important thing to me?" Since the government had been running pretty well without me for a number of years, I called the White House and said, "Ed Young won't be coming." (They recovered from this news beautifully.) Instead I went to the game and had the fun of seeing my son shoot the winning basket.[25]

Bringing Out the Best in Others

If you love someone, you will be loyal to him no matter what the cost. You will always believe in him, always expect the best of him, and always stand your ground in defending him.

1 CORINTHIANS 13:7 TLB

Best-selling author Leo Buscaglia was the youngest son of a very large Italian immigrant family. He grew up speaking Italian at home, learning English as a second language. As a boy, he preferred opera to popular music, and he knew Italian fairy tales rather than the traditional English ones read by his neighbors. His family's home was marked by joyous moments, passionate beliefs, and deep family ties.

Unfortunately, his school psychologist saw him differently. He considered Buscaglia's English language skills to be very low and his view of the world radically unrealistic. The psychologist classified him as mentally deficient, "retarded," and recommended that he be placed in a special class.

In the special class, Buscaglia met Miss Hunt, a caring, warm teacher who paid little attention to the label placed upon him. She saw him and the other students in her class as rich in potential. She conveyed a love of learning to all her students.

Buscaglia soon blossomed, and after several months, Miss Hunt insisted that he be retested. The result was his placement in a regular classroom. Miss Hunt's door remained open to Buscaglia, and she continued to encourage him and convince him that he had a wonderful life ahead.[26]

MY THOUGHTS:

WHAT CAN I DO TO HELP SOMEONE WHO HAS BEEN "WRITTEN OFF" BY OTHERS?

A Mother with a Mission

You will go wherever I send you and speak whatever I tell you to. And don't be afraid of the people, for I, the Lord, will be with you and see you through.

JEREMIAH 1:7-8 TLB

MY THOUGHTS:

_____
_____
_____
_____
_____
_____
_____
_____
_____
_____
_____
_____
_____
_____
_____
_____
_____

ABOUT WHAT CAUSE OR ISSUE DO I FEEL COMPELLED TO SPEAK OUT? HOW SHOULD I GO OUT DOING THAT?

During a long, winding drive through the Italian Alps, two-year-old Alexandra Chalupa slept safely buckled in her backseat car seat. When she awoke, she pleaded to be allowed to sit up front, snuggled between her parents. Tanya Chalupa said no to her toddler's further protests. Moments later, their car skidded in the rain, lurched across traffic lanes, barely missed a deep gorge, and came to rest against a solid wall of rock. Her parents were bruised and shaken, but Alexandra remained firmly fastened and unhurt. Tanya shuddered to think what would have happened if she had been holding her daughter in her lap.

After the family returned to California, Tanya began a one-woman campaign to enact legislation requiring automobile safety seats for children under four years old or weighing less than forty pounds. The memory of the accident and a conviction that such a law would save lives gave her the courage for a four-year campaign, even though she had no political know-how or financial backing. In 1983, the Child Restraint Law went into effect in California, and by year's end, child-passenger injuries had declined by more than 400 from the previous year!

Rear Them Tenderly

Do not irritate and provoke your children to anger [do not exasperate them to resentment], but rear them [tenderly].

EPHESIANS 6:4 AMP

Little Edward misbehaved during dinner one evening. His father, a strict but fair disciplinarian, reprimanded him. Still, such a way Eddy didn't change his ways. The father finally said, "Eddy, if you do not behave, you will be sent to your room, and there will be no more food for you tonight."

Eddy didn't listen but continued to misbehave. At that, he was ordered to march to his bedroom, change into his nightclothes, and climb into bed.

As he lay in bed, Eddy's every thought turned to food. He couldn't remember ever having felt more hungry, alone, or alienated from the family. He began to cry. Then he heard a noise on the stairs and footsteps walking closer and closer to his room. The door opened, and in came his father.

Closing the door behind him, he came over to Eddy's bed and said, "I love you, Eddy, and I've come to spend the night with you."

Not all *behavior* is worthy of applause. But every moment of a child's life and every ounce of a child's *being* is worthy of love.

MY THOUGHTS:

HOW CAN I DISCIPLINE IN SUCH A WAY THAT MY CHILD STILL FEELS LOVED?

Words Paint Pictures

Your words are filled with grace; God himself is blessing you forever.
PSALM 45:2 TLB

MY THOUGHTS:

_____
_____
_____
_____
_____
_____
_____
_____
_____
_____
_____
_____
_____
_____
_____

WHAT WORD PICTURES AM I PAINTING FOR MY CHILDREN?

Her letters to her son Johannes give a strong impression of her clear common sense and her great kindheartedness. In these long letters that have been carefully preserved, she tells her son all the interesting news from Hamburg and never speaks ill of anybody. When son Fritz lost an excellent job, she wrote to Johannes: "Fritz must put his trust in God, who guides all human destinies. He will lead him out of this darkness." She remembered Johannes daily in her prayers, as well as Elise and Fritz, and she tried to keep a tight bond among her children, reminding Johannes to remember their birthdays. There is no sign in her letters of any disharmony in her marriage, which lasted thirty-four years, and generally speaking, peace and cheerfulness seemed to prevail in her household.

In sharp contrast was the world outside their home: a poverty-stricken slum with narrow, crooked streets and grime-encrusted, "blackened" frame houses. Disease was rampant, and if fire broke out, the effects in the neighborhood were devastating.

What was the impact of this mother's goodness and nurture on her son? There's no telling. However, through the centuries, the compelling, beautiful music of Johannes Brahms has touched countless millions.

Vacation from the Kids

Children are a gift from God; they are his reward.
PSALM 127:3 TLB

A couple returned home after a week's vacation to the mountains, feeling more exhausted than ever. All week they ran up and down mountain trails, valiantly struggling to keep their four children in line and safe from danger. Their tent had afforded them no privacy, and they were exhausted from playing referee around the campfire. The children, however, had had a great time. They bubbled over with enthusiasm as they told their grandparents about all the new sights, sounds, and experiences they had encountered—from roasting marshmallows to sleeping under the stars. The grandparents took one look at the parents, however, and said, "You need a vacation." The parents agreed, and with the grandparents volunteering to babysit, they headed for a few days of rest at the beach.

They were sunning themselves one afternoon after they had been there three days, and the wife said dreamily, "Three whole days without the kids. That must be a record. I can't remember three whole days without the kids since the first one was born."

"Right," sighed her husband and then added, "Believe it or not, I kind of miss them. Throw some sand in my face, will you?"

MY THOUGHTS:

WHAT CAN MY SPOUSE AND I DO TO ENSURE TIME TOGETHER AWAY FROM THE KIDS?

Little Ears Are Listening

Say the right thing at the right time and help others by what you say.
EPHESIANS 4:29 CEV

MY THOUGHTS:

_____
_____
_____
_____
_____
_____
_____
_____
_____
_____
_____
_____
_____
_____
_____
_____
_____
_____

*HOW DO I FEEL
WHEN MY CHILDREN
REPEAT WHAT I SAY?
AN EXAMPLE
WOULD BE . . .*

If you ever question whether your children are listening and learning from your life, consider these examples:

A mother and her five-year-old son were driving down the street when the little boy asked, "Mommy, why do the idiots only come out when Daddy drives?"

After the church service, a little boy said to the pastor, "When I grow up, I'm going to give you money." "Thank you," the pastor replied, "but why?" "Because," the little boy explained, "my daddy says you're one of the poorest preachers we've ever had."

A wife invited several family friends to dinner. At the table, she turned to their six-year-old daughter and said, "Would you like to say the blessing?" The girl answered, "I don't know what to say." The mother insisted, "Just say what you hear Mommy say." The daughter bowed her head and said, "Lord, why on earth did I invite all these people to dinner?"

As a parent, you never know when little eyes are watching your actions and little ears are hearing what you say. If you want to avoid embarrassment, don't let your kids hear what you don't want repeated.[27]

Courage

He who covers and forgives an offense seeks love, but he who repeats or harps on a matter separates even close friends.

PROVERBS 17:9 AMP

In *Helping Kids Cope with the Stress, Strains, and Pressures of Life,* Dr. Bettie Youngs writes about a five-year-old girl named Norma. On the first day of kindergarten, too shy to ask the teacher to use the bathroom and too timid to use it without first getting permission, she wet herself. It wasn't long before all the other students were aware of what had happened. Most laughed, some thinking her predicament funny and others nervously relieved that this had happened to her and not to them. But one brave boy named Norm did not laugh. He got up from his desk, walked over to Norma, and said softly, "I will help you." Norma said later, "We were all sitting, and he was standing, so his presence seemed almost majestic." "And I won't let them make fun of you," he added.

Norma looked up at Norm and smiled in admiration. She no longer felt alone and afraid. She had found a new friend. Still holding her hand, Norm turned to the rest of the class and kindly asked, "How would you feel if it happened to you?" The children sat motionless. Then Norm added, "Let's not laugh at her anymore, okay?" Norma concluded, "We knew we were in the presence of courage."

MY THOUGHTS:

HOW CAN I DEVELOP THIS KIND OF COURAGE IN MY CHILDREN?

You Have Something I Don't Have

february 6

Do not be quick in spirit to be angry or vexed, for anger and vexation lodge in the bosom of fools.

ECCLESIASTES 7:9 AMP

MY THOUGHTS:

_____
_____
_____
_____
_____
_____
_____
_____
_____
_____
_____
_____
_____
_____
_____
_____
_____

WHAT QUALITIES DO
I POSSESS THAT
WOULD ENCOURAGE
ANOTHER PERSON
TO WANT TO KNOW
GOD?

The story is told of two farmers who lived next to each other, with nothing but a river dividing their properties. One day when the corn was ripe, the cows of one neighbor got out of their pasture and crossed the river into the other farmer's waving field of corn. They trampled and ruined about half an acre of the crop. The farmer who owned the damaged corn crop rounded up the cattle and put them in his barn. He made his neighbor pay dearly for every ear of corn the cows had destroyed before he would return them to him.

That fall, the hogs of the man whose corn had been eaten got out and crossed the river into the potato patch of the neighbor. They obliterated it. The hog owner saw his hogs and the damage they were doing, so he got his gun and hid himself. He vowed that if his neighbor harmed his hogs, he would shoot him. When he saw that his neighbor had no intention of hurting the hogs, he was surprised. He said to him, "You have something I do not have. What is it?"

The neighbor replied, "I am a Christian."

That night the unregenerate man and his wife crossed the river and visited their neighbors. Both were converted before they left his home.[28]

I Hear You

Let the wise listen.
PROVERBS 1:5 NIV

A young boy came down to a pier on the mighty Mississippi River where an old man was fishing. He began to ask the man a myriad of questions, and with patience, the old man answered him. Their conversation was interrupted, however, by the shrill whistle of the *River Queen* as she came paddling down river. Both the old man and boy stopped to stare in wonder as the gleaming ship splashed spray into the sunshine.

Above the noise of the paddle wheel, the boy began to call across the water, "Let me ride! Let me ride!" The old man tried to calm him, explaining that the *River Queen* didn't just stop anywhere and give rides to little boys. The boy cried all the louder, "Let me ride!" The old man stared in amazement as the great ship pulled toward shore and lowered a gangplank to the pier. In a flash the boy scampered onto the deck. As the gangplank was pulled aboard and the ship began to pull back into the mainstream, the boy called back to his newfound friend, "I knew this ship would stop for me, Mister. The captain is my father!"

The young boy was confident in his relationship with his father. As your children become confident that you will listen to them, they will be able to understand that their Heavenly Father will listen to them as well.

MY THOUGHTS:

_____
_____
_____
_____
_____
_____
_____
_____
_____
_____
_____
_____
_____
_____
_____
_____
_____
_____
_____

WHAT STEPS CAN I TAKE TO DEVELOP THIS TYPE OF CONFIDENCE IN MY CHILDREN?

Be Quick to Apologize

Confess your faults one to another, and pray one for another.
JAMES 5:16

MY THOUGHTS:

_____
_____
_____
_____
_____
_____
_____
_____
_____
_____
_____
_____
_____
_____
_____
_____

WHEN I MAKE MISTAKES, I TYPICALLY . . .

In 1957, Ford bragged about producing "the car of the decade": the Edsel. In reality, however, one analyst likened its sales graph to a very dangerous ski slope, and there is only one recorded case of an Edsel being stolen. These and many other such "failures" are listed in a book entitled *The Incomplete Book of Failures,* which, ironically, had two pages missing when it was printed! The book reports mistakes and errors in a variety of categories, including a memo from a record company that turned down the Beatles in 1962: "We don't like their sound. Groups of guitars are on their way out."

On a more personal note, Maxie Baughan, a former all-pro linebacker, once came off the field and disgustedly threw his helmet to the ground. What he didn't know was that cameras had caught his display of bad temper. A few days later, he was watching his five-year-old son play, and suddenly the boy took off his helmet and gave it a heave. Baughan scolded him for poor sportsmanship, but then the boy told his dad about watching him do the same thing . . . on TV.

Baughan promptly apologized!

Not apologizing for a mistake . . . is to make two mistakes, and the second can be far more damaging!

Diamond in the Rough

february 9

The value of wisdom is far above rubies; nothing can be compared with it.

PROVERBS 8:11 TLB

Many years ago in South Africa, a man sold his farm so that he might spend his days in search of diamonds. He was consumed with dreams of becoming wealthy. When he had finally exhausted his resources and his health and was no closer to his fortune than the day he sold his farm, he threw himself into a river and drowned.

One day, the man who had bought his farm spotted an unusual-looking stone in a creek bed. He placed it on his fireplace mantle as a conversation piece. A visitor noticed the stone and examined it closely. He then stated his suspicion that the stone was actually a diamond. The farmer, very discreetly, had the stone analyzed, and sure enough, it was one of the largest and finest diamonds ever found.

Still operating under great secrecy, the farmer searched his stream, gathering similar stones. They were all diamonds. In fact, his farm was covered with diamonds just waiting to be picked up! The farm the diamond-seeker had sold turned out to be one of the richest diamond deposits in the world.[29]

The lessons of wisdom can often be learned in the relationships and experiences we encounter every day. Ask God to reveal to you what you need to know in order to live the life He desires for you to live. The resources you need are probably right there in front of you.

MY THOUGHTS:

WHAT RESOURCES DO I NEED? WHERE HAVE I LOOKED FOR THEM?

47

Your Child's Destiny

I knew you before I formed you in your mother's womb. Before you were born I set you apart and appointed you.

JEREMIAH 1:5 NLT

MY THOUGHTS:

_____
_____
_____
_____
_____
_____
_____
_____
_____
_____
_____
_____
_____
_____
_____
_____

WHAT STEPS CAN I TAKE TO INSTILL A SENSE OF DESTINY IN MY CHILD?

Dr. Walter L. Wilson tells the story of a woman who attended one of his meetings. She waited after the service, so she could have a few private moments to talk with him. She felt as if her life had no meaning and no purpose—that she was invisible to God. As part of his counseling, Dr. Wilson asked the woman if she could quote any of the Scriptures. She replied that she had once learned John 3:16 in Sunday school.

Dr. Wilson then asked the woman to recite the verse. She said, "For God so loved the world that He gave His only forgotten Son, that whosoever believeth in Him should not perish but have everlasting life."

Immediately Dr. Wilson noticed that she had used the word *forgotten* instead of *begotten* in quoting the verse. He asked, "Do you know why God forgot His Son?"

She said, "No, I don't."

He replied, "It was because He wanted to remember you."

Apart from your personal and family reasons for bearing your child, the Lord has a divine reason for your child's birth. He has a place for your child to fill and a role for your child to fulfill. Every child is planned and wanted from God's perspective!

A Mother Will Conquer for Her Child

By your power I can crush an army; By your strength I leap over a wall.

2 SAMUEL 22:30 TLB

There were once two warring tribes in the Andes, one living in the lowlands and the other high in the mountains. One day the mountain people invaded the lowlanders, kidnapping a baby. They took the infant with them back up into the mountains.

The lowlanders didn't know how to climb the mountain or how to track the mountain people in the steep terrain. Even so, they sent out their best party of fighting men to climb the mountain and bring the baby home. After several days of striving, however, they had climbed only several hundred feet.

Feeling hopeless and helpless, the lowlander men decided that the cause was lost. As they prepared to return to their village below, they saw the baby's mother walking toward them. They realized that she was coming down the mountain that they hadn't figured out how to climb. And then they saw that she had the baby strapped to her back. How could that be?

One man greeted her and said, "We couldn't climb this mountain. How did you do this when we, the strongest and most able men in the village, couldn't do it?"

She shrugged her shoulders and said, "It wasn't your baby."[30]

MY THOUGHTS:

_____
_____
_____
_____
_____
_____
_____
_____
_____
_____
_____
_____
_____
_____
_____

WHAT SEEMINGLY IMPOSSIBLE SITUATION DO I NEED GOD'S GRACE TO OVERCOME?

49

Acceptance

Accept each other just as Christ has accepted you; then God will be glorified.

ROMANS 15:7 NLT

MY THOUGHTS:

_____

_____

_____

_____

_____

_____

_____

_____

_____

_____

_____

_____

_____

_____

_____

_____

IN WHAT WAYS CAN I SHOW MY CHILDREN THE APPROVAL THEY DESERVE?

Samuel Blackwell was an intelligent, warm-hearted man and an enthusiastic supporter of religious tolerance, women's rights, and the abolition of slavery. When his children were barred from public schools because of his religious convictions, he hired private tutors for them. As a result, they received an even better education than they would have had—the girls pursuing the same course of study as the boys. His wife, Hannah, encouraged a love of music and reading in her children. Their home was a magnet for intellectuals of the period; and from their earliest years, the children were exposed to people who valued clear thinking, social awareness, and new ideas. Above all, the Blackwell children were accepted as equals by their parents and given major doses of loving approval.

Five Blackwell girls developed careers: Elizabeth and Emily became doctors, Anna became a newspaper correspondent, Marian became a teacher, and Ellen became an author and artist. One son, Samuel, married America's first woman minister, Antoinette Brown. Son Henry married Lucy Stone, the women's rights leader. All this took place in an age when women were not allowed to serve on juries, cast ballots, or testify in courts, and they were barred from most higher education and from many professions!

When parents show their approval of their children and their talents, the children never learn to limit their abilities.

Encouraging the Gifts in Your Child

A man's gift maketh room for him, and bringeth him before great men.

PROVERBS 18:16

As a boy in Naples, he worked long hours in a factory, all the while yearning to become a singer. When he was ten years old, he took his first voice lesson. The teacher promptly concluded, "You can't sing. You haven't any voice at all. Your voice sounds like the wind in the shutters."

The boy's mother, however, heard greatness in her son's voice. She believed in his talent, and even though they were poor, she put her arms around him and said encouragingly, "My boy, I am going to make every sacrifice to pay for your voice lessons."

This mother's confidence in her son and her constant encouragement of him through the years paid off! Her boy became one of the most widely acclaimed singers around the world. His name? Enrico Caruso.

- What is your child's special talent and desire?
- What are your child's unique gifts—mentally, physically, spiritually?
- What more can you do to nurture them, even as you nurture your child?
- Unearth and foster your child's gifts, and you truly will bring rare riches to the world.

MY THOUGHTS:

WHAT STEPS CAN I TAKE TO ENCOURAGE THE DEVELOPMENT OF MY CHILD'S GIFTS?

Your Example is Your Legacy

february 14

My life is an example to many, because you have been my strength and protection.

PSALM 71:7 NLT

MY THOUGHTS:

_____
_____
_____
_____
_____
_____
_____
_____
_____
_____
_____
_____
_____
_____
_____
_____

WHAT STEPS CAN I TAKE TO LEAD MY CHILDREN TO HEAVEN THROUGH MY EXAMPLE?

In *Values from the Heartland*, Bettie Youngs writes about her father, who got his start in fanning on a rented farm near Vincent, Iowa. In need of financial backing to expand his operation, he turned to Art Swasand at the Farmer's Savings Bank. Art did business the old-fashioned way: a client's character was an important part of the deal.

Art had a reputation for going the extra mile and doing whatever it took to develop and maintain successful working relationships. When her father's tractor broke down one day, Art drove out to visit him. Once he understood what was needed to get the tractor running again, Art financed the parts on the spot.

Says Youngs, "Over the years, these two men financed and paid off machinery, created financial security, purchased land . . . and raised their families. Without fanfare, they became prosperous men doing what they each loved best, with integrity." Youngs's father said of Art after his death, "In more ways than one he was a father, a brother, a confidant, a friend. He was my ideal of a man." [31]

The way you travel through life is the greatest legacy you can leave to those who follow you. In living a life of upright values and strong faith, you are not only making a path through life, you are leading the way to Heaven.

A Mother at Heart

Here am I, and the children the Lord has given me. We are signs and symbols in Israel from the Lord Almighty.

ISAIAH 8:18 NIV

Rachel had a close relationship with her mother, Maria, and after graduating from what areas college, she invited her mother to live with her. When her sister died, Rachel took in her two young daughters and later, her young nephew Roger, and she raised them as her own children. During this time, Maria kept house and typed Rachel's first two books, *Under the Sea-Wind* and *The Sea Around Us.*

When her mother died in 1958, Rachel wrote: "Her love of life and of all living things was her outstanding quality . . . And while gentle and compassionate, she could fight fiercely against anything she believed wrong, as in our present Crusade! Knowing how she felt about that will help me to return to it soon, and to carry it through to completion." Return, she did, writing *Silent Spring*, a book about the dangers of chemical pesticides—taking time out only to explore the woods with Roger, read to him, and play with him. The Environmental Protection Agency was formed in 1970, largely as a result of public outcry in the wake of her book.

Although she never married or bore children of her own, Rachel Carson is called by many the "mother of the age of ecology"—a genuine mother at heart.

MY THOUGHTS:

_____
_____
_____
_____
_____
_____
_____
_____
_____
_____
_____
_____
_____
_____
_____
_____
_____
_____

IN WHAT AREAS DO I NEED GOD'S HELP TO BE A BETTER MOTHER TO MY CHILDREN?

Heavenly Voyage

From birth I have relied on you; you brought me forth from my mother's womb. I will ever praise you.

PSALM 71:6 NIV

MY THOUGHTS:

_____
_____
_____
_____
_____
_____
_____
_____
_____
_____
_____
_____
_____
_____
_____
_____
_____
_____

WHAT DESTINY DO I PERCEIVE WILL BE PART OF MY CHILD'S VOYAGE?

Henry Ward Beecher, considered by many to be one of the most effective and powerful pulpit orators in the history of the United States, not only had a reputation for having an extremely sensitive heart, but also for having a great love of the sea. Many of his sermons were laced with loving anecdotes that had seafaring flavor.

Not only did Beecher make the statement at the bottom of this page, but he had this to say about a mother's relationship with her child: "A babe is a mother's anchor. She cannot swing far from her moorings. And yet a true mother never lives so little in the present as when by the side of the cradle. Her thoughts follow the imagined future of her child. That babe is the boldest of pilots, and guides her fearless thoughts down through scenes of coming years. The old ark never made such voyages as the cradle daily makes."

What a wonderful image to think of a child as being on a voyage from Heaven, traveling through life to return to Heaven's port one day. What a challenge to think that our children have not come along to join us in our sail through life, but rather, we to join in their voyage!

Loving Discipline

A youngster's heart is filled with foolishness, but discipline will drive it away.

PROVERBS 22:15 NLT

Dr. Albert Siegel was quoted by the *Stanford Observer* as saying: "When it comes to rearing children, every society is only twenty years away from barbarism. Twenty years is all we have to accomplish the task of civilizing the infants who are born into our midst each year. These savages know nothing of our language, our culture, our religion, our values, our customs of interpersonal relations...communism, fascism, democracy, civil liberties, the rights of the minority, respect, decency, honesty, customs, conventions, and manners. *The barbarian must be tamed if civilization is to survive.*"

A report from the Minnesota Crime Commission echoes this sentiment: "Every baby . . . wants what he wants when he wants it: his bottle, his mother's attention, his playmate's toy, his uncle's watch. Deny these, and he seethes with rage and aggressiveness which would be murderous were he not so helpless. This means that all children, not just certain children, are born delinquent. If permitted to continue in the self- centered world of infancy . . . every child would grow up a criminal."

The parent who caters to the demands of an infant will reap the fallout of an out-of- control teenager.

MY THOUGHTS:

_____
_____
_____
_____
_____
_____
_____
_____
_____
_____
_____
_____
_____
_____
_____
_____
_____
_____
_____
_____

IN WHAT AREAS DO I NEED TO INSTITUTE MORE DISCIPLINE OF MY CHILDREN?

The Circular Pattern of Love

"Give, and it will be given to you . . . For by your standard of measure it will be measured to you in return."

LUKE 6:38 NASB

MY THOUGHTS:

_____
_____
_____
_____
_____
_____
_____
_____
_____
_____
_____
_____
_____
_____
_____

IN WHAT WAYS ARE WE PERPETUATING THE CIRCLE OF LOVE IN OUR FAMILY?

A reporter once interviewed the famous contralto Marian Anderson and asked her to name the greatest moment in her life. The reporter knew she had many big moments to choose from. He expected her to name the private concert she gave at the White House for the Roosevelts and the king and queen of England. He thought she might name the night she received the ten-thousand-dollar Bok Award as the person who had done the most for her hometown, Philadelphia. Instead, Marian Anderson shocked him by responding quickly, "The greatest moment in my life was the day I went home and told my mother she wouldn't have to take in washing anymore."

The circular pattern of love between a parent and child is more than a matter of "what goes around, comes around." Rather, it stems from the principle that what a child sees, a child copies. Children are not born to be selfless and generous. Their more common cries are rooted in "Me first! Mine! I want." A child must learn to share, to sacrifice for others, and to give spontaneously from the heart. And a child learns that lesson quickly and most easily by copying someone else . . . usually his or her mother!

Correct and Encourage

Tell them when they are wrong. Encourage them with great patience and careful teaching.

2 TIMOTHY 4:2 NCV

MY THOUGHTS:

Beth Raby once competed in a high-school vocal competition in which the songs were to be sung in a foreign language. She had four weeks in which to prepare, but since she had a great deal going on in her life at the time, she didn't prepare as well as she might have. When the time came for her to perform for the judges, she couldn't remember some of the German words in her song. She threw in every German word she could think of! As a result, she did not receive her usual high marks. She felt awful.

On the way home, her teacher said to the group of students, "Don't worry. You did your best." That was all he expected. When they stopped to have lunch, however, Beth remained on the bus, where she burst into tears. She knew that she had not given her best. As she sobbed with her head down, she felt a hand on her back and looked up to see her teacher. He had big tears in his eyes too.

Those tears, far more than any words spoken, brought healing to her heart. While she knew by his words he believed she could do better in the future, she knew by his touch that he would be there to help her. More than any other single thing, that touch helped Beth to become a compassionate teacher herself.[32]

I CAN EXTEND A GOOD MIX OF CORRECTION AND ENCOURAGEMENT TO MY CHILDREN BY . . .

Laugh or Cry

God has brought me laughter, and everyone who hears about this will laugh with me.

GENESIS 21:6 NIV

MY THOUGHTS:

_____
_____
_____
_____
_____
_____
_____
_____
_____
_____
_____
_____
_____
_____
_____
_____

I NEED TO SEE THE
HUMOR IN
SITUATIONS SUCH
AS . . .

In *The Christian Mother*, Jacky Hertz writes:

However sweet and lovable, babies are still very inconsiderate and often dirty creatures. Will I ever forget one day as we were living in Sitka, Alaska? All I had to do while Bill worked eight hours a day on a new naval base nearby was to keep up the tiny two-room house and care for our first baby, then eleven months old. Surely, some would say, I could have cleaned the entire 20-by-20-foot house in two hours a day and had leisure to spare. But life doesn't give us what we'd like.

One day the baby had been quiet too long. I went to the bedroom to see if all that silence was really sleep . . . The view that met my eyes made me want to turn and run crying, or beat my head against the wall . . . But I only began to laugh, and then to dissolve in hysterical giggles. Being fairly new to motherhood, I'd carelessly pinned his diaper with only two pins, one on either side. Now I saw he had soiled the diaper and, being wide awake, had begun to play . . . He'd smeared the sheet . . . the mattress . . . the bars of the crib . . . the bottoms of his feet . . . between his toes . . . his hands . . . his clothes . . . his face . . . his hair. Yet from the middle of all this unholy mess his eyes were so innocent!

The Future Begins Now

The wise man looks ahead. The fool attempts to fool himself and won't face facts.

PROVERBS 14:8 TLB

A man in Vermont once was invited to join a friend of his for a ride through the investments timberland in their area. His friend, a lumberjack, drove him up Mount Cushman in a jeep. Near the top of the mountain, he noticed some six-inch deciduous seedlings that had been planted by the lumberjack.

The man asked his friend when the seedlings would be ready to harvest for lumber, and the lumberjack replied, "In the year 2015." Noting that this was some sixty years into the future and that his friend was well into middle age, he asked his friend why he had planted the trees, since he would never see the harvest.

He replied, "Because my grandfather planted some on the other side of the mountain for me."[33]

Building for a successful future always requires:

F—faith that God will help you in your endeavor

U—unction to get started and stay motivated

T—thoughtful planning

U—undying persistence

R—reliance upon help from others

E—endurance through tough times

When we focus on God's plan for the future, it helps us make the right decisions today.

MY THOUGHTS:

WHAT INVESTMENTS CAN I MAKE IN MY CHILD'S FUTURE TODAY?

february 22

Little Eyes Are Watching

We wanted to set an example for you.
2 THESSALONIANS 3:9 CEV

MY THOUGHTS:

_____
_____
_____
_____
_____
_____
_____
_____
_____
_____
_____
_____
_____
_____
_____
_____
_____
_____

IN WHAT AREAS DO I NEED TO WORK ON SETTING A GOOD EXAMPLE?

Benjamin Franklin came to a personal conclusion that the lighting of streets would not only add gentility to his city but also make his city safer. In seeking to interest the people of his native Philadelphia in street lighting, however, he didn't try to persuade them by *talking* about it. Instead, he hung a beautiful lantern on a long bracket before his own door. Then he kept the glass brightly polished and carefully and diligently lit the wick every evening just as dusk approached.

People wandering down the dark street saw Franklin's light a long way off. They found its glow not only friendly and beautiful but a point of helpful guidance. Before long, other neighbors began placing lights on long brackets before their own homes. Soon, the entire city was dotted with such lights, and the people became aware of the value of street lighting. The matter was taken up with interest and enthusiasm as a city-wide, city-sponsored endeavor.

Just as Franklin's home was a beacon for his city, so, too, our actions as parents are like beacons to our children. What they see, they copy. And when what they see is good, what they copy is also *good*!

A Quiver Full

Like arrows in the hand of a warrior are the sons of one's youth. Happy is the man who has his quiver full of them.

PSALMS 127:4-5 NRSV

A mother already had five children under the age of ten when she gave birth to twins. The minister who came to see her in the hospital said, "I see the Lord has smiled on you again."

"Smiled?" the woman shrieked. "He laughed right out loud!"

Another woman once said to her visiting minister, "I thank God for my sons."

The minister replied, "I'm sure they're all good, productive citizens."

She replied, "Oh, yes. The firstborn is a doctor, the second became a lawyer, the third is a chemist, the fourth an artist, and the fifth a writer." The minister was obviously impressed, and then she added, "But thank God my husband and I had a dry goods store. Not a big one, mind you, but it was still enough for us to be able to support them all."

And finally there was the mother who remarked, "When I was young, my parents told me what to do. Now my children all tell me what to do. When is it that I get to do what I want to do?"

MY THOUGHTS:

_____
_____
_____
_____
_____
_____
_____
_____
_____
_____
_____
_____
_____
_____
_____
_____

WHAT STEPS CAN I TAKE TO ENSURE A PROPER ATTITUDE TOWARD MY CHILDREN?

For Love

Inasmuch as ye have done it unto one of the least of these . . . ye have done it unto me.

MATTHEW 25:40

MY THOUGHTS:

_____
_____
_____
_____
_____
_____
_____
_____
_____
_____
_____
_____
_____
_____
_____
_____
_____

LOVE FOR MY CHILDREN MOTIVATES ME TO . .
.

Perhaps the most famous "mother" in the world was Mother Teresa. As Sister Teresa in 1948, she was given permission to leave her order of nearly twenty years and travel to India. On her first day in Calcutta, Teresa picked up five abandoned children and brought them to her "school." Before the year ended, she had forty-one students learning about hygiene in her classroom in a public park. Shortly thereafter, a new congregation was approved. Mother Teresa quickly named it "Missionaries of Charity." Within two years, their attention had turned to the care of the dying.

Once a poor beggar was picked up as he was dying in a pile of rubbish. He was reduced by suffering and hunger to a mere specter. Mother Teresa took him to the Home for the Dying and put him in bed. When she tried to wash him, she discovered his body was covered with worms. Pieces of skin came off as she washed him. For a brief moment, the man revived. In his semi-conscious state, he asked, "Why do you do it?"

Mother Teresa responded with the two words that are her hallmark: "For love."

Ask any mother why she does what she does, and you are likely to receive the same answer. Love is both a mother's work . . . and a mother's reward.

A Well-Rounded Family

Be an example to the believers in word, in conduct, in love, in spirit, in faith, in purity.

1 TIMOTHY 4:12 NKJV

Behavioral pediatrician John Obedzinski saw two types of families in his practice. On one hand were well-educated parents who raised their children "progressively," allowing them total freedom of choice and expression. Their children were often sullen, arrogant, and totally self-absorbed. On the other hand were parents who were harsh disciplinarians and who made all their children's decisions. These children were often rebellious. Obedzinski set out to study resilient, happy families that seemed to weather life's ups and downs with loyalty and love. In doing so, he found these seven traits to be common:

- The children know their place—a family is not a democracy, and children do not have total freedom.
- The family values tradition and keeps treasured rituals, especially at holiday time.
- Family members admit their mistakes openly.
- Family members acknowledge their differences and try to accommodate them.
- Children are taught to compete against each other in ways that are fair and friendly.
- Children have chores and responsibilities.
- Family members tease one another and laugh at their own foibles, but the humor is never malicious.

MY THOUGHTS:

WHAT ADJUSTMENTS DO WE NEED TO MAKE TO CREATE A WELL-BALANCED FAMILY?

Seek God's Way

A man's own folly ruins his life, yet his heart rages against the Lord.
PROVERBS 19:3 NIV

MY THOUGHTS:

_____
_____
_____
_____
_____
_____
_____
_____
_____
_____
_____
_____
_____
_____
_____
_____

WHICH OF MY GOALS AM I CONFIDENT ARE PART OF GOD'S PLAN FOR MY LIFE? WHY DO I THINK SO?

Many years ago when Egyptian troops conquered Nubia, a regiment of soldiers was crossing the Nubian desert with an Arab guide.

Recognizing that they had limited water and were suffering from great thirst, the soldiers were deceived by the appearance of a beautiful lake on the horizon. They insisted that their guide take them to its banks. The guide, who knew the desert well, knew that what they saw was just a mirage. In vain, he told the men that the lake was not real. He refused to lose precious time by wandering from the designated course.

Angry words led to blows, and in the end, the soldiers killed the guide. As they moved toward the lake, it receded into the distance. Finally, they recognized their delusion—the lake was only burning sand. Raging thirst and horrible despair engulfed the soldiers. Without their guide, the pathless desert was a mystery. They were lost and without water. Not one of them survived.[34]

Be sure that what you seek today is not only within the realm of reality, but even more importantly, that it is part of God's plan for your life. Any other goal is likely to be unworthy of pursuit and may even be deadly.

A Good Name

A sterling reputation is better than striking it rich.
PROVERBS 22:1 MSG

The children of a prominent family thought long and hard about what they could give to their father as a present. They finally decided to commission a professional biographer to write a book detailing the family history. In meeting with the biographer, the children gave him numerous documents and anecdotes to weave into the account, as well as scores of photographs. Then one of the children said, "We have one more matter we need to discuss with you—the family's black sheep." In hushed whispers, they told about an uncle who had been convicted of first-degree murder and executed in the electric chair.

"No problem," the biographer assured the children, "I can handle this situation, so there will be no embarrassment."

"We don't want to lie," said one of the children.

The biographer agreed, "I'll merely say that Uncle Samuel occupied a chair of applied electronics at an important government institution. He was attached to his position by the strongest of ties, and his death came as a real shock."

A good reputation is something that can never be purchased or traded. It can only be acquired by choices rooted in integrity and morality.

MY THOUGHTS:

_____
_____
_____
_____
_____
_____
_____
_____
_____
_____
_____
_____
_____
_____
_____
_____
_____

WHAT STEPS CAN I TAKE TO TEACH MY CHILDREN THE IMPORTANCE OF HAVING A GOOD REPUTATION?

65

Love Isn't Denial

Every wise person acts with good sense, but fools show how foolish they are.

PROVERBS 13:16 NCV

MY THOUGHTS:

_____
_____
_____
_____
_____
_____
_____
_____
_____
_____
_____
_____
_____
_____
_____
_____
_____
_____

HOW DO I REACT TO THE MISTAKES AND WEAKNESSES OF MY CHILDREN? HOW CAN I IMPROVE?

During World War I, one of the most popular songs was about a rookie named Jim. The song recounts a mother telling a friend how she stood on the sidewalk and watched her son's regiment march by. Oh, how proud she was of him! But, as Jim came marching by, she noticed something amiss. All the other young men were putting down their right foot when Jim was putting down his left. When all the others were going right-left, Jim was marching left-right. She concludes, as many a proud mother might: "Were you there? And tell me did you notice? They were all out of step but Jim!"

Mothers should never live in denial about their children's mistakes or faults. Teaching our children to face their weaknesses is a wonderful way to help them grow strong. At the same time, the Scriptures tell us that "love covers a multitude of sins" (1 Peter 4:8). In truly loving people, we are not to deny their flaws but to say instead, "I choose to love them in spite of their mistakes and flaws and to focus instead on all the things that make them beautiful, wonderful, and lovable!"

Each Day Better than the Last

The path of the righteous is like the light of dawn, which shines brighter and brighter until full day.

PROVERBS 4:18 NRSV

A parable has been told about a young mother who asked her guide in life, "Is the way long?"

The guide said, "Yes and hard. You will be old before you reach the end of it, but the end will be better than the beginning." The young mother was happy at that news but and trust couldn't imagine any time being better than the days when she played with her children, gathered flowers for them, and bathed with them in clear streams.

Then night came and with it a storm. Her children shook with fear and cold, and their mother drew them close. They said, "We are not afraid, for you are near."

The mother said, "This is better than the brightness of day, for I have taught my children courage."

The next day, the mother and her children climbed a steep hill. When they reached the top, the children said, "We could not have done it without you, Mother."

She said, "This is a better day than the last, for my children have learned fortitude. I have given them strength."

The next day brought strange clouds of darkness—of war, hate, and evil. The children groped and stumbled, but their mother said, "Lift your eyes to the Light." That night she said, "This is the best day of all, for I have shown my children God."

And so it was, each day was better than the one before, until she died and began her most glorious day of all.[35]

MY THOUGHTS:

HOW CAN I INSTILL IN MY CHILDREN A CONFIDENT EXPECTATION AND TRUST IN GOD?

The Power of a Mother's Love

Love is always supportive, loyal, hopeful, and trusting.
1 CORINTHIANS 13:7 CEV

MY THOUGHTS:

_____
_____
_____
_____
_____
_____
_____
_____
_____
_____
_____
_____
_____
_____
_____
_____

WHAT STEPS CAN I TAKE TO INSPIRE MY CHILDREN TO TURN THEIR WEAKNESSES INTO STRENGTHS?

Sarah's second child was born with a clubfoot, just as her first child had been. At that time, such a child was called a "child of the devil." But that wasn't true in Sarah's thinking. When she saw that her son had a quick mind, she worked night and day for many years as a maid in other people's homes to pay for his education. She taught her son Thad to keep on fighting, no matter how great the odds against him, and she loved him with all her heart.

When young Thad was cruelly taunted as a "cripple" by his classmates, Sarah comforted and encouraged him, and with each passing year, he became more confident. Thaddeus eventually went to law school. His interest turned to those he saw as less fortunate than himself, especially black slaves.

He often paid the doctor bills of crippled boys, and he once spent three hundred dollars of his savings, intended for law books, to buy the freedom of a black man about to be sold away from his family. Over the years, Thaddeus Stevens became loved by American blacks as a hero second only to Abraham Lincoln, and he was considered the greatest defender of former slaves.

A mother's love truly can redeem a child's weakness and turn it into a strength!

Taking a Stand

In my integrity you uphold me and set me in your presence forever.

PSALM 41:12 NIV

Thirty years ago, Sandy Koufax—a Jewish pitcher for the Los Angeles situations Dodgers—announced that he wouldn't play on what he considered the holiest day of his year, Yom Kippur. Koufax's employer pointed out that it was the first game of the 1965 World Series. Couldn't he pitch just a little? "No," Koufax said. But he pitched a shutout in games five and seven, and the Dodgers won the series 4-3.

In 1996, Eli Herring, a 340-pound offensive tackle, who sported a 3.5 grade-point average, was expected to be the top senior offensive tackle in the pro draft. However, he turned down a possible multi-million-dollar deal with the Oakland Raiders because he wouldn't play on his holy day, Sunday.

Unfortunately, most of the Raiders' games were scheduled for Sundays. Herring could either sign up with the NFL and enjoy a very prosperous life or teach math for $20,000 a year, keep the Sabbath, and enjoy a very honorable life. He chose honor and conviction over riches.[36]

An old country-gospel song states the conviction underlying both men's decisions: "You can't be a beacon if your light don't shine."

MY THOUGHTS:

IN WHAT SITUATIONS CAN I SET AN EXAMPLE OF INTEGRITY FOR MY CHILDREN?

Time is Precious

Don't be fools; be wise: make the most of every opportunity you have for doing good.

EPHESIANS 5:16 TLB

MY THOUGHTS:

_____

_____

_____

_____

_____

_____

_____

_____

_____

_____

_____

_____

_____

_____

_____

_____

_____

WHAT STEPS CAN I TAKE TO ENSURE THAT I SPEND TIME EACH DAY WITH EACH OF MY CHILDREN?

While out of town on business, a father called his young son and asked, "What would you like for me to bring you?"

The two-year-old whispered, "Come out clock." The father wasn't sure he had understood him, so he asked his son to repeat his request. Again the boy said, "Come out clock." The man thought this fairly odd, but the next day on his way to the airport, he bought a large toy clock for his son. His son happily opened the present, played with it a few minutes, and then returned to doing what he had done virtually nonstop since his father had walked in the door: tug at his pants leg. The man looked at his wife as if to say, *What's going on? I don't get it.*

At that moment their cuckoo clock began to strike the hour, and on cue, figurines of a woodcutter and his wife popped out, chasing a little boy and girl, with all four then retreating into their cottage. The little boy looked up at the clock, then beamed at his father. The mother suddenly understood. "Each time the clock has struck the hour," she explained, "I've been telling our son, 'It's about time for Daddy to come home.' I think he must have been waiting for you to come out of the clock and chase him around the house!" The father promptly did, to glees of laughter!

Children soon learn how *precious* time is—that's why when a parent gives it to them, they feel so loved!

A Mother's Insight

They are wise and filled with insight.
PSALM 49:3 TLB

Jane Goodall spent more than thirty years in Africa and became the world's top authority on chimpanzees. She writes about the support that helped her get started:

When I decided that the place for me was Africa, everybody said to my mother, "Why don't you tell Jane to concentrate on something attainable?" But I have a truly remarkable mother. When I was two years old, I took a crowd of earthworms to bed to watch how they wriggled in the bedclothes. How many mothers would have said "ugh" and thrown them out the window? But mine said, "Jane, if you leave the worms here, they'll be dead in the morning. They need the earth." So I quickly gathered them up and ran with them into the garden. My mother always looked at things from my point of view.

Seeing things from your child's point of view is one of the most valuable ways to interact with your child! Periodically get down on the floor, and play with your child. As you do, show by example how to play, how to share, how to interact, how to cooperate, how to compete in a friendly manner, and how to put away toys or organize a play space. What you do, your child will do!

MY THOUGHTS:

HOW AM I DOING AT SEEING THINGS FROM MY CHILD'S PERSPECTIVE? HOW CAN I IMPROVE?

Learning to Diffuse Anger

The discretion of a man deferreth his anger; and it is his glory to pass over a transgression.

PROVERBS 19:11

MY THOUGHTS:

_____
_____
_____
_____
_____
_____
_____
_____
_____
_____
_____
_____
_____
_____
_____
_____
_____

WHAT POSITIVE STEPS CAN I TAKE TO DIFFUSE ANGER WHEN I FEEL IT RISING UP IN ME?

The great maestro Toscanini was as well known for his ferocious temper as he was for his outstanding musicianship. When members of his orchestra played badly, he often picked up whatever was within reach and hurled it to the floor in disgust. During one rehearsal, someone misplayed a flat note, causing the genius to grab his valuable watch and smash it. The watch was broken beyond repair.

Shortly afterward, Toscanini received a luxurious velvet-lined box from his devoted musicians. The box contained two watches—one a beautiful gold timepiece, the other a cheap watch. On the back of the cheap watch was inscribed the words, "For rehearsals only."

While Toscanini's temper affected material things, Homer's was quite different. Legend has it that Homer encountered a group of boys on their way home from a fishing trip. When he asked them about their luck, they replied, "What we caught, we threw away; what we didn't catch, we have." The boys were referring to fleas and their bites—not to fish. Homer, however, could not guess their riddle and became so enraged that he killed himself.[37]

Anger rarely has a positive outcome, in your own life or in the lives of those around you. Learn how to diffuse it!

Commandments for Parents

We were gentle among you, like a mother caring for her little children.

1 THESSALONIANS 2:7 NIV

Consider these "Commandments for Parents," written from a child's point of view!

· My hands are small; please don't expect perfection whenever I make a bed, draw a picture, or throw a ball. My legs are of these short; slow down, so I can keep up with you.

· My eyes have not seen the world as yours have; let me explore it safely; don't restrict me unnecessarily.

· Housework will always be there; I'm little only for a short time. Take time to explain things to me about this wonderful world, and do so willingly.

· My feelings are tender; don't nag me all day long (you would not want to be nagged for your inquisitiveness). Treat me as you would like to be treated.

· I am a special gift from God; treasure me as God intended you to do—holding me accountable for my actions, giving me guidelines to live by, and disciplining me in a loving manner.

· I need your encouragement (but not your empty praise) to grow. Go easy on the criticism; remember, you can criticize the things I do without criticizing me.

MY THOUGHTS:

_____
_____
_____
_____
_____
_____
_____
_____
_____
_____
_____
_____
_____
_____
_____
_____
_____

HOW WOULD MY CHILDREN RATE MY PERFORMANCE OF THESE COMMANDMENTS?

Attitude Adjustment

march 7

Each of you should look not only to your own interests, but also to the interests of others.

PHILIPPIANS 2:4 NIV

MY THOUGHTS:

_____
_____
_____
_____
_____
_____
_____
_____
_____
_____
_____
_____
_____
_____
_____
_____
_____

IN WHAT WAYS AM I MORE SELF-CENTERED THAN OTHER-CENTERED? HOW CAN I IMPROVE?

Edmond once vowed that he and his family would never be homeless. But a short time later, he lost his job, and then fire destroyed their home. Suddenly, they were homeless. Their only option was a shelter.

At the end of the first day there, Edmond's prayer was, "Lord, get me out of here." Elis attitude was extremely negative. In his opinion, the shelter's rules were humiliating. Residents had to be escorted across the street to the mission hall for their meals. They had to attend a church that helped support the shelter. When residents found work, they were expected to put 70 percent of their paycheck into a savings fund toward the day when they could move out of the shelter.

After pouring out all his complaints to the shelter's director, Edmond had a restless night. Tie realized that he had been focusing all his attention on getting out rather than on what he could be doing to make things easier for his family. That night, he changed his attitude. He started by taking a glass of water to a coughing man in the next room.

Nine months later, Edmond and his family had a home again. But he didn't forget what he had learned. He still visits the shelter, saying, "Wherever you are, God is there too." Attitude, not circumstances, made the real difference in his life.[38]

Parenting Will Keep You Humble

Boast not thyself of to morrow; for thou knowest not what a day may bring forth.

PROVERBS 27:1

After picking up their three-year-old daughter from her first day of nursery school, Rosanna Smith's husband left this message for her on the voice mail system at her office: "Hi, honey. The good news is that Amanda got through her first day at school. The bad news is the principal wants to meet with us."

A second message, recorded awhile later, updated the story: "The good news is that the parents of the boy she bit aren't suing. The bad news is that he had to go to the doctor because of it, and we'll be paying the bill."

Yet a third message, recorded minutes later, added: "The good news is that once we see her teacher, the school will accept Amanda back. The bad news is that Amanda has decided to drop out."

The message ended, "Have a good day!"

A mother once noted that her favorite saying was this: "And this, too, shall pass." It's a good thought to keep in mind when life takes unexpected twists and turns!

MY THOUGHTS:

_____
_____
_____
_____
_____
_____
_____
_____
_____
_____
_____
_____
_____
_____
_____
_____
_____

WHAT SITUATIONS DO I NEED TO VIEW AS A "THIS TOO, SHALL PASS" PHASE?

Does Your Mother Know?

march 9

Honor (esteem and value as precious) your father and your mother—
this is the first commandment with a promise—that all may he well
with you and that you may live long on the earth.

EPHESIANS 6:2-3 AMP

MY THOUGHTS:

_____
_____
_____
_____
_____
_____
_____
_____
_____
_____
_____
_____
_____
_____
_____
_____

*WHAT CAN I DO TO
SHOW MY MOTHER
HOW MUCH I
APPRECIATE HER?*

Leonard Pitts Jr. has described the feeling he had when business took him to Natchez, Mississippi, where his mother was born and raised. Driving the streets of the town, he recalled how he had dreamed of the riches he had once hoped to give his mother. He said:

The costliest gift I ever gave [her] was a plane ticket. Actually, my sisters and brother and I all chipped in on that . . . The ticket was a gift for what was to be her final birthday before cancer won its years-long battle. It seemed woefully inadequate in light of what she had given us: spirit riches in the shadow of poverty; security on the edge of apprehension; a home in a city jungle. Sick from heart disease and hypertension, abused by a husband who'd sold his soul to the bottle, she gave us ourselves. She made us women and men. What's a plane ticket compared with that?

Pitts had all but forgotten the gift until he stopped at the home of his mother's lifelong friend Isabel. She told him that his mother had said, "My life has been really rough. But if I didn't have my children, I don't know what I'd have done. My children sent me home for my birthday. I'd been wanting to come home one more time." Pitts reflected, "I had always wondered if she knew how grateful we were . . . She knew."[39]

Wise Person or Fool?

He who restrains his lips is wise.
PROVERBS 10:19 NASB

An evangelist from the early-American period once generalized that all infidels were fools. Furthermore, he said he could prove speech say his statement to be true for any given case within ten minutes.

A man in the audience stood up and proclaimed himself to be an infidel but no fool.

The preacher looked him over and said, "So you are an infidel?"

"Certainly, sir; I deny that there is anything at all in religion."

"Nothing at all in religion? Are you willing to go on record as saying that?"

"Go on record?" the infidel replied. "Why, I have been writing and lecturing against religion for twenty years."

The evangelist glanced at his watch and said, "Well, I said I could prove an infidel a fool in ten minutes, and I still have seven minutes left. I'll leave it to the audience to decide if a man isn't a fool to write and lecture for twenty years against a thing that supposedly has nothing whatever in it!"[40]

Before you speak your mind, make certain that there's something in your mind worth speaking.

MY THOUGHTS:

WHAT DOES MY SPEECH SAY ABOUT ME?

A Prayer Covering for Your Children

march 11

Each morning I will look to you in heaven and lay my requests before you, praying earnestly.

PSALM 5:3 TLB

MY THOUGHTS:

_____
_____
_____
_____
_____
_____
_____
_____
_____
_____
_____
_____
_____
_____
_____
_____
_____
_____
_____

IN WHAT AREAS DO I NEED TO PROVIDE MORE PRAYER COVERING FOR MY FAMILY?

The great preacher Billy Sunday told the story of a minister who was making calls one day. He came to one home, and when a child answered the door, he asked for her mother. She replied, "You cannot see Mother, for she prays from nine to ten." The minister waited forty minutes. When the woman finally came out of her "prayer closet," her face was filled with such light and glory that the minister said he knew immediately why her home was so peaceful, a haven of strength and light, and why her elder daughter was a missionary and her two sons were in the ministry. Billy Sunday added his comment, "All hell cannot tear a boy or girl away from a praying mother."

Remember to pray these things for your child:

- physical, emotional, and spiritual health
- an abiding sense of safety and security
- courage to face the problems of each day
- a calm spirit to hear the voice of the Lord
- a willingness to obey a clear mind, both to learn and to recall
- a generous spirit toward family and friends
- wise teachers, mentors, and counselors
- unshakable self-worth and personal dignity
- eternal salvation and a home in Heaven one day

Anything Standing in the Way?

Be ye reconciled to God. For he hath made him to he sin for us, who knew no sin; that we might be made the righteousness of God in him.

2 CORINTHIANS 5:20-21

For years, an atheist in a Greek village envied the serenity of a Christian friend. Finally, he asked his friend if he thought God would give him the same peace of mind. The Christian said, "Yes, I believe so, if you get to know Him."

The atheist asked, "But where can I meet this God?" The Christian said that he customarily went out several miles beyond the village and there met and talked with God.

The next morning the atheist walked out away from the village until he stood before a mountain. He cried, "Lord God Almighty, show me the kind of being You are!" He received no answer, although he cried out several times.

A few days later, he said to his Christian friend, "There is no God! I stood before the mountain day after day and called out to your God, but there was no answer. I asked Him to tell me the kind of being He is."

The Christian replied, "Well, my friend, when I go out there, I tell God the kind of person I am. I confess I am sinful and cannot exist apart from Him. Then God appears to me, and I understand Him better."

The atheist decided to try that approach and fell before the mountain, saying, "Lord, I am a sinful man. Forgive me." When he looked up, the mountain was gone. It had been only a shadow of himself, and once he was out of the way, he could see the Lord.[41]

MY THOUGHTS:

_____
_____
_____
_____
_____
_____
_____
_____
_____
_____
_____
_____
_____
_____
_____
_____
_____
_____

WHAT MOUNTAINS TRY TO STAND BETWEEN ME AND GOD? WHAT STEPS CAN I TAKE TO CHANGE THAT?

79

Open Heart, Open Home

Do not forget ... to extend hospitality ... being friendly, cordial, and gracious, sharing the comforts of your home ... for through it some have entertained angels without knowing it.

HEBREWS 13:2 AMP

MY THOUGHTS:

_____
_____
_____
_____
_____
_____
_____
_____
_____
_____
_____
_____
_____
_____
_____
_____
_____

WHAT STEPS CAN I TAKE TO CREATE A WARM AND INVITING ATMOSPHERE IN OUR HOME?

Corrie ten Boom's character was shaped to a great extent by the people who visited her home. Her mother, a gentle and compassionate woman, was able to bring harmony even to cramped quarters filled with divergent personalities. She loved guests and had a gift for "stretching a guilder until it cried." Those who came to their home found music, fun, food, and interesting conversations. Corrie kept a "blessing box" to collect coins for missionary projects, and she always gave guests an opportunity to be a blessing, even as they were blessed by her family's hospitality. The soup may have been watered down, but the oval table always had room for unexpected guests who arrived just before mealtime. The atmosphere was one of *gezellig*, of warm exuding friendship, and it wove its way into the very fabric of Corrie's personality.

In later years as Corrie ten Boom traveled the world and was dependent upon the invitations of other Christians, she seldom stayed in hotels. Instead, she graciously accepted food and lodging from others. She once said, "I think that I am enjoying the reward for the wide-open doors and hearts of our home." To those she visited, however, she was now the angel unaware, bringing with her welcome *gezellig*.

Encouraging Words

Hold them in very high and most affectionate esteem.
1 THESSALONIANS 5:13 AMP

Children's stories often provide profound insights into life. The tales of Winnie the Pooh are a good source for friendly and warm words, as evidenced by the following story told on a Pooh Bear recording:

One day Pooh Bear is about to go for a walk in the Hundred Acre Wood. It's about 11:30 in the morning. It is a fine time to go calling—just before lunch. So Pooh sets out across the stream, stepping on the stones, and when he gets right in the middle of the stream, he sits down on a warm stone and thinks about just where would be the best place of all to make a call.

He says to himself, "I think I'll go see Tigger." No, he dismisses that. Then he says, "Owl!" Then, "No, Owl uses big words, hard-to-understand words."

At last he brightens up! "I know! I think I'll go see Rabbit. I like Rabbit. Rabbit uses encouraging words like, 'How's about lunch?' and 'Help yourself, Pooh!' Yes, I think I'll go see Rabbit."

Give some oxygen—in the form of encouragement—to your child daily.

MY THOUGHTS:

_____

_____

_____

_____

_____

_____

_____

_____

_____

_____

_____

_____

_____

_____

TODAY I WILL GIVE AN ENCOURAGING WORD TO MY CHILD REGARDING . . .

The Whole Truth

We keep everything we do and say out in the open, the whole truth on display, so that those who want to can see and judge for themselves in the presence of God.

2 CORINTHIANS 4:2 MSG

MY THOUGHTS:

_____
_____
_____
_____
_____
_____
_____
_____
_____
_____
_____
_____
_____
_____
_____
_____
_____
_____

HOW DO I HANDLE THINGS I'D RATHER NOT HEAR?

A missionary in Brazil once ran a camp near the Parana river. On days when the temperature reached a scorching 120 degrees, he was tempted to swim in the cool river waters but was leery because of the man-eating fish that he knew inhabited them. His neighbors assured him, however, that piranhas only bite people while swimming in schools and that they never swam in schools in that part of the river. So each afternoon for the rest of the summer, the missionary enjoyed a swim.

Months later, the missionary heard a report that a local fisherman had fallen out of his boat and had not been found. Alarmed, he asked his neighbors if perhaps the man had been eaten by piranhas. "Oh, no," they said. "Only while swimming in schools do piranhas bite people, and they never swim in schools around here."

"But why not around here?" the missionary pressed.

"Oh," his neighbor casually replied, "they never swim in schools in places where there are alligators."[42]

It's always important when hearing things you want to hear—especially statements that offer reassurance, flattery, or approval—that you question what is not being said. The whole truth always acknowledges the negative.

See the Humor in Everything

A cheerful heart fills the day with song.
PROVERBS 15:15 MSG

In his best-seller *Fatherhood*, Bill Cosby tells of a decision that he and his wife made about their children using the family car: "We would not allow any of the children to have a driver's license as long as he or she was living with us." He asks, "Does this sound unreasonable to you?" Cosby goes on to write:

One memorable day, one of these children did drive to town just to see if she could do it while unencumbered by a license. It was a Saturday morning, and my wife and I had just finished breakfast. I walked over to the sink to rinse out a glass, and there I suddenly saw our car going past the kitchen window. Turning to my wife, I said, "Dear, did you just drive by here?"

"No," she replied.

"Well, am I in this kitchen?"

"As far as I can tell."

"Then why did I just go by in the car?"

MY THOUGHTS:

_____
_____
_____
_____
_____
_____
_____
_____
_____
_____
_____
_____
_____
_____
_____
_____

HOW CAN I MAINTAIN A GOOD SENSE OF HUMOR WITHOUT COMPROMISING DISCIPLINE IN OUR HOME?

People Are Watching You

Abstain from all appearance of evil.
1 THESSALONIANS 5:22

MY THOUGHTS:

_____
_____
_____
_____
_____
_____
_____
_____
_____
_____
_____
_____
_____
_____
_____
_____
_____
_____

WHAT DO MY ACTIONS SAY ABOUT ME?

A young farmer in the West had a reputation for frequenting the local bar, which was located in the town's hotel. Then, he became a Christian. Whenever he visited town, however, he continued to tie his team of horses to the hotel hitching post. An elderly deacon from the town church couldn't help but notice this practice. He said, "George, I'm a good deal older than you, and I know you will pardon me if I make a suggestion from my experience. No matter how strong you think you are, take my advice and change your hitching post at once."[43]

There are times when "changing your hitching post" is an important part of your Christian witness. A couple in a sophisticated urban area discovered this in a slightly different way after their conversion. They had long been part of a social set in which alcohol freely flowed. After becoming Christians, they discovered that when they tried to tell their friends about Christ, they were highly ineffective as long as they were holding glasses in their hands—even though their glasses contained soft drinks. When they switched to holding coffee cups, however, people noticed the changes in the rest of their behavior, which gave credibility to their testimony.

When you proclaim Christ in your life, people expect to see a difference in how you act.

A Wise Answer

All I want is a reasonable answer—then I will keep quiet.

JOB 6:24 TLB

A little girl once asked her grandmother, "How old are you?"

The grandmother replied, "Now dear, you shouldn't ask people that question. Most grown-ups don't like to tell their age."

The next day the little girl had another question. She asked, "Grandma, how much do you weigh?"

The grandmother said, "Oh, honey, you shouldn't ask grown-ups how much they weigh. It isn't polite."

The third day the little girl came to her grandmother with a big smile and announced, "Grandma, I know how old you are. You're sixty-two. And I also know that you weigh 140 pounds."

"My goodness," the grandmother said, "how do you know all that?"

The little girl replied, "You left your driver's license on the table, and I read it." And then the little girl added, "And I also saw on your driver's license that you flunked sex."

Three of the greatest things you can do as a parent are:

1. Answer your children's questions as completely as possible.

2. Give your children information they need to have, and spare them knowledge they don't need.

3. Take time to converse with your children.

Each of these things is a genuine act of love!

MY THOUGHTS:

_____
_____
_____
_____
_____
_____
_____
_____
_____
_____
_____
_____
_____
_____
_____
_____
_____
_____

HOW WELL AM I ANSWERING MY CHILD'S QUESTIONS?

Love Cultivates

I made you grow like a plant of the field. You grew up and developed and became the most beautiful of jewels.

EZEKIEL 16:7 NIV

MY THOUGHTS:

_____
_____
_____
_____
_____
_____
_____
_____
_____
_____
_____
_____
_____
_____

TODAY I WILL CULTIVATE MY CHILD'S CONFIDENCE BY . . .

Jane lavished on her children the kind of love that empowered not enslaved. She taught all four of her children how to play baseball, bake a cake, and play fair. Her daughter Janet recalls, "She loved us with all her heart. She taught us her favorite poets. And there is no child care in the world that will ever be a substitute for what that lady was in our lives . . . My mother always told me to do my best, to think my best, and to do right and consider myself a person."

Maggy, another daughter, recalls, "What gave us our self-confidence was the absolute certainty that every adult in our world loved us absolutely. They weren't always perfect, and we weren't always perfect. But we could count on that love."

Jane received love in return. Her daughter Janet declined to be considered for a job in President Clinton's administration until after her mother's death, so she might remain by her ailing mother's side. When Janet Reno finally did accept a position, it was as attorney general of the United States —the first woman to head the Justice Department.

Take All in Stride

Do everything without complaining or arguing.
PHILIPPIANS 2:14 NIV

Astronaut Shannon Lucid was not supposed to set an American record for time spent in space. However, her assignment was extended almost two months because of technical difficulties with shuttle booster rockets and two hurricanes. The result was that Lucid stayed in space 188 days, setting a United States space endurance record and a world record for a woman. She returned to earth to high accolades from politicians and NASA officials, as well as to the loving arms of her family members.

What many reports failed to note in the wake of Lucid's record-setting stay on the Russian space station Mir was the excellent reputation that Lucid had with her Russian hosts. That reputation was based not only on her technical expertise as an astronaut but also on the fact that her Russian counterparts never once heard her complain during her six-month stay. Every time Lucid was notified of a shuttle delay, she took the news in stride.

Valery Ryumin, a Russian space manager, noted that Lucid reacted like Russian cosmonauts do when their missions are extended: Russians deliberately choose cosmonauts "who are strong enough not to show any feelings" when receiving bad news.[44]

Complaining not only makes you feel negative, but it spreads your negativity to others. Even an unpleasant or disappointing situation can become positive when you have a good attitude and speak uplifting words.

MY THOUGHTS:

HOW DO I REACT WHEN ENCOUNTERING UNPLEASANT SITUATIONS? AN EXAMPLE WOULD BE . . .

Outlook and Outcome

Today I have given you the choice between life and death, between blessings and curses. I call on heaven and earth to witness the choice you make. Oh, that you would choose life, that you and your descendants might live!

DEUTERONOMY 30:19 NLT

MY THOUGHTS:

_____
_____
_____
_____
_____
_____
_____
_____
_____
_____
_____
_____
_____
_____
_____
_____
_____

WHAT IS MY OUTLOOK ON LIFE TODAY?

Kenneth was a high-school football star and later, an avid wrestler, boxer, hunter, and skin-diver. Then, a broken neck sustained in a wrestling match left him paralyzed from the chest down. He underwent therapy, and his doctors were hopeful that one day he would be able to walk with the help of braces and crutches.

The former athlete could not reconcile himself to his physical limitations, however, so he prevailed upon two of his best friends to take him in his wheelchair to a wooded area. They left him alone there with a twelve-gauge shotgun. After they left, he held the shotgun to his abdomen and pulled the trigger. He committed suicide at the age of twenty-four.

At the age of nineteen, Jim was stabbed, leaving him paralyzed from the middle of his chest down. Although confined to a wheelchair, he lives alone, cooks his own meals, washes his clothes, and cleans his house. He drives himself in his specially equipped automobile. He has written three books and was the photographer for the first book on the history of wheelchair sports. Thirty years after his injury, he made a successful parachute jump, landing precisely on his target.[45]

Kenneth and Jim had nearly identical injuries and physical limitations. Their outlooks, however, led to vastly different outcomes.

Selflessness

"He that is greatest among you shall be your servant."

MATTHEW 23:11

C harles Lamb was once deeply in love with a woman, but he never married. Rather, he willingly chose to fill the role of "guardian angel" of his childhood home and especially of his sister Mary who at times was mentally deranged. He saw his foremost responsibilities in life as those of son and brother.

After Mary stabbed their mother to death in one of her mad spells, Charles turned away from any pursuits that might have furthered or enhanced his own life, and for thirty-eight years he watched over Mary with tender care. A friend has told how he sometimes would see the brother and sister walking hand in hand across the field to the old asylum, their faces bathed in tears.

The story of Charles Lamb is a sad story yet a grand one. He had a purpose in life; he had a role—and it was never left empty.[46]

In our self-centered world, we tend to dismiss the greatness of people like Charles Lamb. And yet without those who make such sacrifices, there is little we could count as noble or admirable in our culture. It is the willingness to take on responsibilities that require selfless giving that truly makes a person great.

MY THOUGHTS:

_____
_____
_____
_____
_____
_____
_____
_____
_____
_____
_____
_____
_____
_____
_____
_____
_____
_____

TODAY I WILL CHOOSE SELFLESSNESS BY . . .

A Mother's Influence

Reject not nor forsake the teaching of your mother.
PROVERBS 1:8 AMP

MY THOUGHTS:

_____
_____
_____
_____
_____
_____
_____
_____
_____
_____
_____
_____
_____
_____
_____
_____
_____

WHAT CHARACTER
TRAITS DO I FEEL
IMPRESSED TO
TEACH MY
CHILDREN AT THIS
TIME?

Lech Walesa, the first freely elected president of Poland in fifty years and the 1983 winner of the Nobel Peace Prize, credits his mother for teaching him the values that led to his success. He writes the following about her in his book, *Lech Walesa: A Way of Hope.*

She is the only person from my childhood I still have a really clear recollection of. She took an interest in history and current affairs, and read a great deal. In the evenings, she would sometimes read to us. We took great pleasure in these moments. All the stories our mother told us had a moral in them: they taught one to be honest, to strive always to better oneself, to be just, and to call white white and black black. Mother was very religious. My faith can be said almost to have flowed into me with my mother's milk.

The children in the Walesa home were kept on a "tight rein," he recalls. Even the youngest had jobs to do—tending geese, taking the cows out to pasture, doing a variety of manual jobs.

Wisdom, faith, and discipline all have a mother's knee as their first foundation—and what a strong and wonderful foundation it can be if the mother is a woman who seeks those same qualities in her own life!

Talking Their Language

How wonderful to be wise, to understand things, to be able to analyze them and interpret them. Wisdom lights up a man's face, softening its hardness.

ECCLESIASTES 8:1 TLB

The name Albert Einstein is synonymous with that of "genius." Many don't know, however, that Einstein was a late talker. His parents grew quite worried about this. Then, at supper one night, he broke his silence with a full sentence, saying, "The soup is too hot." Overjoyed, his greatly relieved parents asked him why he hadn't with my spoken before. He said, "Because up to now everything was in order."

Oftentimes, it is a struggle for parents to get their children to talk—not just their babies but also their teens. Babies are busy learning their parents' language, but as they grow older, a shift occurs, and suddenly the parents are trying to understand the language of their teens! This shift happens in several stages. First, children go through the "Why?" stage. When their parents don't have answers, the children enter their own "I know" stage. Next, they add vocabulary words they don't learn from their parents. "Jam" and "cool" take on new meanings. The children then ask more questions, using these new words, such as "Why are you jammin' fifty in a school zone?" and "Is it ever cool to break the law?" Finding that their parents *still* don't have answers, teens take to the telephone to talk to someone who does—another teen. The solution to the communication gap with your teenagers may very well be: *Make up some answers!*

MY THOUGHTS:

_____
_____
_____
_____
_____
_____
_____
_____
_____
_____
_____
_____
_____
_____
_____

WHAT STEPS CAN I TAKE TO BEGIN NARROWING THE COMMUNICATION GAP WITH MY CHILDREN?

Too Much of a Good Thing

"Wear my yoke—for it fits perfectly—and let me teach you; for I am gentle and humble, and you shall find rest for your souls; for I give you only light burdens."

MATTHEW 11:29-30 TLB

MY THOUGHTS:

_____
_____
_____
_____
_____
_____
_____
_____
_____
_____
_____
_____
_____
_____
_____

WHAT THINGS DO I NEED TO SAY "NO" TO IN ORDER TO GIVE MORE ATTENTION TO MY FAMILY?

Linda was a perfectionist as a wife and mother. She kept a spotless house; served excellent meals; and was a willing volunteer at church, her children's school, and in the community. She tried to be all things to all people and was often frustrated and physically exhausted. Still, she was unwilling to give up any of her commitments or lower her standards. She felt she needed to be perfect and do everything she did in order to keep her husband's love.

A crisis came for Linda when her husband told her he would leave her if she didn't slow down and give up some of her responsibilities. She responded in anger and assumed even more responsibility than before. She was eventually hospitalized for exhaustion.

While in the hospital, Linda feared things would go to pieces in her absence from her home and community. When she saw that the world did indeed go on without her—her children still wore clean clothes, meals were still cooked, the various boards and committees continued to function—Linda began to relax for the first time in years. The result was not only the restoration of her own health but the strengthening of her relationship with her family.[47]

Choose to do what you do well, but make your choices wisely, and limit them to what is truly required.

Giving Love Away

"God so loved the world, that he gave his only begotten Son, that whosoever believeth in him should not perish, but have everlasting life."

JOHN 3:16

One evening just before Mary Martin, the great Broadway musical star, was to go on stage in *South Pacific*, a note was handed to her. It was from Oscar Hammerstein, who had written this to her from his deathbed: "Dear Mary, A bell's not a bell till you ring it. A song's not a song till you sing it. Love in your heart is not put there to stay. Love isn't love till you give it away."

After her performance that night, a number of people rushed backstage, exclaiming, "Mary, what happened to you out there tonight? We have never heard anything like that performance! You sang with more power than you've ever sung!"

Blinking back tears, Mary then read them the note from Hammerstein and added, "Tonight, I gave my love away!"

Even the poorest people have something to give to others if they have love in their hearts. Love's gifts take many forms—a smile, a hug, a note of thanks, "just being there" in tough times. Love is the one gift that always fits, is always appropriate, and is always in season and in fashion.

MY THOUGHTS:

TO WHOM CAN I GIVE A SPECIAL GIFT OF LOVE TODAY? AN EXAMPLE WOULD BE . . .

The Two-Sided Coin

march 27

"When you do a kindness to someone, do it secretly—don't tell your left hand what your right hand is doing. And your Father, who knows all secrets, will reward you."

MATTHEW 6:3-4 TLB

MY THOUGHTS:

_____
_____
_____
_____
_____
_____
_____
_____
_____
_____
_____
_____
_____
_____
_____
_____
_____
_____
_____

WHAT THINGS CAN I GIVE IN SECRET TODAY?

Giving is like a two-sided coin. The more we "open up" in our attitude toward giving, the more our attitude toward seeing the blessings that God has and is pouring into our lives "opens up." But the secret to activating this principle appears to be giving without desiring public acclaim. Our giving must be "pride free." This principle is captured well in the following poem by an unknown author:

> I did a favor yesterday,
> A kindly little deed,
> And then I called to all the world
> To stop and look and heed.
> They stopped and looked and flattered me
> In words I could not trust,
> And when the world had gone away,
> My good deed turned to dust.
> A very tiny courtesy I found to do today;
> Twas quickly done with none to see,
> And then I ran away
> But someone must have witnessed it,
> For—truly—I declare
> As I sped back the stony path
> Roses were blooming there.[48]

94

Rich in Memories

Her children arise up, and call her blessed.
PROVERBS 31:28

In 1932, Violet married a union organizer and within a few years, had four sons. When she was pregnant a fifth time, gangsters moved to take over the union, and her husband left her, feeling his family was safer without him. Violet and her sons moved into a tiny apartment, and a few months later, a daughter was born. To feed her family, Violet worked days at the National Silver Company and nights at a drugstore. She would work, have bouillon for lunch, finish her first job, pick up a kidney for twenty-five cents to make soup, tell the children not to mind the taste, go to the second job, come home and wash out the children's socks and shirts, catch a couple of hours of sleep, and begin her next day. On days off, she waited tables, and on holidays, she worked at a department store.

Over the years, she worked in a cracker factory, hawked ice cream, labeled medicine bottles, cleaned offices, and pushed a coffee cart. In 1959, she became an orderly in a home for the aged, and seventeen years later she retired with a pension of $31.78 a month. For the first time since 1946, she had a week off! Thomas, her son, perhaps paid her the highest tribute possible, saying he had only "happy memories" of his childhood: "We didn't even know we were poor until years later."

MY THOUGHTS:

WHAT KIND OF MEMORIES AM I CREATING FOR MY CHILDREN?

Build Them Up

I want to use the authority the Lord has given me to build you up, not to tear you down.

2 CORINTHIANS 13:10 NLT

MY THOUGHTS:

_____
_____
_____
_____
_____
_____
_____
_____
_____
_____
_____
_____
_____
_____
_____

WHAT KIND OF MARK AM I LEAVING ON MY CHILDREN?

The following poem, first published in *The Bible Friend*, speaks about the great influence that a mother has:

> I took a piece of plastic clay
> And idly fashioned it one day;
> And as my fingers pressed it still,
> It moved and yielded at my will.
> I came again when days were past,
> The form I gave it still it bore,
> And as my fingers pressed it still,
> I could change that form no more.
> I took a piece of living clay,
> And gently formed it day by day,
> And molded with my power and art,
> A young child's soft and yielding heart.
> I came again when days were gone;
> It was a man I looked upon,
> He still that early impress bore,
> And I could change it never more.

Every word . . . every action . . . leaves a mark upon your child, for good or for bad. Little things to an adult sometimes loom large for a child. What may seem to you an insignificant comment or deed may turn out to be the one thing your child remembers!

Cancel the Date

I keep under my body, and bring it into subjection: lest that by any means, when I have preached to others, I myself should be a castaway.

1 CORINTHIANS 9:27

In *Sin, Sex and Self-Control*, Norman Vincent Peale writes:

Martha took the kids away to the mountains for a month, so I was a summer bachelor. And about mid-way through that month I met a girl, a beautiful girl looking for excitement. She made it clear that I had a green light . . . so for one weekend I put my conscience in mothballs and arranged a meeting with her for Saturday night.

I woke up early Saturday morning with a bit of a hangover; I'd played poker until late the night before. I decided to get up, put on my swimming trunks, and take a walk on the beach to clear my head. I took an ax along, because the wreck of an old barge had come ashore down the beach, and there was a lot of tangled rope that was worth salvaging . . . There was something about the freshness of the morning and the feel of the ax that made me want to keep on swinging it. So I began to chop in earnest.

I felt as if I were outside myself, looking at myself through a kind of fog that was gradually clearing. And suddenly I knew that what I had been planning for that evening was so wrong, so out of key with my standards and my loyalties and the innermost me that it was out of the question.[49]

Step back, and take a good look at yourself. Is there something you need to get a clear view on today?

MY THOUGHTS:

_____
_____
_____
_____
_____
_____
_____
_____
_____
_____
_____
_____
_____
_____
_____
_____

HOW AM I DOING WHEN IT COMES TO DISCIPLING MY DESIRES? AN EXAMPLE WOULD BE . . .

march 31

I will forget my complaint, I will change my expression, and smile.
JOB 9:27 NIV

MY THOUGHTS:

----

*I NEED TO DEVELOP
A SENSE OF HUMOR
WHEN IT COMES TO .
. .*

Kathy and Jim were longing for the day when their precious baby would eventually sleep all the way through the night. Originally they had agreed to take turns getting up when she cried. But Jim frequently gave in to the urge to prompt his wife into taking his turn by saying, "Honey, she's probably hungry." That, of course, was a problem only a nursing mother could address.

Their fatigue, however, was greatly mitigated by the considerable joy they had in watching little Anna grow and gain new skills, not the least of which was her attempt at learning to talk. Kathy knew that most babies speak "Dada" as their first word, and she knew that her beloved husband would be thrilled if Anna's first word was, indeed, for him. So, day after day, she worked with her bright baby to teach her to say what she was sure would be a magical word to Daddy's ears.

One night, all of Kathy's diligence paid off. At 2:15am, Anna awoke and cried "Dada" at the top of her lungs. Kathy turned over and said softly to her husband beside her, "She's calling for you, dear, and I'm sure this is something only you can handle."

Do Them Right

"If someone grabs your shirt, gift-wrap your best coat and make a present of it. If someone takes unfair advantage of you, use the occasion to practice the servant life. No more tit-for-tat stuff. Live generously."

LUKE 6:29-30 MSG

Ben was disgusted with himself for having let the bill grow so large. He was a home-delivery milkman and had allowed a pretty young woman with six children and another on the way to fall seventy-nine dollars behind on her account. She told him repeatedly, "I'm going to pay you soon, when my husband gets a second job." Ben believed her. But eventually she moved away and left no forwarding address. He was angry that he had been so gullible and even more angry about the loss of the seventy-nine dollars, which would have to come from his own pocket.

A friend made an unusual suggestion: "Give the milk to the woman. Make it a Christmas present to the kids who needed it."

Ben replied, "Are you kidding? I don't even get my wife a Christmas gift that expensive."

"Perhaps not," the friend said, "but you've already lost the income. What do you have to lose?"

Ben resisted the idea, but in the end, he told his friend, "I did it! I gave her the milk as a Christmas present. It wasn't easy, but I really do feel better. Those kids had lots of milk on their cereal just because of me." He not only felt better toward the woman but toward all his other customers. His cheerful nature was restored.[50]

MY THOUGHTS:

_____
_____
_____
_____
_____
_____
_____
_____
_____
_____
_____
_____
_____
_____
_____
_____
_____
_____

WHOM DO I NEED TO RELEASE FROM A DEBT THEY OWE?

april 2

Influencing for All Eternity

What a woman your mother was—like a lioness! Her children were like lion's cubs!

EZEKIEL 19:2 TLB

MY THOUGHTS:

_____
_____
_____
_____
_____
_____
_____
_____
_____
_____
_____
_____
_____
_____
_____

WHAT ARE THE CHARACTER TRAITS I MOST DESIRE TO INSTILL IN MY CHILDREN? I CAN DO THIS BY . . .

"Whenever I held my new-born baby in my arms," Rose once said, "I used to think that what I said and did to him could have an influence not only on him, but on all whom he met, not only for a day or a month or a year, but for all eternity— a very, very challenging and exciting thought for a mother." Feeling this duty, Rose became a natural and determined teacher of her children, leading them by discovery, story, example, and inspiration to fulfill their own destinies.

Rose engaged her children in conversation about history and politics, and when guests visited their home, she expected her children to ask questions and offer opinions. Even though the family was wealthy, the boys were expected to fix their own bicycles and were required to earn their own pocket money. She gave each child a sense of independence and privacy yet dressed them with similar clothes, so they would feel a part of a whole family unit. Rose expected her children to be self-confident adults and independent thinkers, with compassion for those less fortunate.

And she succeeded. Among Rose Kennedy's children, son John became president of the United States; son Robert, attorney general; and son Edward, a United States senator.

Practice What You Preach

If we say that we have fellowship with Him, and walk in darkness, we lie and do not practice the truth.

1 JOHN 1:6 NKJV

Two boys were walking home from church one day. They began talking about the Sunday school lesson they had heard earlier in the morning.

"That would really be something," one of the boys said, "to be out in a wilderness for forty days and nights."

"Yeah," said the other boy, "and not eat. Jesus must have been real strong."

"It would have been kind of scary, too," said the first boy, "to have the devil show up and tempt you."

The second little boy didn't respond, so the first boy asked, "Do you believe that stuff about the devil? Do you think there really is a devil?"

The second little boy looked at his friend and said, "Naaah, he's probably just like Santa Claus—it's really just your dad."

Not only do children copy the mannerisms of their parents, they are quick to zero in on their parents' traits, beliefs, and values. Would your child call you a Christian today? Does your child know what you believe and why? Does your child know how important your faith is to you?

The most important person to whom you can witness about your faith is your own child.

MY THOUGHTS:

_____
_____
_____
_____
_____
_____
_____
_____
_____
_____
_____
_____
_____
_____
_____
_____
_____

WHAT STEPS CAN I TAKE TO BECOME A MORE EFFECTIVE CHRISTIAN WITNESS TO MY CHILDREN?

Honeycomb Givers

"Whosoever drinketh of the water that I shall give him shall never thirst; but the water that I shall give him shall be in him a well of water springing up into everlasting life."

JOHN 4:14

MY THOUGHTS:

_____
_____
_____
_____
_____
_____
_____
_____
_____
_____
_____
_____
_____
_____
_____
_____

WHAT TYPE OF GIVER AM I? AN EXAMPLE WOULD BE
. . .

There are three kinds of givers: the flint, the sponge, and the honeycomb.

To get anything from the flint, you must hammer it. And even then, you generally get only chips and sparks. It gives nothing away if it can help it and even then only with a great display.

To get anything from the sponge, you must squeeze it. It is good-natured. It readily yields to pressure, and the more it is pressed, the more it gives. Still, you must press.

To get anything from the honeycomb, you must only take what flows from it. It takes delight in giving, without pressure, without begging or badgering. It gives its sweetness freely.

There is another difference in the honeycomb. It is a renewable resource. Unlike the flint or sponge, the honeycomb is connected to life—it is the product of ongoing work and creative energy.

One of the reasons "honeycomb givers" are able to give freely is that they are aware that their lives are continually being replenished. They believe that what they give away will soon be regenerated.[51]

As long as you are connected to the Source of all giving, you can never run dry. When you give freely, you will receive in like manner.

A Living Letter

You show that you are a letter from Christ . . . not written with ink but with the Spirit of the living God. It is not written on stone tablets but on human hearts.

2 CORINTHIANS 3:3 NCV

The story is told of four scholars who were arguing over the beauty and accuracy of various Bible translations.

One scholar argued for the *King James Version*, citing its beautiful, eloquent old English.

The second scholar advocated the *American Standard Bible*. He cited its literalism—the way it moved a reader from passage to passage with confident feelings of accuracy from the original texts.

The third scholar said he preferred the translation by Moffatt. He praised its quaint, penetrating use of words, the turn of a phrase that captured the attention of the reader.

After giving thought to each of the lengthy and impassioned arguments presented, the fourth scholar said, "Frankly, I have always preferred my mother's translation."

Knowing that his mother was not a Bible translator nor a scholar, the other three chuckled and said, "No, seriously . . ."

The man did not waver. "I stand by my claim," he said. "My mother translated each page of the Bible into life. And it was the most convincing translation I have ever seen."

MY THOUGHTS:

WHAT KIND OF TRANSLATION DO MY CHILDREN SEE IN ME? AN EXAMPLE WOULD BE . . .

103

An Overactive Imagination

april 6

We are destroying speculations and every lofty thing raised up against the knowledge of God, and we are taking every thought captive to the obedience of Christ.

2 CORINTHIANS 10:5 NASB

MY THOUGHTS:

_____

_____

_____

_____

_____

_____

_____

_____

_____

_____

_____

_____

_____

_____

_____

_____

_____

WHAT STEPS CAN I TAKE TO GAIN BETTER CONTROL OVER MY IMAGINATION?

A man was driving down a country road late one night when his tire blew out. He opened his trunk only to discover he had forgotten to replace the jack the last time he saw light from a farmhouse in the distance and began walking toward it, hoping to borrow a jack. On the way, he mused, *I'll knock on the door and say, "I'm in trouble and would you please lend me a jack." He'll say, "Sure."*

As he walked, however, he noticed that the light in the house had gone out. He thought to himself, *Now he's gone to bed, and he'll be mad because I've awakened him. I'd better offer him a dollar for his trouble.*

The man continued the imaginary conversation in his head as he walked. *What if he is away and his wife is alone? She'll be afraid to open the door. I'd better offer five dollars.* This amount, however, seemed too high. *Five dollars! All right but not a cent more. What are you trying to do, rob a man?* By this time he was on the porch of the farmhouse.

He knocked loudly. When the farmer in residence leaned out the upstairs window and asked, "Who's there?" the stranger yelled back at him, "You and your stupid jack! You can keep the wretched thing!"[52]

Much of the struggle in life comes not from actual circumstances we encounter but from our overactive imaginations.

A Mother's Life

She looketh well to the ways of her household, and eateth not the bread of idleness.

PROVERBS 31:27

Harriet Rukenbrod Day's poem "A Mother's Dilemma" humorously depicts the chaos of motherhood:

Baby's in the cookie jar
Sister's in the glue
Kitty's in the birdie's cage
And I am in a stew!
Time for dad to come to lunch
Someone's spilled the roses
Breakfast dishes still undone
The twins have drippy noses.
Junior has the stove apart
Dinner guests at eight
Neighbors' kids swoop in like flies
How can I concentrate?
Telephone keeps ringing wildly
Someone's in the hall
Fido's chewed the rug to bits
The preacher's come to call!
Would mothers like to chuck their load?
They couldn't stand the rap
Easy mild existences
Would cause their nerves to snap!

MY THOUGHTS:

_____
_____
_____
_____
_____
_____
_____
_____
_____
_____
_____
_____
_____
_____
_____
_____
_____
_____

WHAT THINGS CAN I DO TO EXPERIENCE PEACE IN THE MIDST OF CHAOS?

Who Will Your Baby Become?

She conceived . . . and said, I have gotten a man from the Lord.
GENESIS 4:1

MY THOUGHTS:

_____

_____

_____

_____

_____

_____

_____

_____

_____

_____

_____

_____

_____

_____

_____

_____

_____

_____

WHAT THINGS CAN I DO TODAY TO SHOW MY CHILDREN MY BELIEF IN THEIR POTENTIAL?

Henry Kendall from Boston, and Richard Taylor from Medicine Hat, Canada, achieved a breakthrough in people's understanding of matter and furthered the theory of the structure of protons and neutrons.

Mikhail Gorbachev from Privolnoye, U.S.S.R., contributed to a breakthrough in people's understanding about how East and West might better relate through *glasnost*, a policy of open political coexistence.

Octavio Paz from Mexico City, was a political commentator, diplomat, essayist, and poet who wrote passionately throughout his life about people's need for "wider horizons."

Edward Donnall Thomas from Mart, Texas, proved that it was possible to transplant organs to save the lives of dying patients.

Harry M. Markowitz from Chicago, developed the theory that combinations of economic assets of differing risks could decrease the overall risk of investment.

What did these five men have in common? Two things. First, although they represent vastly diverse heritages, interests, and talents, they all won Nobel Prizes in 1990. And second, nobody could have predicted their success *before* they were born.

A Ray of Sunshine

In thy presence is fulness of joy; at thy right hand there are pleasures for evermore.

PSALM 16:11

One Christmas Eve, a man was driving two young women to a church youth group celebration when they came upon a multiple-car collision. They were unable to stop on the slick road before they slammed into the back of a car. One of the girls, Donna, was thrown face-first through the windshield. The jagged edges of the broken windshield made two deep gashes in her left cheek.

At the hospital, the doctor on duty happened to be a plastic surgeon. He took great care in stitching Donna's face. Nevertheless, the driver was devastated by what had happened and dreaded visiting Donna on Christmas Day He expected to find her sad and depressed. Instead, he found her happy and bright, asking many questions of her doctors and nurses. A nurse confided to him that all the nurses were making excuses to go into Donna's room—they called her a "ray of sunshine." She refused to let the accident destroy her Christmas joy.

The man moved to another city shortly thereafter and lost touch with the family—for fifteen years. When he saw Donna's mother again, he fearfully asked how Donna was doing. Her mother told him that Donna had been so intrigued by her hospital stay that she became a nurse, got a good job at a hospital, met a young doctor, married him, and then had two children.

The mother said, "Donna told me to tell you that the accident was the best thing that could have happened to her!"[53]

We have the freedom to choose our attitude in any and every circumstance of life. We can choose to let trouble leave us depressed and weak, or we can choose to be happy and strong in spite of our trials. When we choose to have joy, our worst moments can be turned into our greatest triumphs.

MY THOUGHTS:

_____
_____
_____
_____
_____
_____
_____
_____
_____
_____
_____
_____
_____
_____
_____
_____
_____
_____

WHAT BIBLE PROMISES CAN HELP ME REACT MORE POSITIVELY TO MY CIRCUMSTANCES?

Too Busy to Gossip

"Let your light so shine before men, that they may see your good works, and glorify your Father which is in heaven."

MATTHEW 5:16

MY THOUGHTS:

_____
_____
_____
_____
_____
_____
_____
_____
_____
_____
_____
_____
_____
_____
_____
_____
_____
_____

WHAT STEPS CAN I TAKE TO AVOID GOSSIP? AN EXAMPLE WOULD BE . . .

Gossip usually begins because a person feels a need for attention or revenge. A better way to get attention, however, is to speak and do good things. The "best" revenge is found in doing good to one's enemies.

If you were busy being kind,
Before you knew it, you would find
You had forgotten to think 'twas true
That someone was unkind to you.
If you were busy, being glad
And cheering people who were sad,
You'd soon forget to notice it,
Although your heart might ache a bit.
If you were busy being good,
And doing just the best you could,
You wouldn't have the time to blame
Someone doing just the best he can.
If you were busy being true
To what you know you ought to do,
You'd be so busy you'd forget
The blunders of the folks you've met.[54]

Choose today to stay busy showing kindness, spreading cheer, and doing your best. You not only will have no time or temptation to gossip, but others will find little to gossip about in your life!

Willing to Step Forward

Little children, let us stop just saying we love people; let us really love them, and show it by our actions.

1 JOHN 3:18 TLB

The story is told of a young man who chose to take on a problem that plagues many American cities: potholes. In his case, the problem was one particular pothole. It was located at an intersection near his home, and it had been there for as long as he could remember. Residents of the neighborhood had developed the habit of driving around it; strangers learned about it the hard way.

One day, the young man decided it was time to fix the problem. He and his brother stopped at a hardware store and purchased sand and cement. Once the store owner learned what they planned to do, he loaned them a shovel and a concrete mixer and even volunteered his son to help out.

As soon as they began filling the pothole, several passing motorists parked their cars and began directing traffic around the three men at work. Some passing children made "Wet Concrete" signs to put around the pothole once the work was done. In all, nearly twenty neighbors participated in the project. Together, they had handled a problem that had bothered all of them for years. All it took was one person willing to step forward and take responsibility for seeing that the problem was fixed.[55]

It's one thing to define a problem or theorize about solutions; it's quite another to actually solve the problem!

MY THOUGHTS:

INSTEAD OF COMPLAINING, I'LL BE A PART OF THE SOLUTION BY . . .

A Fruitful Home

The Spirit produces the fruit of love, joy, peace, patience, kindness, goodness, faithfulness, gentleness, self-control.

GALATIANS 5:22-23 NCV

MY THOUGHTS:

_____
_____
_____
_____
_____
_____
_____
_____
_____
_____
_____
_____
_____
_____

WHAT QUALITIES IS
MY CHILD LIVING
WITH?

If a child lives with criticism,
He learns to condemn;
If a child lives with hostility,
He learns to fight;
If a child lives with ridicule,
He learns to be shy;
If a child lives with shame,
He learns to feel guilty.
BUT
If a child lives with tolerance,
He learns to be patient;
If a child lives with encouragement,
He learns confidence;
If a child lives with praise,
He learns to appreciate;
If a child lives with fairness,
He learns justice;
If a child lives with security,
He learns to have faith;
If a child lives with approval,
He learns to like himself;
If a child lives with acceptance and
friendship,
He learns to find LOVE in the world!

DOROTHY LAWE HOLT

Kids Can Be Pretty Clever

There is a right time for everything . . . A time to laugh.
ECCLESIASTES 3:1,4 TLB

A college freshman once wrote the following to her parents:

Dear Mom and Dad,

Just thought I'd drop you a note to clue you in on my plans. I've fallen in love with a guy named Buck. He quit high school between his sophomore and junior year to travel with his motorcycle gang. He was married at eighteen and has two sons. About a year ago he got a divorce.

We've been going steady for two months now and plan to get married in the fall. (He thinks he should be able to find a job by then.) Until then, I've decided to move into his apartment. I think I might be pregnant.

At any rate, I dropped out of school last week. I was just bored with the whole thing. Maybe I'll finish college sometime in the future.

[And then on the next page she continued. . .]

Mom and Dad, everything I've written so far in this letter is false. NONE OF IT IS TRUE! But, Mom and Dad, it IS true that I got a C in French and flunked my math test. And it IS true that I'm overdrawn and need more money for my tuition payments.

Your loving daughter.

MY THOUGHTS:

_____
_____
_____
_____
_____
_____
_____
_____
_____
_____
_____
_____
_____
_____
_____
_____
_____
_____
_____
_____

WHEN MY KIDS TRY TO MANIPULATE ME, I RESPOND BY . . .

Do You Want to Go Where Flattery Will Take You?

They loved the praise of men more than the praise of God.
JOHN 12:43

MY THOUGHTS:

_____
_____
_____
_____
_____
_____
_____
_____
_____
_____
_____
_____
_____
_____
_____
_____
_____
_____
_____

*HOW COMMITTED
AM I TO SPEAKING
THE TRUTH IN LOVE?
AN EXAMPLE
WOULD BE . . .*

In ancient Greece, one of the most politically crafty philosophers was Aristippus. He also had a hearty appetite for the "good life." Although Aristippus disagreed with the tyrant Denys, who ruled over the region, he had learned how to get along with him in court by flattering him on all occasions. Aristippus looked down his nose at some of the less prosperous philosophers and wise men who refused to stoop that low.

One day, Aristippus saw his colleague Diogenes washing some vegetables. He said to him disdainfully, "If you would only learn to flatter King Denys you would not have to be washing lentils."

Diogenes looked up slowly and in the same tone of voice replied, "And you, if you had only learned to live on lentils, would not have to flatter King Denys."[55]

Flattery is a two-edged sword: lying and manipulation. A genuine compliment is always in order, but flattery is telling people something that isn't true in hopes of gaining their favor. What flatterers don't realize, of course, is that with each falsehood, they are diminishing their own value. Eventually their words have no meaning, and their flattery sounds hollow, even to the one who has been flattered.

Choose instead to be a person of principle—one who always speaks the truth with love.

Something She'll Really Appreciate

Children, obey your parents; this is the right thing to do because God has placed them in authority over you.

EPHESIANS 6:1 TLB

For all the "trouble" children can cause, they can also keep life "fun" with their unrehearsed quips and candid observations about life. Consider, for example, the little boy who was in a quandary about what to get his mother for Mother's Day. The little girl next door asked, "You have any money?"

"Na-a-a," the boy said.

"What about making her something?" the girl asked.

"I'm not very good at arts and crafts," the boy admitted.

"I know!" the little girl said. "You could promise to keep your room clean and neat for a whole week. And if you really want to make it a special gift, you could remember to clean your goldfish bowl and put your dirty clothes in the laundry basket."

The little boy just shrugged, unimpressed by her ideas. "Or," she continued doggedly, "you could go home the first time she calls you. Or . . . you could quit fighting with your brothers and sisters, especially at the dinner table."

The boy continued to shake his head. "No," he said. "I want to get my mom something she will really use—and something she'll really *appreciate!*"

MY THOUGHTS:

_____
_____
_____
_____
_____
_____
_____
_____
_____
_____
_____
_____
_____
_____
_____
_____
_____

TODAY I WILL COMMUNICATE TO MY CHILDREN THAT I REALLY APPRECIATE . . .

Convincing Evidence

Choose for yourselves this day whom you will serve ... As for me and my house, we will serve the Lord.

JOSHUA 24:15

MY THOUGHTS:

_____
_____
_____
_____
_____
_____
_____
_____
_____
_____
_____
_____
_____
_____
_____
_____
_____

WHAT DO MY
ACTIONS REVEAL
ABOUT MY HEART?
AN EXAMPLE
WOULD BE . . .

The oldest; sister of Daniel Webster was married to John Colby who was considered the most wicked, Godless man in his neighborhood when it came to swearing and impiety. Then news came to Webster that there was a change in Colby. He decided to call on him to see if it was true.

On entering his sister's home, he noticed a large-print Bible opened on a table. Colby had been reading it before he answered the knock on the door. The first question Colby asked him was, "Are you a Christian?" When he was assured of Webster's faith, he suggested that they kneel together and pray.

After the visit, Webster told a friend, "I would like to hear what enemies of religion say of Colby's conversion. Here was a man as unlikely to be a Christian as any I ever saw; and he had gone his Godless way until now, with old age and habits hard to change! Yet see him—a penitent, trusting, humble believer! Nothing short of the grace of Almighty God."[56]

The fruit of your faith is always found in your behavior. You cannot hide what you believe or don't believe. Your actions will always give away the secrets of your heart.

Why Worry?

Whoever exalts himself will be humbled, and he who humbles himself will be exalted.

LUKE 14:11

In *A Man Called Peter*, Catherine Marshall writes the following about the angst her son felt in moving from kindergarten to the first grade:

> *Peter John was stunned to discover that something new had been added. The first grade was no longer all play. He was expected to learn to read and write. He questioned us sharply about this none-too-welcome change. "You might as well get used to it, Peter," his father said bluntly; "you'll have to go to school for a long time—eleven years, then four more years of college, then maybe more."*
>
> *Peter looked crushed, and went away disconsolate. It took him several weeks to get used to this new and awful revelation. He would be sitting on the floor playing with his wooden trains and blocks, apparently quite content, when suddenly his lower lip would begin to tremble, and tears would overflow. "Peter, what on earth is the matter?" we would question. Between sobs he would say, "I'm worryin' about when I'll have to go to college..."*

Marshall felt her son's behavior could reveal something about worry to all of us. She wrote, "The next time you start fretting about something, rather than trusting God to take care of it, remember that an all-wise God knows your worrying to be just as futile— just as silly—as our six-year-old worrying about when he will go to college."[57]

MY THOUGHTS:

_____
_____
_____
_____
_____
_____
_____
_____
_____
_____
_____
_____
_____
_____
_____
_____
_____

OVER WHAT AREAS DO I TEND TO WORRY MOST?

Partnering With God

For this child I prayed; and the Lord hath given me my petition which I asked of him: Therefore also I have lent him to the Lord; as long as he liveth he shall be lent to the Lord.

1 SAMUEL 1:27-28

MY THOUGHTS:

_____
_____
_____
_____
_____
_____
_____
_____
_____
_____
_____
_____
_____
_____
_____
_____

DAILY I WILL PRAY FOR MY CHILD REGARDING . . .

Wesley L. Gustafson once related that when he was a boy—and as long as he was living at home as a young man—his mother would never go to bed until he was safely in the house. Even if he was traveling and didn't get home until near dawn, he would creep up the stairs to his room, only to find that the light was still on in his mother's room. Putting his head against the door of her room, he would hear her praying for him. Then, after he was in bed, she would come into his room. "Wes," she would call his name softly again and again.

He would pretend to be asleep and would not respond. Feeling assured that her son was asleep, she would stand by the window and pray audibly, "O God, save my boy."

Gustafson said about this, "I myself am quite sure that the prayers of a good mother never die."

Another mother, Susanna Wesley, spent one hour each day praying for her children—even though she had seventeen children to care for! Two of her sons are credited with bringing revival to England.

Perhaps the most beneficial thing you can do for your children is to pray for them diligently, faithfully, daily, and with detail.

God Will Cause Even Disaster to Work for Our Good

We know that all things work together for good to them that love God, to them who are the called according to his purpose.

ROMANS 8:28

Robert and his wife were in shock when their dream cabin—10,000 square feet of luxurious space overlooking Mount Timpanogos—was crushed in an avalanche. It took nature only ten seconds to destroy what had taken them several years to design, plan, build, and furnish. They had a very difficult time seeing God in the situation as they picked through the smashed bits of their belongings.

Eight months later, Robert was at a business meeting when a colleague told him about an accident their wives had almost had on the day of the avalanche. Before leaving their cabin, one of this man's sons had offered a prayer for a safe trip home. Then, as they drove down the narrow road, they met Robert's wife, but when they slammed on their brakes, the car skidded on the ice. Just before the two vehicles collided, the man's wife turned her Suburban into a deep snow bank. It took almost an hour to get the vehicle unstuck—all that time it blocked Robert's wife and son from passing. Had the accident not occurred, Robert's wife and child would very likely have been at home, killed in the avalanche![58]

Be slow to judge devastating circumstances in your life. Trouble does not come from God, but He is ever-present to turn those things around for your good. Ask God to show you His hand in the situation, and you will see that He was there helping you all along.

MY THOUGHTS:

_____
_____
_____
_____
_____
_____
_____
_____
_____
_____
_____
_____
_____
_____
_____
_____
_____
_____
_____

WHAT DISASTROUS SITUATIONS IN MY LIFE HAS GOD TURNED AROUND FOR MY GOOD?

An Empty Sack

Young people are prone to foolishness.
PROVERBS 22:15 MSG

MY THOUGHTS:

WHAT SITUATIONS
HAVE I ASSUMED
ARE FINE, BUT I
FEEL I NEED TO
CHECK ON?

Every morning a mother announced, "This is not a restaurant; there are no menus." She still got orders as she packed school lunches for all her children.

"Peanut butter and jelly?" one would cry. "Oh no! Why can't we ever have cheese?" That child seemed to have totally forgotten that yesterday's sandwich was cheese and he had complained it wasn't peanut butter.

"Grape jelly?" another asked. "Can't we ever get strawberry?"

Yet another would say, "Leave the jelly off mine, but can I have two sandwiches?"

Over the years, the mother felt confident that she had finally learned what each child liked. Her youngest, Jim, always seemed to return home with an empty sack—a fact she took as a high compliment. Until one day ... when she handed Jim his sack and said, "Enjoy your lunch."

He replied, "Oh, I'm not gonna eat this, Mom. I'm trading with Josh. His Mom bakes cookies, and he told me he'd trade lunches today if I let him play with my football. Isn't that great? I can hardly wait!"

"Does anybody ever want to trade for your lunch?" the mother asked hopefully.

"Naw," the boy replied. "But don't worry about me. I still eat well. Nobody else in my class has a football."

The "Favorite" Child

When they were discouraged, I smiled and that encouraged them and lightened their spirits.

JOB 29:24 TLB

Humorist Erma Bombeck once wrote:

Every mother has a favorite child. She cannot help it. She is only human. I have mine—the child for whom I feel a special closeness, with whom I share a love that no one else could possibly understand. My favorite child is the one who was too sick to eat ice cream at his birthday party . . . who had measles at Christmas . . . who wore leg braces to bed because he toed in . . . who had a fever in the middle of the night, the asthma attack, the child in my arms at the emergency ward.

My favorite child is the one who messed up the piano recital, misspelled committee in a spelling bee, ran the wrong way with the football, and had his bike stolen because he was careless.

My favorite child was selfish, immature, bad-tempered and self-centered. He was vulnerable, lonely, unsure of what he was doing in this world—and quite wonderful.

All mothers have their favorite child. It is always the same one: the one who needs you at the moment. Who needs you for whatever reason—to cling to, to shout at, to hurt, to hug, to flatter, to reverse charges to, to unload on—but mostly just to be there.

MY THOUGHTS:

_____
_____
_____
_____
_____
_____
_____
_____
_____
_____
_____
_____
_____
_____
_____
_____
_____

WHICH OF MY CHILDREN NEEDS ME THE MOST RIGHT NOW? WHY DO I FEEL THAT WAY?

A Gratitude Attitude

It is a good thing to give thanks unto the Lord, and to sing praises unto thy name, O most High.

PSALM 92:1

MY THOUGHTS:

_____
_____
_____
_____
_____
_____
_____
_____
_____
_____
_____
_____
_____
_____
_____
_____

WHAT BLESSINGS OF GOD HAVE I TAKEN FOR GRANTED?

The World Health Organization has estimated that approximately one-third of the world is well fed, one-third is underfed, and one-third is starving. Worldwide, four million people die of starvation each year, and 70 percent of children under age six are undernourished. At this rate, 30 people die of starvation every minute.

The United Nations Food and Agricultural Organization has reported: "About 460 million people are at the brink of starvation daily, and some 200 million children slip into some form of mental retardation and blindness due to lack of food, another ten million or so give way finally to hunger-related diseases."

In 1975, United States Senator Mark O. Hatfield presented a resolution designating the Monday before Thanksgiving Day as a "National Day of Fasting." He and Stan Mooneyham, then president of World Vision International, called on all Americans to willingly experience hunger and reevaluate their own lifestyles and habits.[59]

When you are tempted to complain about something you don't have, stop and remind yourself to be thankful for what you do have. God will reward your thankfulness.

The Gift of Presence

We loved you dearly—so dearly that we gave you not only God's message, but our own lives too.

1 THESSALONIANS 2:8 TLB

In 1971, child-care expert Penelope Leach had a crisis that changed her life as well as many of her opinions about the needs and growth of children. Leach was well launched into a promising career as a child-development researcher when her two-year-old son, Matthew, nearly died of viral meningitis. Although he allowed her time to care for her sick child, Leach's employer also pressed her to return to work as quickly as possible. So as soon as Matthew was out of danger, Leach left him with a babysitter and returned to her job. She says, "I just took it for granted that's what I had to do."

Physically, Matthew was well, but Leach found that "you could reduce him to tears playing peekaboo. The only person he was okay with was me." So, two months later, Leach made another decision—this time to quit her job and devote herself to the "total health" of her child. Today, she looks back with embarrassment that she ever allowed her son to reach such a low point in his emotional growth. She recalls, "Quitting was tough, but it wasn't as if we were going to starve." What *did* happen as the result of her quitting was that Matthew didn't starve . . . for the assurance, comfort, attention, and love he needed.

MY THOUGHTS:

_____
_____
_____
_____
_____
_____
_____
_____
_____
_____
_____
_____
_____
_____
_____
_____
_____
_____
_____

WHAT IS THE CURRENT STATE OF MY CHILD'S EMOTIONAL HEALTH AND WELL-BEING? AN EXAMPLE WOULD BE . . .

The Ripple Effect

april 24

Children become spoiled when we substitute "presents" for "presence."
Death and life are in the power of the tongue: and they that love it
shall eat the fruit thereof.

PROVERBS 18:21

MY THOUGHTS:

_____
_____
_____
_____
_____
_____
_____
_____
_____
_____
_____
_____
_____
_____
_____
_____

TODAY I WILL START
A LIFE-GIVING
RIPPLE EFFECT BY . .
.

It's not easy to control our tongues. But as these words from the poem "Drop a Pebble in the Water" by James W Foley illustrate, a careless word can have far-reaching effects. Fortunately, so can a careful word!

Drop a pebble in the water: just a
splash, and it is gone;
But there's half-a-hundred ripples
circling on and on and on,
Spreading, spreading from the
center, flowing on out to the sea.
And there is no way of telling where
the end is going to be.
Drop an unkind word, or careless: in
a minute it is gone;
But there's half-a-hundred ripples
circling on and on and on.
They keep spreading, spreading,
spreading from the center as they
go,
And there is no way to stop them,
once you've started them to flow.
Drop a word of cheer and kindness:
in a minute you forget;
But there's gladness still a-swelling,
and there's joy a-circling yet,
And you've rolled a wave of comfort
whose sweet music can be heard
Over miles and miles of water just by
dropping one kind word.[60]

"I'm a Present"

Lo, children are am heritage of the Lord: and the fruit of the womb is his reward.

PSALM 127:3

During the Christmas season, a bubbly four-year-old girl became caught up in the excitement of the season, especially as she saw the number of presents under the tree slowly increasing as Christmas Day approached. Several times during a day, she would pick up various gifts, examine the boxes closely—shaking them and looking at them from all angles—and then try to guess what was inside each package.

One evening as she picked up a box, its big red bow fell from it. In a burst of inspiration, she picked up the bow and stuck it on top of her head. With a twinkle in her eyes and a smile as bright as the star atop the Christmas tree, she twirled and announced to her parents, "Mommy and Daddy, look at me! I'm a present!"

This little girl's words were truer than she realized. After the gift of God's own Son, our children are the most wonderful gifts God has ever given to us. Take time today not only to admire your child's talents and achievements . . . not only to enjoy your child's personality . . . but to truly delight in the fact that your child is a present from the Creator to you and your family!

MY THOUGHTS:

_____
_____
_____
_____
_____
_____
_____
_____
_____
_____
_____
_____
_____
_____
_____
_____
_____
_____

WHAT THINGS CAN I DO TO CONVEY TO MY CHILDREN WHAT PRECIOUS GIFTS THEY ARE TO ME?

Examine Yourself First

april 26

"First take the beam out of your own eye, and then you will see clearly to take out the speck that is in your brother's eye."

LUKE 6:42 AMP

MY THOUGHTS:

_____
_____
_____
_____
_____
_____
_____
_____
_____
_____
_____
_____
_____
_____
_____
_____
_____
_____

WHAT THINGS
ABOUT ME NEED TO
BE CHANGED FOR
THE GOOD OF MY
CHILDREN?

Coming down the main walk from the capitol in Washington, D.C., toward Pennsylvania Avenue, one encounters a group of steps. In watching the crowds go up and down those steps, a man once observed that people were continually stumbling on them, while they didn't seem to stumble on any other flights of stairs in the city.

He called the attention of the capitol architect to the matter. The architect couldn't believe this was so until he observed the situation for himself. He was amazed at the number of people who stumbled in going up the steps. "I cannot account for it," he said. "I spent weeks in arranging those steps. I had wooden models of them put down at my own place, and I walked over them day after day until I felt sure they were perfect.

A person hearing him speak asked, "Isn't one of your legs shorter than the other, Mr. Olmstead?" Sure enough . . . the architect had designed the steps of the capitol based on his own inequality of limbs and had thus made the stairs truly suitable only for those with a similar condition!

Life After Death

Jesus said unto [Martha], "I am the resurrection, and the life: he that believeth in me, though he were dead, yet shall he live: And whosoever liveth and believeth in me shall never die."

JOHN 11:25-26

One of the most ancient books in the Bible is the book of Job. In it, Job poses a question that has been in people's hearts from the beginning: "If a man die, shall he live again?"

Many answers have been offered through the centuries:

- Science says, "People may live again."
- Philosophy says, "People hope to live again."
- Ethics says, "People ought to live again."
- Atheism says, "People will never live again."
- Reincarnationists say, "People will live again but in another form, not as themselves."
- Judaism says, "People will live on in their children and in the memory of all they have befriended."
- Jesus Christ said, "He shall live again if he believes in Me. I am the resurrection and the life."[61]

Regardless of your religious persuasion, death is something you will face—either with or without the hope of eternal life. When eternal life is your hope, you can face every day with joy.

MY THOUGHTS:

WHERE WILL I SPEND ETERNITY? WHAT MAKES ME THINK SO?

125

A Tribute to a Mother's Prayers

Follow God's example in every thing you do just as a much loved child imitates his father.

EPHESIANS 5:1 TLB

MY THOUGHTS:

_____

_____

_____

_____

_____

_____

_____

_____

_____

_____

_____

_____

_____

_____

_____

_____

_____

_____

TODAY MY CHILDREN WILL HEAR ME PRAYING ABOUT . . .

Abraham Lincoln is not the only president who has paid tribute to his mother's faith. President Reagan was also reverential about his mother, calling her "one of the kindliest persons I've ever known."

After an assassination attempt on President Reagan's life in March, 1981, he spoke of his mother in a letter: "I found myself remembering that my mother's strongest belief was that all things happen for a reason. She would say we may not understand the why of such things, but if we accept them and go forward, we find, down the road a ways, there was a reason and that everything happens for the best. Her greatest gift to me was an abiding and unshakable faith in God."

There are many things that children *don't* remember. They rarely remember every scraped knee, every reprimand, every home-cooked meal. What children tend to remember are character traits of a parent and the way they manifested themselves in a pattern of consistency. Make prayer a daily habit—and let your children overhear you praying for them on a daily basis. They may not remember each and every prayer . . . but they will remember you as a praying person! And that example will never depart from them.

Wrong Motives

A man's pride shall bring him low: but honour shall uphold the humble in spirit.

PROVERBS 29:23

Antonio Salieri, an ambitious, albeit mediocre, eighteenth-century composer, offers this prayer in the popular film on Mozart's life, *Amadeus*: "Lord, make me a great composer. Let me celebrate Your glory through music. And be celebrated myself. Make me famous through the world, dear God, make me immortal. After I die, let people speak my name forever with love for what I wrote. In return I will give You my chastity, my industry, my deep humility, my life."

When it became obvious to the superficially pious Salieri that he would never be as gifted as the roguish Wolfgang Amadeus Mozart, he became insanely jealous of Mozart and plotted to destroy him. He also turned from God. As far as Salieri was concerned, God had betrayed him. He had failed to answer his prayer. In a very powerful scene in the movie, he takes a crucifix from the wall of his room and places it in the fire.[61]

Even when people seem to be successful in doing great things for God, they may find that they feel unfulfilled. When that happens, pride is generally at work. Those people are desiring God to use them in a special way, for their own glory, without realizing that true fulfillment lies in allowing God to use them in any way He desires, for His glory.

MY THOUGHTS:

HOW DO I FEEL ABOUT THE LIFE TO WHICH GOD HAS CALLED ME?

Girlfriends

A friend loves at all times, and is born, as is a brother, for adversity.
PROVERBS 17:17 AMP

MY THOUGHTS:

_____
_____
_____
_____
_____
_____
_____
_____
_____
_____
_____
_____
_____
_____
_____
_____

WHO ARE THE
LIKE-MINDED
WOMEN IN MY LIFE
FROM WHOM I
DRAW STRENGTH?

They call themselves the "Ladies of the Lake," but they never set out to be a club. Rather, the group began when one of the women returned home exhausted from a business trip and came to the conclusion that she had too much of one thing in her life: MEN! With a husband and two boys at home, a work environment that was mostly male, and an elderly father and uncle to care for, she resolved to set some time aside for herself and a few female friends.

Over the years, Paula hadn't cultivated very many friendships with other women, but she was determined to see that change. Eventually she discovered three like- minded women: one owned a machine shop, one worked for a contractor, and one ran a truck stop. The women pulled out their calendars over dinner one evening and agreed on this schedule—"A trip to the lake at least once a quarter!"

At the lake, the women would listen to Mozart, fix gourmet dinners, and sit on the deck overlooking the water. They would talk for hours—about everything—without an agenda.

Over the years, they have become very close and often refer to each other as "sister." Says Paula, "Nobody understands like another woman."

Keeping the Vow

He who walks with the wise grows wise.
PROVERBS 13:20 NIV

Little Danny, only six months old, was bitten on the hand by a rat as he lay in his crib. His screams awakened everyone in the house, and his parents rushed him to the hospital. Although the doctors did all they could do with the limited medical techniques available at the time, the poor baby was just about given up for dead. His mother fell to her knees and screamed aloud, "Please, God, spare him, and I vow to you that I will beg pennies from door to door for a whole year to give to the poor. Spare my baby. Please, God, spare my baby." His father, too, dropped to his knees, prayed, and vowed that he would never gamble again.

Miraculously, Danny lived, perhaps even with rabies from the rat. And for an entire year, his mother took the streetcar to the end of the line and walked all the way back downtown, begging pennies from door to door. Sometimes doors were slammed in her face, but she persevered for a full year, pleading in her Middle Eastern accent, "Please give pennies to the poor. I promise God." His father never again gambled.

This memory is the chief reason Danny Thomas cites for his generous fundraising on behalf of the Saint Jude Children's Research Hospital in Memphis, Tennessee.

MY THOUGHTS:

_____
_____
_____
_____
_____
_____
_____
_____
_____
_____
_____
_____
_____
_____
_____
_____
_____
_____

HOW AM I TEACHING MY CHILDREN THE IMPORTANCE OF FULFILLING ONE'S VOWS?

Obedience Pays Off

"If anyone serves Me, he must continue to follow Me [to cleave steadfastly to Me, conform wholly to My example in living . . .] and wherever I am, there will My servant he also. If anyone serves Me, the Father will honor him."

JOHN 12:26 AMP

MY THOUGHTS:

_____
_____
_____
_____
_____
_____
_____
_____
_____
_____
_____
_____
_____
_____
_____
_____
_____

HOW QUICK AM I TO OBEY THE PROMPTING OF GOD? AN EXAMPLE WOULD BE . . .

It was late, and she was tired. She had been working all day, and she needed to leave town early the following morning. She was scheduled to give three talks in two cities in one day. But Eugenia Price was prevailed upon to talk with someone—an actor who couldn't overcome his addiction to alcohol.

Before she agreed to meet with the man, Eugenia struggled with doubts. Was it fair to the people she'd be speaking to the next day to exhaust herself now and not give her best? The actor lived near her home—perhaps she could talk with him after she returned from her trip.

Finally, she asked God to reveal to her His will for the man for that night. After praying quietly for several minutes, she knew what to do. She spoke with the actor, believing God had asked her to do so.

On his way home from their meeting that night, the actor stopped his car on the side of the road and asked Jesus to be his Savior and Lord. What had brought him to that point? He said he was impressed by the fact that despite her weariness and doubts, Eugenia had been mastered by Jesus. She had put her will into His hands and trusted Him to lead her in the right direction.[62]

For one actor, one woman's decision to do God's will on one night made an eternal difference.

Getting Their Attention

may 3

He will yet fill your mouth with laughter.

JOB 8:21 NIV

Teresa Bloomingdale offers these humorous suggestions for improving family communication:

· If you have tiny children who won't give you their attention, simply place a long-distance telephone call to somebody important, preferably their grandmother. Your toddlers will immediately climb up on your lap and become all ears.

· If you have older children who avoid you like the plague, buy yourself some expensive bath salts, run a hot tub, and settle in . . . Teenagers who haven't talked to you since their tenth birthday will bang on the door, demanding your immediate attention.

· Lure your husband into the bedroom, and lock the door. The entire family will immediately converge in the hallway, insisting they must talk to you.

· Get a job in an office, which discourages personal phone calls. Your kids will then call you every hour on the hour.

· Send them away to college, or let them move into an apartment. They can then be counted on . . . for long chats, during which they will expound at length on what wonderful parents you were, and what happened, because you certainly are spoiling their younger siblings rotten.

MY THOUGHTS:

HOW EFFECTIVE AM I AT GETTING MY CHILDREN'S ATTENTION? AN EXAMPLE WOULD BE . . .

131

The Sweetness of a Mother's Love

may 4

Your loving-kindness is wonderful; your mercy is so plentiful, so tender and so kind.

PSALM 69:16 TLB

MY THOUGHTS:

_____
_____
_____
_____
_____
_____
_____
_____
_____
_____
_____
_____
_____
_____
_____
_____
_____

WHAT STEPS CAN I TAKE TO KEEP THE SWEETNESS IN MY LOVE FOR MY CHILDREN?

An angel strolled out of Heaven one beautiful day and winged his way to earth. On a quest for beauty he wandered through both fields and cities, beholding the glories of nature and the finest works of art. As sunset approached, he thought, *What memento can I take hack to show my Heavenly friends the beauty of earth?*

He noticed a patch of beautiful and fragrant wildflowers in the field where he was standing, and he decided to pluck them to make a bouquet. Then, passing a home, he saw through the open door a baby smiling from his crib. He took the smile with him too. At another home, he saw through an open window a mother pouring out her love to her precious child as she stooped to kiss him good night. The angel decided to take the mother's love too.

As the angel flew homeward through the pearly gates, he noticed to his astonishment that the flowers in his hand had withered. The baby's smile had changed into a frown. Only the mother's love remained as he had found it. He said to those who greeted him, "Here is the only thing I found today on earth that could retain its beauty and goodness all the way to Heaven—the sweetness of a mother's love!"

Something Good to Say

Don't shoot off your mouth, or speak before you think.

ECCLESIASTES 5:2 MSG

A young preacher had announced to his congregation that he was leaving the church to accept another call. He was standing at the door after the service to greet the people, as preachers often do, when one of the elderly saints approached him. Her eyes were swimming with tears as she said, "Oh, pastor, I'm so sorry you've decided to leave. Things will never be the same again."

The young man was flattered. Taking her hands in his, he replied with as much kindness as possible, "Bless you, dear sister, but I'm sure that God will send you a new pastor even better than I."

She choked back a sob as she said, "That's what they all say, but they keep getting worse and worse."

Another woman was overheard telling her pastor after a worship service, "I'm deaf, and I hardly hear a word you preach, but I still come to get my plate full."

Hoping to console her, this pastor said, "Well, maybe you haven't missed much."

She replied, "Yes, that's what they all tell me."[63]

The old adage "think before you speak" is still the best way to fulfill the equally longstanding advice, "If you can't say something good, don't say anything at all."

MY THOUGHTS:

WHAT IS THE VALUE OF THE WORDS THAT COME OUT OF MY MOUTH?

133

A Team Effort

Behold, how good and how pleasant it is for brethren to dwell together in unity!

PSALM 133:1

MY THOUGHTS:

_____
_____
_____
_____
_____
_____
_____
_____
_____
_____
_____
_____
_____
_____
_____
_____

WHAT STEPS CAN I TAKE TO CULTIVATE A TEAM SPIRIT WITHIN OUR FAMILY?

It was a long hard road that took the Chandler children out of the cotton fields and out of poverty in Mississippi. All nine children have memories of a sharecropper's cabin and nothing to wear and nothing to eat. But today, all nine are college graduates! Their parents borrowed two dollars to buy a bus ticket for son Cleveland. He worked his way through school and became chairman of the economics department at Howard University. Luther went to the University of Omaha and became the public service employment manager for Kansas City. He helped brother James get to Omaha and then to Yale for graduate work. James, in turn, helped Herman, who is now a technical manager in Dallas. Donald works in Minneapolis.

The children also helped themselves—picking cotton, pulling corn, stripping millet, and digging potatoes. Fortson went to Morehouse and is a Baptist minister in Colorado. Princess has an M.A. from Indiana, and is a schoolteacher. Gloria is also a teacher. Bessie has an M.A. and is the dietitian at a veterans' hospital.

Together, the children bought a house for their parents in 1984. Nine players make a baseball team, but nine Chandler children have made an unbeatable team for the game of life!

Peace or a Trouble Heart

God's peace [shall be yours . . . that peace] which transcends all understanding shall garrison and mount guard over your hearts and minds in Christ Jesus.

PHILIPPIANS 4:7 AMP

In deep despair, William Cowper tried to end his life one morning by swallowing poison. His attempt at suicide failed. He that will then hired a coach and asked to be driven to the Thames River. He intended to hurl himself over the bridge into the icy waters below but felt "strangely restrained."

The next morning, still immersed in inner darkness, he tried again to end his life by falling on a sharp knife, but he only succeeded in breaking the blade! In one last desperate attempt, he tried to hang himself but was found and taken down unconscious, still alive.

Some time later Cowper picked up a Bible and began to read the book of Romans. It was there that he finally met the God who could speak peace to the storm in his soul. After many years of following the Lord, he wrote:

God moves in a mysterious way
His wonders to perform;
He plants His footsteps in the sea,
And rides upon the storm.
Deep in unfathomable mines
Of never-failing skill
He treasures up His bright designs
And works His sovereign will.[63]

Ask the Lord to speak peace to your troubled heart today. He alone is the Author of a peace that holds firm.

MY THOUGHTS:

WHAT STEPS CAN I TAKE THAT WILL HELP ME RECEIVE GOD'S PEACE?

may 8

"Let us eat, and be merry."
LUKE 15:23

MY THOUGHTS:

_____
_____
_____
_____
_____
_____
_____
_____
_____
_____
_____
_____
_____
_____
_____
_____
_____

I CAN MAKE MEALTIME A MORE ENJOYABLE FAMILY AFFAIR BY . . .

In *Family The Ties That Bind and Gag!* Erma Bombeck writes:

"In retrospect, it was only a matter of time before the Family Dinner Hour passed into history and fast foods took over . . . My pot roast gave way to pizza . . . My burgers couldn't compete with the changing numbers under the Golden Arches. I couldn't even do chicken . . . right! The old rules for eating at home—sit up straight, chew your food, and don't laugh with cottage cheese in your mouth— didn't fit the new ambiance. A new set of rules emerged."

Bombeck suggests these among the new rules:

· When ordering from the back seat of the car, do not cup your mouth over Daddy's ear and shout.

· Never order more than you can balance between your knees.

· Front-of-the-car seating is better than back seat if you have a choice. The dashboard offers space for holding beverages.

· Afterward, each person should be responsible for his/her trash and should contain it in a bag. Two-week-old onion rings in the ashtray are not a pretty sight.

Enlarge Our Hearts

Whatsoever ye do in word or deed, do all in the name of the Lord Jesus.

COLOSSIANS 3:17

In 1981, Elizabeth Glaser gave birth to a girl, Ariel. But moments after Ari was born, Elizabeth began to hemorrhage. She remembers watching silently as she received a transfusion of seven pints of blood . . . blood contaminated by HIV Four years later, Ariel began to suffer baffling stomach pains and draining fatigue. She underwent a battery of tests, one of which gave a name to her illness: AIDS.

After Ariel's death, Elizabeth became a leading AIDS activist, cofounding the Pediatric AIDS Foundation. Many consider her to be the most effective AIDS lobbyist in the nation. She says of Ariel: "It was Ari who taught me to love when all I wanted to do was hate. She taught me to be brave when all I felt was fear. And she taught me to help others when all I wanted to do was help myself. I am active in fighting AIDS because I want to be a person she would be proud of; I was so proud of her . . . I think about her courage, and I am able to go on."

About living with HIV Elizabeth said, "Everything—from making peanut-butter sandwiches and watching Jake [her son] play ball to planting the garden—has significance to me."

Children add another dimension to our lives—one that focuses on someone else besides ourselves.

MY THOUGHTS:

WHAT LESSONS ARE MY CHILDREN TEACHING ME?

When It Comes to Love, Speak It Often

I had to show you how very much I loved you and cared about what was happening to you.

2 CORINTHIANS 2:4 TLB

MY THOUGHTS:

_____
_____
_____
_____
_____
_____
_____
_____
_____
_____
_____
_____
_____
_____
_____
_____
_____

TO WHOM DO I NEED TO VOICE MY LOVE TODAY? HOW CAN I MAKE THIS A HABIT IN MY LIFE?

A teacher once gave his class this assignment: "This week, go to someone you whom you have never, or have not in a long time, said, 'I love you' to and tell them you love them."

The next week, he asked if anyone wanted to share what had happened. One student rose and said:

Five years ago, my father and I had a vicious argument and never really resolved it. We avoided each other as much as possible. Once I made the decision to tell him I loved him, however, it was as if a heavy load lifted from my chest. When I told my wife what I was going to do, she didn't just get out of bed, she catapulted out and hugged me. We stayed up half the night talking. It was great!

The next morning I got to the office two hours early and got more done than most days. After work, I went to see Dad. When he answered the door, I didn't waste any time. I took one step in the door and said, "Dad, I just came over to tell you that I love you." His face softened and he began to cry. He reached out and hugged me and said, "I love you too, son, but I've never been able to say it."

Two days later my dad had a heart attack. He's still unconscious, and I don't know if he'll make it. The lesson I learned is this: Don't wait to do the things you know need to be done. Do them now.[64]

Patience

Let patience have her perfect work, that ye may be perfect and entire, wanting nothing.

JAMES 1:4

One of the most beautiful descriptions especially of patience in all of classic literature is the need to be following from Bishop Horne:

Patience is the guardian of faith, the preserver of peace, the cherisher of love, the teacher of humility. Patience governs the flesh, strengthens the spirit, sweetens the temper, stifles anger, extinguishes envy, subdues pride: she bridles the tongue, restrains the hand, tramples upon temptations, endures persecutions, consummates martyrdom.

Patience produces unity in the church, loyalty in the state, harmony in families and societies: she comforts the poor, and moderates the rich; she makes us humble in prosperity, cheerful in adversity, unmoved by calumny and reproach; she teaches us to forgive those who have injured us, and to be the first in asking forgiveness of those whom we have injured; she delights the faithful, and invites the unbelieving; she adorns the woman, and approves the man; she is beautiful in either sex and every age . . .

She rides not in the whirlwind and stormy tempest of passion, but her throne is the humble and contrite heart, and her kingdom is the kingdom of peace.

Remember, when the opportunity arises to be patient with your child, consider how you would want God to respond to you in a We need to be patient with our children in similar circumstance.

MY THOUGHTS:

_____

_____

_____

_____

_____

_____

_____

_____

_____

_____

_____

_____

_____

_____

_____

_____

_____

I ESPECIALLY NEED TO BE PATIENT WITH MY CHILD WHEN . . .

Love Me, Love My Rag Dolls

"Love one another. As I have loved you, so you must love one another."
JOHN 13:34 NIV

MY THOUGHTS:

_____
_____
_____
_____
_____
_____
_____
_____
_____
_____
_____
_____
_____
_____
_____
_____

WHO ARE THE RAG
DOLLS IN MY LIFE
WHOM GOD WANTS
TO LOVE THROUGH
ME?

Ian Pitt-Watson has adapted the following portion from *A Primer for Preachers:*

There is a natural, logical kind of loving that loves lovely things and lovely people. That's logical. But there is another kind of loving that doesn't look for value in what it loves, but that "creates" value in what it loves. Like Rosemary's rag doll.

When Rosemary, my youngest child, was three, she was given a little rag doll, which quickly became an inseparable companion. She had other toys that were intrinsically far more valuable, but none that she loved like she loved the rag doll. Soon the rag doll became more and more rag and less and less doll. It also became more and more dirty. If you tried to clean the rag doll, it became more ragged still. And if you didn't try to clean the rag doll, it became dirtier still.

The sensible thing to do was to trash the rag doll. But that was unthinkable for anyone who loved my child. If you loved Rosemary, you loved the rag doll—it was part of the package . . . "Love me, love my rag dolls," says God, "including the one you see when you look in the mirror. This is the finest and greatest commandment."[65]

Invited into the World

Jesus said, "Let the little children come to me, and don't prevent them."
MATTHEW 19:14 TLB

Margaret Bourke-White, one of the innovators of the photo essay in the field of photojournalism, was one of the first four staff photographers of *Life* magazine when it began in 1936. She was also the first woman photographer ever attached to United States armed forces in World War II. From early years, Margaret knew that she was counted as a "gift" to her parents. She recalls her mother telling her, "Margaret, you can always be proud that you were invited into the world."

In her autobiography, aptly titled *Portrait of Myself*, she writes: "I don't know where she got this fine philosophy that children should come because they were wanted and should not be the result of accidents . . . When each of her own three children was on the way, Mother would say to those closest to her, 'I don't know whether this will be a boy or girl and I don't care. But this child was invited into the world and it will be a wonderful child.' She was explicit about the invitation and believed the child should be the welcomed result of a known and definite act of love between man and woman."

Have you told your child today that he or she is a gift—a child you wanted and "invited" into the world?

MY THOUGHTS:

_____
_____
_____
_____
_____
_____
_____
_____
_____
_____
_____
_____
_____
_____
_____
_____
_____
_____

HOW CAN I COMMUNICATE TO MY CHILD THAT HE OR SHE IS WELCOME IN MY WORLD?

Encourage Their Potential

We are God's workmanship, created in Christ Jesus to do good works, which God prepared in advance for us to do.

EPHESIANS 2:10 NIV

MY THOUGHTS:

_____
_____
_____
_____
_____
_____
_____
_____
_____
_____
_____
_____
_____
_____
_____
_____

TODAY I CAN INSPIRE MY CHILD'S POTENTIAL BY . . .

Shortly after arriving in the major leagues, pitcher Orel Hershiser was called to the office of Dodgers General Manager Tommy Lasorda. Orel knew the news wasn't going to be good. He had had a disappointing start as a relief pitcher. Lasorda, however, didn't focus on his record. He said instead, "You don't believe in yourself! You're scared to pitch in the big leagues! Who do you think these hitters are, Babe Ruth? Ruth's dead! You've got good stuff. If you didn't, I wouldn't have brought you up. I've seen guys come and go, son, and you've got it! You gotta go out there and do it on the mound. Be a bulldog out there. That's gonna be your new name: Bulldog. Bulldog Hershiser. I want you, starting today, to believe you are the best pitcher in baseball. I want you to look at that hitter and say, 'There's no way you can ever hit me.'"

Hershiser writes in his autobiography, *Out of the Blue*, "I couldn't get over that Tommy Lasorda felt I was worth this much time and effort . . . He believed I had more potential. He believed I had big league stuff." The next game, Hershiser pitched for three innings and gave up only one hit.

Talk more to your children about their potential than their track records. They have more potential than history!

Divine Intervention

We can make our plans, but the final outcome is in God's hands.
PROVERBS 16:1 TLB

Denis Waitley writes the following in *The New Dynamics of Winning*:

In 1979, I was booked on a flight from Chicago to Los Angeles. I was on my way to a speaking engagement before going home for the weekend. I had to run for the plane, and became very upset when I saw the gate agent lock the door and then saw the mobile ramp pull away from the plane. I argued and begged and told her I had to be on that nonstop DC 10, Flight 191 to L.A., or I would miss my speech. The plane taxied away from the ramp and out toward the runway despite my protests. I stormed out of the boarding area and back to the ticket counter to register my complaint.

Standing in line at the counter, about twenty minutes later, I heard the news that the plane had crashed on takeoff with no survivors. I left the ticket line, booked a room at the airport hotel, knelt down beside my bed in prayer, and tried to get some sleep. It's been over a decade since then, but I still have my unvalidated ticket for Flight 191. I never turned it in to my travel agent for a refund. Instead, I tacked it on a bulletin board in my office at home as a silent reminder. About once a year I get a little annoyed with some injustice in the world that has made me a victim... My wife, Susan, gently takes me by the hand to my bulletin board.[66]

MY THOUGHTS:

_____
_____
_____
_____
_____
_____
_____
_____
_____
_____
_____
_____
_____
_____
_____
_____
_____
_____

THE NEXT TIME SOMETHING SEEMS TO TURN OUT BADLY, MY ATTITUDE WILL BE . . .

may 16

"Thou shalt . . ."
MATTHEW 4:7

MY THOUGHTS:

_____
_____
_____
_____
_____
_____
_____
_____
_____
_____
_____
_____
_____
_____
_____

*WHAT STEPS CAN I
TAKE TO TEACH MY
CHILDREN TO BE
CONSIDERATE OF
OTHERS?*

Parents have a few habits that children never seem to understand or copy—such as my flipping off lights in rooms with no one in them and turning off faucets in a bathroom. In *Family: The Ties That Bind and Gag!* author Erma Bombeck offers these "Commandments for the Utilities":

· Thou shalt flush. Especially if thou is fifteen years old and has the use of both arms.

· Thou shalt hang up the phone when thou has been on it long enough for the rates to change.

· Thou shalt not stand in front of the refrigerator door waiting for something to dance.

· Thou shalt not covet the rest of the family's hot water.

· Thou shalt honor thy father's and mother's thermostat and keep it on normal.

· Thou shalt remember last month's electricity bill and rejoice in darkness.

Unfortunately, notes Bombeck, these commandments generally are kept in a family like broken stone tablets amidst wet towels and melting soap!

Actions Speak Louder than Words

Show me your faith without deeds, and I will show you my faith by what I do.

JAMES 2:18 NIV

The story is told of a missionary who was lost at sea and by chance, washed up on an island near a remote native village. Finding him half-dead from starvation and exposure, the people of the village nursed him back to health. He subsequently lived among the people for some twenty years. During that time he confessed no faith, sang no Gospel songs, and preached no sermons. He neither read nor recited Scripture and made no claim of personal faith.

However, when the people were sick, he attended them. When they were hungry, he gave them food. When they were lonely, he kept them company. He taught the ignorant and came to the aid of those who were wronged.

One day missionaries came to the village and began talking to the people about a man called Jesus. After hearing what they had to say of Jesus' ministry and teachings, they insisted that He had been living among them for twenty years. "Come, we will introduce you to the man about whom you have been speaking." They led the missionaries to a hut where they found a long-lost friend, the missionary, whom all had thought dead.[67]

Your true witness for Christ is the sum of all you do—not just what you say.

MY THOUGHTS:

IF I WERE THIS LONG-LOST MISSIONARY, WHAT WOULD BE SAID ABOUT ME?

A Poor Example

In everything set them an example by doing what is good.
TITUS 2:7 NIV

MY THOUGHTS:

_____
_____
_____
_____
_____
_____
_____
_____
_____
_____
_____
_____
_____
_____
_____
_____
_____

WHAT ARE SOME OF THE WAYS THAT I CAN SET A BETTER EXAMPLE FOR MY CHILDREN?

According to an old legend, there once was a man who had an only son to whom he gave everything he owned. When his son grew up, he was unkind to his father, refused to support him, and turned him out of his own house.

As the old man prepared to leave his home, he turned to his young grandson and said, "Go and fetch the covering from my bed, that I may go and sit by the wayside and wrap myself in it and beg for alms."

The child burst into tears and ran for the covering. But rather than take it to his grandfather, he ran to his father and said, "Oh Father, Grandfather has asked for this, so he can keep himself warm as he sits by the road and begs. Please cut it into two pieces. Half of it will be large enough for Grandfather. And you may want the other half when I am grown to be a man and turn you out of doors."

The child's words struck to the very core of the uncaring son, and he ran to his father, asked his forgiveness, and took care of him until his death.

What we *do* always comes across to our children as the loudest and clearest of messages.

An Excellent Example

He must have a well-behaved family, with children who obey quickly and quietly.

1 TIMOTHY 3:4 TLB

Sarah Edwards, wife of revivalist and theologian Jonathan Edwards, bore eleven children. At her death, Samuel Hopkins eulogized her in this way:

> She had an excellent way of governing her children. She knew how to make them regard and obey her cheerfully, without loud, angry words, much less heavy blows . . . If any correction was necessary, she did not administer it in a passion . . . In her directions in matters of importance, she would address herself to the reason of her children, that they might not only know her will, but at the same time be convinced of the reasonableness of it . . . Her system of discipline was begun at a very early age and it was her rule to resist the first as well as every subsequent exhibition of temper or disobedience in the child . . . wisely reflecting that until a child will obey his parents, he can never be brought to obey God.

At the close of each day, after all in the family were in bed, Sarah and her husband shared a devotional time together in his study. With eleven children to "tuck into bed," Sarah did not allow any of them leeway in keeping her from this cherished time with her husband!

MY THOUGHTS:

_____
_____
_____
_____
_____
_____
_____
_____
_____
_____
_____
_____
_____
_____
_____

OF THE DISCIPLINARY AREAS MENTIONED, I NEED TO WORK MOST ON . . .

147

Major on the Majors

Now you've got my feet on the life path, all radiant from the shining of your face. Ever since you took my hand, I'm on the right way.

PSALM 16:11 MSG

MY THOUGHTS:

_____
_____
_____
_____
_____
_____
_____
_____
_____
_____
_____
_____
_____
_____
_____
_____
_____

WHAT ARE THE "MAJORS" IN MY LIFE? WHY ARE THOSE THINGS IMPORTANT TO ME?

Two friends landed in New York City, and finding they had a nine-hour layover between flights, they decided to hire a taxi to drive them around to see some of the city's famous landmarks. The driver took them to various noteworthy places, taking time to tell the significance of each.

One of the friends was eager to take in all that he could see and hear. He noticed, however, that his friend seemed a bit oblivious to the sights. Instead, his eyes were firmly fixed upon the driver. Finally, he whispered to his friend, "Look, he has his sweater on inside out."

Many a person has been known to major on the minors or to pursue something that is of little significance once it is attained. A dog once chased a freight train, but when it had succeeded in stopping the train, it didn't know what to do with it. In the end, "catching" the train did not bring near the reward the dog had thought it would. It would have been much more fulfilled as a dog if it had gone after a cat or a rabbit.[68]

Today, make sure that what you are pursuing is truly what you want, should you attain it. Every success has some degree of difficulty. Be certain you can endure the trials without compromising your values or identity.

Beautiful to Your Children

Charm is deceptive, and beauty is fleeting; but a woman who fears the Lord is to be praised.

PROVERBS 31:30 NIV

For more than a century, the majestic statue titled *Liberty Enlightening the World* has towered near the entrance to New York Harbor as a symbol of America's freedom.

The famous sculptor of the statue, Bartholdi, spent twenty years supervising the construction of his masterpiece. He personally helped raise the four million dollars needed to pay for the statue, which was presented by France as a gift to the United States. When the fund-raising program for the statue lagged, Bartholdi pledged his own private fortune to keep the project funded and practically impoverished himself in the process.

At the start, when Bartholdi was seeking for a model on whom to pattern "Liberty," he received a great deal of advice from art experts. Most of the leading authorities advised him to find a grand heroic figure as his pattern. After examining countless heroes, however, Bartholdi chose as his model . . . his own mother. Just as no other statue in the world so eloquently lights the way to freedom, so no other woman so beautifully lighted Bartholdi's own world.

Remember, your children are watching even the very expressions on your face—be sure a fair amount of the time your face is wearing a smile.

MY THOUGHTS:

_____
_____
_____
_____
_____
_____
_____
_____
_____
_____
_____
_____
_____
_____
_____
_____
_____
_____

WHAT DO MY CHILDREN SEE WHEN THEY LOOK AT ME? HOW DO I FEEL ABOUT THAT?

Making a Man Out of a Boy

Teach me good judgment as well as knowledge.
PSALM 119:66 TLB

MY THOUGHTS:

_____
_____
_____
_____
_____
_____
_____
_____
_____
_____
_____
_____
_____
_____
_____
_____

WHAT STEPS CAN I TAKE TO SEE THAT MY CHILD HAS ENOUGH FREEDOM TO LEARN RESPONSIBILITY?

Entrepreneur and public speaker Wilson Harrell has recalled his best teacher this way:

When I was eleven, my father made me a cotton buyer at his gin. Now I knew cotton, but I was well aware that my father was entrusting an eleven-year-old with an awesome responsibility. When I cut a bale, I pulled out a wad, examined the sample, identified the grade and set the price. I'll never forget the first farmer I faced. He looked at me, called my father over and said, "Elias, I've worked too hard to have an eleven-year-old boy decide what I'll live on next year."

My father was a man of few words. "His grade stands," he answered and walked away. Over the years my father never publicly changed my grade. However, when we were alone, he'd check my work. If I'd under-graded (and paid too little), I'd have to go tell the farmer I'd made a mistake and pay him the difference. If I'd over-graded, my father wouldn't say a word—he'd just look at me . . .

I'm not sure my father knew anything about entrepreneurship, but he understood an awful lot about making a man out of a boy. He gave me responsibility and then backed my hand. He also taught me that fairness builds a business and that the willingness to admit and correct mistakes is a sure way to bring customers back.[69]

When you do what is right, there's not much you have to say.

Analysis of a Childs Room

In the fear of the Lord is strong confidence: and his children shall have a place of refuge.

PROVERBS 14:26

E linor Goulding Smith offers this analysis of a child's room:

The child's room is a sight to make strong men faint, and induces in mothers a condition characterized by trembling, pallor, dysphasia, weakness... The room is characterized by litter to a depth of two to three feet, except under the bed where it is perhaps only six inches deep. You can see no article of furniture, each being buried completely, and emerging as simply a higher mound of rubbish. You once, many years before, saw an occasional bureau top (let me see, was it maple?) or a desk top (birch—I think) but alas, they are only a memory now.

A few bits of furniture stick up above the level of the rubbish—the very top of a desk lamp protrudes above a mountain of papers, books, crayons, hedge shears, gym sneakers, the remains of a tongue sandwich, two peach pits, a camera, a microscope, some jars of extremely aromatic pond water, a deck of marked cards, coping saw, overdue library books, bicycle tire pumps, a Siamese fighting fish no longer in the prime of life who lives in the bottom half of a cider jug, and so on ... right up to the top of the desk lamp. You look at the top of the lamp happily. "At last," you say, as you totter across the room, "a landmark!"

MY THOUGHTS:

_____
_____
_____
_____
_____
_____
_____
_____
_____
_____
_____
_____
_____
_____
_____
_____
_____

WHAT STEPS CAN I TAKE TO ENSURE THAT MY CHILDREN'S ROOMS ARE THEIR OWN WITHOUT LETTING THEM BECOME HEALTH HAZARDS?

Stay on the Positive Side

All thy children shall be taught of the Lord; and great shall be the peace of thy children.

ISAIAH 54:13

MY THOUGHTS:

_____
_____
_____
_____
_____
_____
_____
_____
_____
_____
_____
_____
_____
_____
_____
_____
_____
_____

WHAT ARE SOME OF THE GOOD THINGS I CAN PRAISE MY CHILDREN FOR?

A mother once left her children with her single sister in order to work for three weeks overseas. Although she missed her children tremendously, she was also glad for a break. She was feeling worn out as a single parent, struggling to juggle her job and her role as a mother. The demands of constant discipline sometimes seemed too much. As she prepared to return to her family, she thought, *I wonder how Sis' coped. I hope she heeded my parting words not to let them get away with murder.* The last thing she looked forward to was a round of arguing and reprimanding.

To her great surprise, she arrived at her sister's home to find her children playing quietly, eager to see her but quick to obey her sister's slightest request. "What did you do?" she whispered to her sister. "They're never this well behaved!"

Her sister replied, "Nothing, really. Before you left, I read a little article about parenting, and I just did what it said."

The woman said, "What was it? Give me the formula!"

The sister picked up the article and read, "Tell children what to do, far more than you tell them what not to do. And then praise them for what they do—instead of criticizing them for what they don't do." Smiling at her sister, she added, "It seemed to work!"

Persist in Prayer

Let us not grow weary while doing good, for in due season we shall reap if we do not lose heart.

GALATIANS 6:9 NKJV

When Jill was a little girl, she visited her grandparents' farm every summer. One day as she came into the farmhouse, she could hear her grandmother talking. She entered the living room cautiously, certain that her grandmother had company. Instead, she found her grandmother alone, in prayer. Jill felt as if she were treading on holy ground.

As she quietly made her way toward the staircase, she was amazed to hear her name. Her grandmother was praying for her! She listened intently as her grandmother pleaded with God to keep her safe and healthy and to give her a desire to follow the Lord and grow up to be a soul-winner. Tears sprang to Jill's eyes as she felt the love expressed in her grandmother's prayer.

A few years later when Jill was in high school, a friend invited her to attend a youth rally. That evening, she gave her life to Christ. Later that night, she recalled the prayers of her grandmother. She suddenly realized, tears flowing down her face—*My grandmother's prayer has been answered!* The answer had taken nearly a decade to manifest, but nevertheless, the answer had come—not only for her grandmother but for Jill.

God knows the seasons of our hearts. Our role is to persist in prayer—planting seeds and watering them—until we reap the harvest!

MY THOUGHTS:

_____
_____
_____
_____
_____
_____
_____
_____
_____
_____
_____
_____
_____
_____
_____
_____
_____
_____

IN WHAT AREAS AND FOR WHAT PEOPLE SHOULD I FOCUS MY PERSISTENCE IN PRAYER?

Creating a Happy Home

Better a dry crust with peace and quiet than a house full of feasting, with strife.

PROVERBS 17:1 NIV

MY THOUGHTS:

_____
_____
_____
_____
_____
_____
_____
_____
_____
_____
_____
_____
_____
_____
_____
_____

WHAT ARE SOME OF THE THINGS I CAN DO TO MAKE OUR HOUSE A HOME?

Women are often tempted to think that their homemaking skills—such as cooking, decorating, and cleaning—are what turn a house into a home. But consider how one of the most famous cooks of all time, Julia Child, recalls her own childhood:

I know I'm happy. I was very fortunate in my family background because I had a very loving, supportive family. We had no conflict. My sister was five years younger, and we had a brother halfway between, so we never had any sibling rivalry. My parents were happy; we were not rich, but comfortably well-off. My mother thought everything we did was absolutely marvelous. I think your background makes an awful lot of difference. I don't know what you do if you've been abused, or haven't been praised enough so that you don't feel that you're okay. I was very fortunate in having such a happy background. I was never brilliant in school, but I never had any problems either, so I didn't feel inferior. I did have the problem of being twice as tall as anyone else, but that didn't seem to make any difference because my mother always said we were so wonderful, no matter what.

Notice . . . Julia didn't make one mention of her mother's cooking skills or food . . . only of praise!

Addicted to Prayer

Devote yourselves to prayer, keeping alert in it with an attitude of thanksgiving.

COLOSSIANS 4:2 NASB

A father was playing ball with his young son one day when his son's best friend appeared in the backyard. "Dad, can I go play with my friend?" the boy asked.

"But son," the father replied, "we're playing ball. Don't you want to play with me?"

His son replied candidly, "Nah, I'd rather play with him."

The father went inside to nurse his wounded ego and suddenly realized that perhaps God felt the same way about his reactions at times. God jealously desires our affection and attention. The father had to admit that all too often, he had a greater interest in cars, television, yard work, sports, hobbies, books, and family activities than in spending time with God.

One of the best ways of determining addictions in our lives is to ask ourselves these two questions:

· What is the first thing I think about in the morning?

· What is the main thing I want to make sure is included in my day tomorrow?[70]

These are good questions to ask about our relationship with the Lord. If God were to examine your heart today, what rivals for His attention and affection would He encounter?

MY THOUGHTS:

_____

_____

_____

_____

_____

_____

_____

_____

_____

_____

_____

_____

_____

_____

_____

TODAY I WILL CULTIVATE AN ADDICTION TO PRAYER BY . . .

Take Time to Listen

may 28

Don't ever forget that it is best to listen much, speak little.
JAMES 1:19 TLB

MY THOUGHTS:

_____
_____
_____
_____
_____
_____
_____
_____
_____
_____
_____
_____
_____
_____
_____

WHAT STEPS CAN I TAKE TO ENSURE THAT I'M EMOTIONALLY AVAILABLE TO MY CHILDREN?

A busy mother of four children found her job as wife and mom a careful balancing act. Each day was filled to the brim with a part-time job, home chores, and chauffeur duty. She had found the most efficient way for her to handle the weekly grocery shopping was to go alone, unhampered by "help" that usually inflated her grocery bill and strained her patience.

On one shopping day, her thirteen-year-old son asked, "Where ya goin', Mom?"

She replied, "To the grocery store. I'll be back soon."

Her son asked, "Can I go with you?"

She almost had the words "some other time" out of her mouth when something inside checked her, and she heard herself say, "OK."

Once in the car, she braced herself for the struggle she anticipated over the use of the radio. Instead, her son began to talk. "When I grow up, I'm going to be rich," he announced.

"Oh?" she said.

"Yeah," he said. "Then I can give my kids everything they want."

She asked, "Do you know any kids who get everything they want?" Her son gave her the name of such a child. "Do you like him?" Mom asked.

After a long pause, he grinned and said, "Naw, he's the meanest, most unhappy kid I know. His dad's never around, and his mom's always too busy."

If you want to know—really know—your children, take time to listen to them.

The Funny Things Kids Do

When I was a child, I spake as a child, I understood as a child, I thought as a child.

1 CORINTHIANS 13:11

A salesman telephoned a household, and a four-year-old boy answered. The salesman said, "May I speak to your mother, please?"

The little boy replied, "She's in the shower right now and can't come to the phone."

The man asked, "Well, is anyone else at home?"

"Yes," the boy said, "my sister is here."

"Well, OK," the salesman continued. "May I speak to her, please?"

"I guess so," the boy said. "I'll go get her."

At this point the man heard a clunk as the boy laid down the receiver. This was followed by a very long silence on the phone.

Finally the little boy came back on the line and said, "Are you still there?"

"Yes," the man said, trying hard to sound patient, "I thought you were going to put your sister on the phone."

The boy replied, "I tried, mister. But she's sound asleep, and I couldn't lift her out of her crib."

MY THOUGHTS:

_____
_____
_____
_____
_____
_____
_____
_____
_____
_____
_____
_____
_____
_____
_____

INSTEAD OF GETTING ANNOYED, I'LL ENJOY MY CHILD BY . . .

Count Your Blessings

I will remember the works of the Lord: surely I will remember thy wonders of old. I will meditate also of all thy work, and talk of thy doings.

PSALMS 77:11-12

MY THOUGHTS:

_____
_____
_____
_____
_____
_____
_____
_____
_____
_____
_____
_____
_____
_____
_____
_____

WHAT ARE THE BLESSINGS I CAN COUNT TODAY?

In some parts of Mexico, hot springs and cold springs are found side by side. Because of this natural phenomenon, local women have the convenience of boiling their clothes in the hot springs, then rinsing them in the adjacent cold springs. While watching this procedure a number of years ago, a tourist said to her guide, "I imagine that they think old Mother Nature is pretty generous to supply such ample, clean hot and cold water here side by side for their free use."

The guide replied, "Well, actually, no. There is much grumbling because Mother Nature supplies no soap! And not only that, the rumor has started to filter in that there are machines that do this work in other parts of the world."

So often we compare our lives to others—what they have, in contrast to what we don't, and what they are, that we aren't. Such comparisons invariably leave us feeling left out, rejected, and cheated. If we aren't careful to put the brakes on such negative emotions, we can become unnecessarily bitter. How much better to count our blessings!

The Key to Fellowship

may 31

Draw near to God and He will draw near to you.

JAMES 4:8 NASB

In *Too Busy Not to Pray*, Bill Hybels admits, "Prayer has not always been my strong suit. For years, even as senior pastor of a large church, I *knew* more about prayer would talk than I ever *practiced* in my own life. I have a racehorse temperament, and the tugs of self- sufficiency and self-reliance are very real to me. I didn't want to get off the fast track long enough to find out what prayer is all about.

"Several years ago the Holy Spirit gave me a leading so direct that I couldn't ignore it, argue against it, or disobey it. The leading was to explore, study, and practice prayer until I finally understood it." Hybels read books on prayer and studied every passage in the Bible on prayer. And then, he says, "I did something absolutely radical: I prayed."

"The greatest fulfillment in my prayer life has not been the list of miraculous answers to prayers I have received, although that has been wonderful. The greatest thrill has been the qualitative difference in my relationship with God."[71]

Are you on a casual, pray-on-the-run basis with your Creator? Or do you know His heart, sense His desires, and feel His presence? The key to ultimate fellowship with God lies in prayer.

MY THOUGHTS:

TODAY I WILL TALK TO GOD LIKE I WOULD TALK TO A FRIEND ABOUT . . .

A Fruitful Vine

Thy wife shall be as a fruitful vine by the sides of thine house: thy children like olive plants round about thy table.

PSALM 128:3

MY THOUGHTS:

_____
_____
_____
_____
_____
_____
_____
_____
_____
_____
_____
_____
_____
_____
_____
_____

HOW CAN I RECEIVE AND APPLY MORE OF GOD'S GRACE TO MEET THE NEEDS I FACE?

Lillian Gilbreth took an active role in Sunday school work. She didn't teach a class, but she served on a number of committees. Once she called on a woman who had just moved to town to ask her to serve on a fund-raising committee. "I'd be glad to if I had the time," the woman said, "but I have three young sons, and they keep me on the run. I'm sure if you have a boy of your own, you'll understand how much trouble three can be."

Lillian replied, "Of course, that's quite all right. And I do understand."

"Have you any children, Mrs. Gilbreth?" the woman asked.

Lillian replied, "Oh, yes."

The woman pursued the line, "Any boys?"

Lillian said, "Yes, indeed."

The woman persisted, "May I ask how many?"

Lillian graciously replied, "Certainly. I have six boys."

The woman gulped, "Six boys? Imagine a family of six!"

Lillian added, "Oh, there are more in the family than that. I have six girls too."

As Frank B. Gilbreth Jr. and Ernestine Gilbreth Carey tell in their book, *Cheaper by the Dozen*, the newcomer then whispered, "I surrender. When is the next meeting of the committee? I'll be there, Mrs. Gilbreth. I'll be there."

Recommended Daily Allowance

"When you pray, go away by yourself, all alone, and shut the door behind you and pray to your Father secretly, and your Father, who knows your secrets, will reward you."

MATTHEW 6:6 TLB

Louis Harris, the pollster, was playing tennis one day when he was struck by sharp pains in both calves. Within moments, both legs were numb. Subsequent medical tests revealed that the problem was poor circulation. Surgery was an option, but his physician preferred to try a less drastic approach first. He advised Harris to walk at least a mile every day. The doctor's hope was that as Harris's muscles demanded more blood flow, the body would bypass the clogged arteries and create new ones called collaterals.

Harris struggled at first, but within a year, he was easily walking more than a mile a day. He has said, "I allow nothing to get in the way of my daily walk."[72]

The same must be true for our prayer life. Some might consider prayer to be an optional exercise, but in fact, prayer is vital to spiritual health. It is a channel of communication that must be kept open—unclogged and free-flowing at all times.

If we deny our souls their "recommended daily allowance" of prayer, we will, over time, damage a precious and vital part of our relationship with God.

MY THOUGHTS:

WHAT OBSTACLES MOST OFTEN TRY TO HINDER MY PRAYER TIME?

Gifts with Purpose

Every good gift and every perfect gift is from above, and cometh down from the Father of lights, with whom is no variableness, neither shadow of turning.

JAMES 1:17

MY THOUGHTS:

_____
_____
_____
_____
_____
_____
_____
_____
_____
_____
_____
_____
_____
_____
_____
_____
_____
_____

WHAT KINDS OF GIFTS CAN I GIVE MY CHILDREN THAT WILL STIMULATE THEIR GROWTH?

Eight-year-old William was appreciative but not enthusiastic when he found skis under the Christmas tree. They had not been high on his wish list, but his father knew he would need them for an upcoming family trip.

As it turned out, the skis were the best gift he ever received. William took to the sport his first day on the slopes, and he joined the resort's junior racer program. For the next ten years, William skied every winter weekend, sometimes getting up in subzero cold to be at the mountain early. The skis taught him self-discipline and persistence. He learned to get up after falling hard. At home, he learned to budget his time to allow for homework. William became a hard-working, focused young adult who was willing to take risks because he wasn't afraid to fail. The skis did for William what the long-gone record player and toy train could not.

Just as you give your children nutritious food and make them wear warm clothing *ultimately for their benefit*, so, too, choose gifts wisely for them. Provide what is most beneficial not necessarily what is desired. Give gifts that challenge them, bring out their talents, and broaden their creativity and horizons. Such gifts last far beyond one season!

Remember to Give Thanks

It is a good thing to give thanks unto the Lord, and to sing praises unto thy name, O most High.

PSALM 92:1

Upon hearing that the pages at his court were neglecting to ask God's blessing on their daily meals, Alfonso XII of Spain invited the boys to a banquet. He served many delicacies, which the boys ate delightedly. Not one of them, however, remembered to ask God's blessing on their food or to thank Him.

During the banquet, a dirty, ill-clad beggar entered the room. He proceeded to eat and drink to his heart's content. The pages were shocked. They expected the king to order him away, but Alfonso spoke not a word. When the beggar arose and left without so much as a word of thanks, the boys could hold back their indignation no longer. "What a despicably mean fellow!" they cried.

The king silenced them and in a calm voice said, "Boys, bolder and more audacious than this beggar have you all been. Every day you sit down to a table supplied by the bounty of your Heavenly Father, yet you ask not His blessing nor express to Him your gratitude."[73]

For what are you failing to give thanks today? As you voice your "overdue" thanks, you will find that the problems you have been grumbling about will pale in comparison to God's graceful goodness.

MY THOUGHTS:

FOR WHAT BLESSINGS DO I OWE GOD MY "OVERDUE" THANKS?

Compelling Love

"Greater love hath no man than this, that a man lay down his life for his friends."

JOHN 15:13

MY THOUGHTS:

_____
_____
_____
_____
_____
_____
_____
_____
_____
_____
_____
_____
_____
_____
_____
_____

WHOM ARE THE PEOPLE IN MY LIFE THAT I COULD LOVE INTO THE KINGDOM OF GOD?

Shortly after Charles Colson received word that he was to be returned to Maxwell prison, he got a call from Al Quie, one of the most respected public figures in Washington. Quie said, "Chuck, I've been thinking about what else we can do to help you . . . There's an old statute someone told me about. I'm going to ask the president if I can serve the rest of your term for you."

Colson was stunned. "I mean it, Chuck," Quie said. "I haven't come to this decision lightly." Overwhelmed, Colson refused his offer. Later that day, he received a note from Al Quie, who wrote, "If I could, I would gladly give my life so you could use the wonderful gifts of God that He has entrusted you with, to the glory of God . . ."

That night Colson completely surrendered his life: "Lord, if this is what it is all about . . . I praise You for giving me Your love through these men, for being God, for just letting me walk with Jesus."

Forty-eight hours later, an order was issued to release Colson from prison. A Christian marshal said to him as he departed, "I kind of knew He would set you free today."

Colson replied, "Thank you, but He did it two nights ago."[74]

He'll Show You What to Do

If you don't know what you're doing, pray to the Father. He loves to help. You'll get his help, and won't he condescended to when you ask for it.

JAMES 1:5 MSG

J ames Gilmour, a missionary to Mongolia, was once asked to treat some wounded soldiers. Although Gilmour was not a doctor, he had some knowledge of first aid, so he felt he should help the men the best he could. He cleaned and dressed the wounds of two of the soldiers, but the third man's leg was badly broken. The missionary had no idea what to do for such an injury.

Kneeling beside the man, he humbly asked the Lord for guidance. He rose, confident that help would be supplied. No sooner had he finished his prayer than a group of beggars came up and asked Gilmour for money. His heart went out to them, and he hurriedly gave them a small gift and a few kind words.

One weary beggar remained behind as the others left. The man was little more than a walking skeleton. Immediately, Gilmour realized the Lord had brought him a living anatomy lesson! He asked the elderly beggar if he might examine him. Carefully tracing the femur bone with his fingers, he discovered what he needed to do to set the soldier's fractured leg![75]

When we come to God with a humble heart, admitting we don't know what to do, He will answer us and show us the way.

MY THOUGHTS:

_____
_____
_____
_____
_____
_____
_____
_____
_____
_____
_____
_____
_____
_____
_____
_____
_____

TODAY I NEED GOD'S WISDOM REGARDING . . .

A Mother's Work Is Never Done

Always be joyful.

1 THESSALONIANS 5:16 TLB

MY THOUGHTS:

_____
_____
_____
_____
_____
_____
_____
_____
_____
_____
_____
_____
_____
_____
_____
_____
_____
_____
_____

THE NEXT TIME I BECOME EXASPERATED, I WILL WORK ON BECOMING JOYFUL BY . . .

A mother once faced the prospect of sixteen trips to church! Various combinations of her children were serving in various roles for three different Sunday services. The one serving the seven o'clock service had to be there fifteen minutes early to robe and light the candles. So Mom doubled back for the kids who were going to attend that service since they weren't ready when she left the first time. And so it went for each service—two trips . . . and the same coming home. With three services, Sunday school, and two different youth-group meetings, the total number of trips was sixteen! Since the church was six miles from their home, she drove ninety-six miles that morning, all before lunch. She moaned to herself more than once, "This is the last time my husband goes out of town on business over a weekend!"

To her dismay, she found a police car in their driveway upon her final trip home. An officer had been sent to check on a fairly large number of past-due parking tickets acquired by her husband. "Been busy this morning?" the officer asked. The woman recounted the litany of her morning. And then the officer asked the worst possible question, "May I see your license?" It had been expired for two months!

Keep Your Inner Vision Clear

If our consciences are clear, we can come to the Lord with perfect assurance and trust.

1 JOHN 3:21 TLB

In *My Utmost for His Highest*, Oswald Chambers wrote:

Conscience is that ability within me that attaches itself to the highest standard I know, and then continually reminds me of what the standard demands that I do. It is the eye of the soul which looks out either toward God or toward what we regard as the highest standard. This explains why conscience is different in different people. If I am in the habit of continually holding God's standard in front of me, my conscience will always direct me to God's perfect law and indicate what I should do. The question is, will I obey? . . .

God always instructs us down to the last detail . . . He does not speak with a voice like thunder—His voice is so gentle that it is easy for us to ignore. And the only thing that keeps our conscience sensitive to Him is the habit of being open to God on the inside. When you begin to debate, stop immediately. Don't ask, "Why can't I do this?" You are on the wrong track. There is no debating possible once your conscience speaks. Whatever it is—drop it, and see that you keep your inner vision clear.[76]

MY THOUGHTS:

WHAT IS THE STATE OF MY CONSCIENCE? AM I HAPPY WITH MY EVALUATION?

167

june 9

Live Honestly

We trust we have a good conscience, in all things willing to live honestly.

HEBREWS 13:18

MY THOUGHTS:

_____
_____
_____
_____
_____
_____
_____
_____
_____
_____
_____
_____
_____
_____
_____
_____

WHAT AREAS OF MY LIFE COULD APPEAR PHONY TO MY CHILDREN? AN EXAMPLE WOULD BE . . .

A little girl shouted with glee at the unexpected appearance of her grandmother in her nursery. "I've come to tuck you into bed and give you a good-night kiss," the grandmother explained.

"Will you read me a story first?" the little girl asked.

Grandma, dressed elegantly for the impending dinner party downstairs, couldn't resist the soulful plea in her granddaughter's eyes "All right," she replied, "but just one."

At the close of the story, the little girl snuggled into her bed, ready for sleep but not before she said, "Thank you, Grandma. You look pretty tonight."

The grandmother smiled and replied, "Yes, I have to be pretty for the dinner party your parents are hosting."

"I know," the little girl said. "Mommy and Daddy are entertaining some very important people downstairs."

"Why, yes," said the grandmother. "But how did you know that? Was it because I surprised you by coming upstairs tonight? Was it my dress that gave it away?" Each time her granddaughter shook her head with a vigorous no. Finally, the grandmother asked, "Was it that I only read one story to you?"

"No," the little girl giggled. "Just listen! Mommy is laughing at all of Daddy's jokes."

Faith Before the Fact

"I tell you, whatever you ask for in prayer, believe that you have received it, and it will be yours."

MARK 11:24 NIV

In *Beyond Ourselves*, author Catherine Marshall tells how one of her first lessons in living by faith came when she faced a problem financing her college education. She and her family lived in a small town in West Virginia that had undergone severe today? financial struggles in the aftermath of the 1929 stock-market crash. The two railroad shops, which were the only industry in town, were nearly shut down. Her father, a minister, suffered along with everyone else.

Even with the promise of a small work scholarship and $125 she had saved, Catherine was several hundred dollars short of what she needed to attend college.

One night her mother came to her room and found her sobbing. Her dreams of college seemed dashed. Her mother said, "You and I are going to pray about this." They went to the guest room, so they wouldn't be disturbed. Her mother said, "Whenever we ask God for something that is His will, He hears us. If He hears us, then He grants the request we have made. So you and I can rest on that promise." The answer came quickly. Catherine's mother was offered a job writing the history of their county. History had long been one of her mother's loves, and she made enough in this job to pay for Catherine's college expenses with a little to spare. Catherine concluded, "I learned that we must have faith before the fact, not after."[77]

MY THOUGHTS:

FOR WHAT THINGS DO I NEED TO TRUST GOD TODAY?

A Mother's Touch

Be patient with each person, attentive to individual needs.
1 THESSALONIANS 5:14 MSG

MY THOUGHTS:

_____
_____
_____
_____
_____
_____
_____
_____
_____
_____
_____
_____
_____
_____
_____
_____
_____
_____
_____

WHAT STEPS CAN I TAKE TO BECOME MORE LIKE THE MOTHER IN THIS STORY?

In her book, *American Girl*, Mary Cantwell tells of her great embarrassment and agony at not being able to do math like the other children in her class at school. She writes:

It was agony to me to be so stupid. The more Miss Fritzi tried to show me how to translate the marks into symbols, the more cotton seemed to be stuffing the corners of my head. The cotton seemed even thicker on the nights Papa sat beside me at the desk in the living room, pencil points breaking under his fierce attack. I snuffled and shook and his voice took on a steel edge, and when at last my mother shyly volunteered, the suffering eyes we turned on her were identical.

For several nights she sat at the desk . . . and summoned up her old schoolteacher's skills. Sniffling at her left, I bent over a scratch pad watching while her small, shapely hand (a hand that could trace a line of gold leaf as fine as a hair) traced swoops and curlicues. Suddenly they assembled themselves into sense and the cotton fled my head, leaving it as clear and clean as a tide-rinsed seashell . . . I knew a triumph second only to that I'd known on the morning I finally succeeded in tying my shoelaces into bows. I could add!

Taking the time to help your children —no matter what the task—can change their world and yours.

Thirsty for God

As a deer longs for flowing streams, so my soul longs for you, O God. My soul thirsts for God, for the living God.

PSALMS 42:1-2 NRSV

J ohn Vianney, who is considered a saint, has written beautifully about the heart's cry of prayer and the need to pray with a pure heart:

Prayer is a fragrant dew, but we must pray with a pure heart to feel this dew. There flows from prayer a delicious sweetness, like the juice of very ripe grapes. Troubles melt away before a fervent prayer like snow before the sun. To approach God one should go straight to him, like a ball from a cannon. Prayer disengages our soul from matter; it raises it on high, like the fire that inflates a balloon. The more we pray, the more we wish to pray. Like a fish which at first swims on the surface of the water, and afterwards plunges down and is always going deeper, the soul plunges, dives, and loses itself in the sweetness of conversing with God. Prayer is the holy water that by its flow makes the plants of our good desires grow green and flourish, that cleanses our souls of the imperfections, and that quenches the thirst of passion in our hearts.[78]

It is out of the deepest recesses of the heart that our most passionate prayers arise. It is about our unspoken dreams and secret desires that we need to pray most. It is in this area of our soul that prayer does its most powerful work.

MY THOUGHTS:

_____
_____
_____
_____
_____
_____
_____
_____
_____
_____
_____
_____
_____
_____
_____
_____
_____
_____

TODAY I WILL START THE FLOW OF LIVING WATER BY . . .

The Joy of Newborns

Children's children are a crown to the aged, and parents are the pride of their children.

PROVERBS 17:6 NIV

MY THOUGHTS:

_____
_____
_____
_____
_____
_____
_____
_____
_____
_____
_____
_____
_____
_____
_____
_____
_____
_____
_____

WHO IN MY LIFE MIGHT BE WILLING TO HELP OUT WITH MY CHILDREN?

In *Murphy Must Have Been a Mother*, Teresa Bloomingdale recalls a conversation she had with her husband, who said, "I love new babies.

"Since when?" I joked. "You were the one who always wished they could be born housebroken and able to play baseball! You had no patience at all with the squalling infants who leaked from both ends and spit up on every shirt you owned. It wasn't until they got into their terrible twos that you thought the kids were worth keeping!"

"That's not true and you know it," he said with a sigh. "I truly loved those infants, even ones who couldn't tell time and kept us up all night . . . Don't tell me you wouldn't just love to start all over again!"

"True, I loved having a new baby every year . . . when I was young and lively and had not yet become addicted to sleep. But at our age? No, thank you."

In planning to help her son and daughter-in-law, Bloomingdale was determined to be the model grandmother —up at night, folding diapers, and making formula. But then she discovered she was out of a job. The baby's *great*-grandmother had arrived to help out!

Is it true that the elderly need less sleep? If so, great-grandmas truly may be best suited for newborns!

Growing Deeper Roots

I pray that Christ will be more and more at home in your hearts, living within you as you trust in him. May your roots go down deep into the soil of God's marvelous love.

EPHESIANS 3:17 TLB

An English minister, Leslie Stokes, once told the following parable:

Once upon a time there was a tree—a lovely tree, shapely, strong, and stately. However, appearances cannot always be trusted. Inwardly, the tree knew that its massive strength was beginning to wane. When the wind was strong, it felt itself shaking ominously. It heard suspicious creaks and groans in its wood. The tree attempted to compensate for this weakness by growing another branch or two. It then looked stronger and safer than ever.

When the next gale blew, however, there was a terrific snapping of roots, and but for the support of a friendly neighboring tree, the stately tree would have crashed to the ground.

Over time, the tree recovered from its shock and began to re-anchor its roots, albeit its shape had been altered, and it now leaned slightly. It looked at its neighbor with curiosity, wondering how it had withstood the storm. The tree asked, "How is it that you not only stood your ground, but were able to help me?"

The neighboring tree replied, "That's easy to answer. When you were busy growing new branches, I was growing deeper roots."[79]

Prayer causes our roots to grow, strengthening us so that our branches are able to support others and produce fruit.

MY THOUGHTS:

_____
_____
_____
_____
_____
_____
_____
_____
_____
_____
_____
_____
_____
_____
_____
_____
_____
_____

WHAT PARTS OF MY LIFE HAVE I BEEN CULTIVATING? AN EXAMPLE WOULD BE . . .

june 15

We show we are servants of God by our pure lives, our understanding, patience, and kindness.

2 CORINTHIANS 6:6 NCV

MY THOUGHTS:

_____
_____
_____
_____
_____
_____
_____
_____
_____
_____
_____
_____
_____
_____
_____
_____

WHAT CHARACTER TRAITS DO I EMPLOY WHEN TRYING TO BRING OUT THE TURTLES IN MY LIFE?

A little girl once paid a visit to relatives who lived in the country. While walking along a country road, she found a turtle also walking on the warmed pavement. As she moved closer to examine it, the turtle closed its shell like a vice. When she tried to pry him open with a stick, her uncle intervened, "No, no. That is not the way. I'll show you what we need to do."

The uncle picked up the small creature and carried it into the house. There he set it on the hearth. Within a few minutes, the turtle began to get warm; he stuck out his head and feet and calmly crawled toward the girl.

"People are sort of like turtles too," her uncle said. "If you try to force them to do anything, they'll usually close up tightly. But if you warm them up with a little kindness, they'll more than likely open up and come your way."

If you had to pick only one trait around which to live all the time, what would it be? Order . . . honors . . . knowledge . . . passion . . . fame? Probably not. The most livable of all traits is one every person can show: kindness.

Just Talk to Him

"This is your Father you are dealing with, and he knows better than you what you need. With a God like this loving you, you can pray very simply."

MATTHEW 6:8-9 MSG

A minister once attended a conference at which a number of notable Christian leaders were present. The conversation was intense, to god just and the minister found it almost impossible to keep up with the theological and philosophical issues being discussed. At lunchtime, several of the ministers gathered at a nearby restaurant, and a seminary professor was asked to pray before the meal. The minister thought to himself as he bowed his head, *This is going to sound like theology class.*

To the minister's great surprise, the professor prayed, "Father, I love being alive today And I love sitting down with my brothers, eating good food and talking about kingdom business. I know You're at this table, and I'm glad. I want to tell You in front of these brothers that I love You, and I'll do anything for You that You ask me to do." His simple prayer came from his heart not his intellect.

So often in prayer we attempt to *sound* like theologians—using "thee" and "thou" language and lofty phrases, as if we are attempting to impress God with our understanding. The fact is, God knows what we *are not* as well as what we *are*. While He is not impressed with our knowledge and understanding, He desires to impress upon us, with His indelible stamp of grace, His identity and righteousness.[80]

MY THOUGHTS:

TODAY I WILL TALK TO GOD JUST LIKE I WOULD TALK TO A TRUSTED FRIEND ABOUT . . .

Know What Love is Not

Teach them the statutes and instructions and make known to them the way they are to go and the things they are to do.

EXODUS 18:20 NRSV

MY THOUGHTS:

_____
_____
_____
_____
_____
_____
_____
_____
_____
_____
_____
_____
_____
_____
_____
_____

WHAT RESPONSIBILITIES DO I NEED TO REQUIRE OF MY CHILDREN AT THIS TIME?

Once upon a time, there was a little boy who was given everything he wanted. As an infant, he was given a bottle at the first little whimper. He was picked up and held whenever he fussed. His parents said, "He'll think we don't love him if we let him cry."

He was never disciplined for leaving the yard, even after being told not to. He suffered no consequence for breaking windows or tearing up flower beds. His parents said, "He'll think we don't love him if we stifle his will."

His mother picked up after him, made his bed, and cleaned up all his messes. His parents said, "He'll think we don't love him if we give him chores."

Nobody ever stopped him from using bad words or telling dirty jokes. He was never reprimanded for scribbling on his bedroom wall. His parents said, "He'll think we don't love him if we stifle his creativity."

He never was required to go to Sunday school. His parents said, "He'll think we don't love him if we force religion down his throat."

One day the parents received news that their son was in jail on a felony charge. They cried to each other, "All we ever did was love him and do for him." Unfortunately, that is, indeed, all they did.

Silence is Golden

Be still, and know that I am God.
PSALM 46:10

Although their denominations and doctrinal positions may differ, nearly all notable Christian leaders seem to agree on this one point: God works within us and speaks to us in stillness. God looks on the heart, and a pure heart attuned to Him is of far more value to Him than many words. Here is what some have said:

"God wants quiet; He works in silence; He needs serenity to act, and time to calm us down. Like present-day servants, He insists on one point: that we treat Him with consideration, that we take time and trouble to think of Him."—Louis Evely in *Teach Us How To Pray*[81]

"There's no use slamming on the brakes and stopping our car on a dime if the motor inside keeps whirling at top speed."— Trappist monk

"Some of the best times in prayer are wordless times. I stop speaking, close my eyes, and meditate upon what I have been reading or upon what I have been saying, and I listen inside of myself."—Charles R. Swindoll in *Three Steps Forward, Two Steps Back*[82]

"We cannot put ourselves directly in the presence of God if we do not practice internal and external silence."—Mother Teresa in *Life in the Spirit*[83]

In prayer, silence is not the absence of sound. It is the sound of being fully submitted to hear God's voice.

MY THOUGHTS:

_____
_____
_____
_____
_____
_____
_____
_____
_____
_____
_____
_____
_____
_____
_____
_____
_____
_____
_____
_____

THE THINGS THAT KEEP ME FROM GETTING QUIET INSIDE ARE . . .

177

An Act of God

God blessed them, and God said unto them, Be fruitful, and multiply, and replenish the earth, and subdue it.

GENESIS 1:28

MY THOUGHTS:

_____
_____
_____
_____
_____
_____
_____
_____
_____
_____
_____
_____
_____
_____
_____
_____
_____
_____
_____

WHAT HAS BEEN GOD'S GREATEST ACT IN MY LIFE? HOW DID IT COME ABOUT?

When ancient men and women witnessed great manifestations of nature's power—such as volcanic eruptions, giant waterfalls, hurricanes, great earthquakes, and lightning bolts—they referred to them as "God's deeds" because they knew that no matter how strong they might be as individual people or collective bands of people, they could not do anything as powerful. Even today, great natural catastrophes are termed "acts of God" by insurance companies.

Unfortunately, these displays of nature were often devastating to people, and thus "deeds of God" became equated in the minds of many as "punishments by God." The thinking developed that when God intervenes in the affairs of mankind, it is generally for the purpose of reprimand.

How unfair to God! The truth is that when God chooses to intervene in the affairs of men and to set history on a new course, He does not send a lightning bolt, tidal wave, or tornado—rather, He causes a baby to be born.

The conception of a baby may not be regarded as earthshaking news to anyone other than the baby's family, but from God's perspective, it is the most powerful "deed" He performs!

Moved to Action

When [Jesus] saw the multitudes, he was moved with compassion on them, because they fainted, and were scattered abroad, as sheep having no shepherd.

MATTHEW 9:36

Amy Carmichael landed in India in 1897. As a missionary, she devoted her first few years there to itinerant evangelism. As she traveled and became acquainted with the people, to her horror she discovered that there was "secret traffic" in the area: little girls were being sold or given for temple prostitution.

With anguished tears, Amy diligently prayed that God would enable her to find a way to rescue some of these girls. No one had ever known such a girl to escape. Nonetheless, Amy continued to pray, believing she was praying the will of Heaven and that God would answer her heart's cry.

Several years passed, but then suddenly her prayer was answered. A little girl escaped and came—led by an angel, Amy believed—straight to her. That first escape opened the way for other girls to be rescued.

Shortly thereafter, Amy discovered that little boys were being used for homosexual purposes by drama societies connected with Hindu temple worship. She prayed for the boys as she had for the girls, with many tears and much faith. Within a few years, Amy had become Amma ("Mother") to a rapidly growing Indian family that eventually numbered nine hundred children![84]

MY THOUGHTS:

WHAT MOVES ME TO TAKE ACTION? WHY?

The Real Mom

The angel said to her, "Rejoice, highly favored one, the Lord is with you; blessed are you among women!"

LUKE 1:28 NKJV

MY THOUGHTS:

_____
_____
_____
_____
_____
_____
_____
_____
_____
_____
_____
_____
_____
_____
_____
_____
_____

WHAT THINGS CAN I DO TO BRING HEALING TO MY CHILD'S HURTING HEART?

A thirteen-year-old girl named Amy was not only struggling with growing into womanhood but also with discovering her "identity." She had been adopted from South Korea and had no information about or remembrance of her birth mother. As much as she loved her adoptive parents, she began to speak frequently about what her "real mother" might be like.

During this time, Amy's dentist determined that she needed braces. On the day her braces were fitted, Amy went home from the dentist's office in pain. As the day wore on, her discomfort grew, and by bedtime she was miserable. Her mother gave her medication and then invited her to snuggle up in her lap in the rocking chair, just as she had done when she was a little girl. As the mother rocked and stroked Amy, she began to relax in comfort. She was nearly asleep when she said to her mother in a drowsy voice, "I know who my real mom is."

"You do?" her mother asked gently.

"Yes," she replied. "She's the one who takes away the hurting."

A mother may not always be able to "kiss it and make it well," but the love she gives her children goes a long way toward making them "whole."

Any Time Is a Good Time to Pray

Pray all the time.

1 THESSALONIANS 5:17 MSG

MY THOUGHTS:

After attending an early church service one Sunday morning, Bill stopped at a cafe for breakfast. The cafe was empty, except for two elderly men sitting at the counter. They were obviously regulars because one of the men became quite upset that his usual waiter was not on duty that morning. When the waitress started to pour him a cup of coffee, he cried, "No, no! I never drink coffee. I drink hot chocolate. Where is my waiter? What are you doing here? He always knows what I want for breakfast."

On the verge of tears, the woman retreated to the kitchen area. Bill, who had overheard their conversation thought, *I've already had my morning devotionals and said my prayers at church, but perhaps it's time to pray again.* He said in a whisper, "God, please make this man's day a little easier for him. Let him find a soft spot in his heart for this hardworking waitress."

A short while later, the young woman returned to bring food to the two men, and the one who had been so rude to her said tenderly, "I'm sorry, my dear. I don't know what came over me. What I said was very rude. I hope I didn't hurt your feelings."[85]

Any time is a good time to pray. Any circumstance is a great opportunity! As Francis de Sales once said, "Give Him your whole soul a thousand times in the day."[86]

TODAY I WILL LOOK FOR OPPORTUNITIES TO PRAY AS I . . .

We Never Outgrow Our Need for Mothers

Near the cross of Jesus stood his mother.
JOHN 19:25 NIV

MY THOUGHTS:

_____
_____
_____
_____
_____
_____
_____
_____
_____
_____
_____
_____
_____
_____
_____

I ESPECIALLY NEED MY MOTHER WHEN . . .

A number of years ago, a popular Mother's Day card summed up what many adult women feel. The cover of the card read, "Now that we have a mature, adult relationship, there's something I'd like to tell you." On the inside were these words: "You're still the first person I think of when I fall down and go boom."

None of us ever get beyond feeling a need for our mothers—the one person who has nurtured us, comforted us, and cared for us as no other person ever has or ever will. It is only when we are mothers ourselves, however, that we tend to realize how important our own mothers were to us. As Victoria Farnsworth has written:

Not until I became a mother did I understand how much my mother had sacrificed for me.

Not until I became a mother did I feel how hurt my mother was when I disobeyed.

Not until I became a mother did I know how proud my mother was when I achieved.

Not until I became a mother did I realize how much my mother loves me.

He Changes Our "Want To"

It is God who works in you to will and to act according to his good purpose.

PHILIPPIANS 2:13 NIV

One day a woman couldn't help but notice that her young nephew was feeling a bit antsy. The boy was generally an even-tempered, attentive child, but on this particular day, he could not seem to keep his mind on the chore she had assigned him. Finally, with genuine concern, she asked, "Is something wrong?" He nodded. "Why don't you tell me about it?" she asked.

"Auntie," he said, "I've lost my favorite marble. It's a cat eye, and it took me forever to get it in the first place. Now it's gone."

"Why don't we pray about it?" she asked.

Together, they knelt by a nearby chair. Immediately after their prayer, the boy seemed to be in a calmer mood, and his chore was finished quickly.

The next day, almost afraid to mention it lest her nephew still be missing his favorite marble, the aunt asked cautiously, "Dear, did you find your missing treasure?"

"No," the boy replied cheerfully, "but God has me not want to."[87]

When we pray, we may find that we don't always get what we thought we wanted. But if we pray sincerely with an open heart, we sometimes find that our heart's desires change to conform to what God truly desires to give us.

MY THOUGHTS:

_____
_____
_____
_____
_____
_____
_____
_____
_____
_____
_____
_____
_____
_____
_____
_____
_____
_____
_____
_____

I'D LIKE GOD TO CHANGE MY "WANT TO" REGARDING . . .

Make an Investment

Sons and daughters, come and listen and let me teach you the importance of trusting and fearing the Lord.

PSALM 34:11 TLB

MY THOUGHTS:

_____
_____
_____
_____
_____
_____
_____
_____
_____
_____
_____
_____
_____
_____
_____
_____
_____
_____

I WANT TO INCREASE THE INVESTMENT IN MY CHILD IN THE AREAS OF . . .

The Lazy B Ranch—all 260 square miles of it—lies on the New Mexico and Arizona border. Most of it is scrub brush, and it has been in the Day family since 1881. When Harry and Ada Mae Day had their first child, they traveled 200 miles to El Paso for the delivery. Ada Mae brought her baby girl home to a difficult life. The four-room adobe house had no running water and no electricity. There was no school within driving distance. One would think that with such limited resources, a little girl's intellectual future might be in question. But Harry and Ada Mae were determined to "stitch learning" into their children.

Ada Mae subscribed to metropolitan newspapers and magazines. She read to her child hour after hour. When her daughter was four years old, she began her on the Calvert method of home schooling, and she later saw that her daughter went to the best boarding schools possible. One summer, the parents took their children on a car trip to visit all the state capitols west of the Mississippi River. When young Sandra was ready for college, she went to Stanford, then on to law school . . . and eventually, she became the first woman justice to sit on the Supreme Court of the United States of America.

Every day you make an investment into the character of your child. Make BIG investments!

Spiritually Fit

Spend your time and energy in the exercise of keeping spiritually fit. Bodily exercise is all right, hut spiritual exercise is much more important and is a tonic for all you do.

1 TIMOTHY 4:7-8 TLB

A middle-aged man looked in the mirror one day and didn't like what he saw. His formerly lean, muscular body had become flabby Although he had enjoyed physical exertion as a young man, he now detested exercise. Not only did he find it a waste of time, but he hated the aches and pains associated with it. He had a long track record of starting, stopping, starting, and stopping exercise programs. The result? He remained unfit.

Then one day, he picked up Kenneth Cooper's book, Aerobics, in which Dr. Cooper documents the importance and benefits of exercising the heart. The man read the book several times and started jogging regularly. He didn't read the book for information or to become convinced. He read the book for motivation. Eventually, exercise became its own motivation. He began to enjoy exercise because he liked the results![88]

We can know prayer is valuable and be convinced it is important. But it is only when we pray in a disciplined manner that we truly become motivated to pray further. Why is this so? Because prayer empowers us. The more we feel empowered by God, the more we desire to become empowered. The net result is spiritual fitness —a greater capacity to serve others and experience abundant life.

MY THOUGHTS:

WHAT STEPS CAN I TAKE TO BECOME MORE DISCIPLINED IN MY PRAYER LIFE?

june 27

Motherhood—A Noble Profession

A capable, intelligent, and virtuous woman . . . She is far more precious than jewels.

PROVERBS 31:10 AMP

MY THOUGHTS:

_____
_____
_____
_____
_____
_____
_____
_____
_____
_____
_____
_____
_____
_____
_____
_____
_____
_____

WHAT VALUE DO I PLACE ON MY ROLE AS A MOTHER? WHY DO I FEEL THAT WAY?

Popular writer and speaker Tony Campolo tells a story about his wife. When he was on the faculty of the University of Pennsylvania, his wife was often invited to faculty gatherings, and inevitably a woman lawyer or sociologist would confront her with the question, often framed in a condescending tone of voice, "And what is it that you do, my dear?"

Mrs. Campolo gave this as her response: "I am socializing two homo-sapiens in the dominant values of the Judeo-Christian tradition in order that they might be instruments for the transformation of the social order into the teleologically prescribed utopia inherent in the echelon." Then she would politely and kindly ask the other person, "And what is it that you do?" The other person's response was rarely as overpowering!

Too often women feel as if they should apologize for being mothers or wives who "work at home" for the betterment of their families and husbands. In reality, these roles are noble callings—ones with far-reaching impact and eternal consequences!

Imploring the Assistance of Heaven

Unless the Lord builds the house, its builders labor in vain.

PSALM 127:1 NIV

In 1787, the Constitutional Convention was on the brink of failure over the issue of whether small states should have the same representation as the larger states. The situation seemed hopeless, and many of the delegates were making plans to return home when eighty-one-year-old Benjamin Franklin offered a suggestion. He was convinced that Scripture is right when it says, "Except the Lord build the house, they labour in vain that build it" (Psalm 127:1). He rose to address the delegates:

"Gentlemen, I have lived a long time and am convinced that God governs in the affairs of men. If a sparrow cannot fall to the ground without His notice, is it probable that an empire can rise without His aid? I move that prayer imploring the assistance of Heaven be held every morning before we proceed to business."

His motion carried. Every morning thereafter, the sessions opened with prayer. In a short while, a compromise was forged. It is still in effect today—a fixed representation for states in the Senate, representation according to population in the House.[89]

The best building material for constructing any solution you may need today is prayer.

MY THOUGHTS:

_____
_____
_____
_____
_____
_____
_____
_____
_____
_____
_____
_____
_____
_____
_____
_____

I CAN ENSURE THAT PRAYER HOLDS ITS RIGHTFUL PLACE IN OUR FAMILY BY . . .

Let the Children Come

june 29

"I tell you the truth, unless you change and become like little children, you will never enter the kingdom of heaven."

MATTHEW 18:3 NIV

MY THOUGHTS:

_____
_____
_____
_____
_____
_____
_____
_____
_____
_____
_____
_____
_____
_____
_____

WHAT STEPS CAN I TAKE TO STEER MY CHILD TOWARD FOLLOWING CHRIST?

A little girl, only three years old, had just learned she was adopted, but she had failed to react one way or the other to that news. Her mother was at a loss as to how to explain the adoption any further.

The next day at church the little girl watched as a number of people came forward at the close of the service to accept Jesus Christ as their Savior and Lord. She asked her mother, "What are they doing?"

Her mother was quick to reply, "God has offered to adopt all of them as His children, and they are taking Him up on His offer, so they can live with Him forever in Heaven and always know that He loves them with all His heart." The little girl nodded and watched in awe as the pastor prayed with each person.

The next day, the mother overheard her little girl speak into her cocker spaniel's silky ear, "I just wanted you to know I'm 'dopting you 'cause God and Mommy and Daddy have 'dopted me. And that way we can live together forever."

Never assume that your children are too young to follow Christ. As much they are able, let them accept and follow. Give approval and full acceptance to their decisions. Eventually, "following" will seem to be the only desirable choice for them to make!

A Great Paradox

He who refreshes others will himself by refreshed.

PROVERBS 11:25 NIV

Everywhere the minister went that day, he encountered crises. He had offered a listening ear, a consoling word, and patient understanding until he was completely drained. Arriving home late in the day, he put on his jogging shoes and headed out for a run. He hoped the exercise would restore his sense of well-being and balance.

As he put on his shoes, he reached into the pocket of his sweatshirt and pulled out a frayed devotional book he often read before his run. He felt like screaming as he read the "thought for today": *Pray for others.*

"Pray for others?" he said. "All I've done today is give to others. What about me? Who cares about my needs?"

He felt angry that God was calling him to still more giving, but eventually he yielded. As his feet rhythmically hit the pavement, he prayed for his neighbors and the people he had met during the day. As he turned his steps toward home, he prayed for his family.

Upon arriving home, the minister realized he was refreshed both spiritually and physically, and he was ready to "give some more."[90]

Is there power in prayer? Most assuredly! It is God's power bestowed *to us* and *in us* so that we might serve others.

MY THOUGHTS:

_____
_____
_____
_____
_____
_____
_____
_____
_____
_____
_____
_____
_____
_____
_____
_____
_____
_____

TODAY I FEEL LED TO PRAY FOR . . .

A Suitable Mother

Being strengthened with all power according to his glorious might so that you may have great endurance and patience.

COLOSSIANS 1:11 NIV

MY THOUGHTS:

_____
_____
_____
_____
_____
_____
_____
_____
_____
_____
_____
_____
_____
_____
_____
_____

WHAT QUALITIES DO I NEED TO DEVELOP IN ORDER TO BE THE KIND OF MOTHER I WOULD LIKE TO BE?

According to a fable, a woman showed up one snowy morning at 5am at the home of an "examiner" of "suitable mother" candidates. Ushered in, she was asked to sit for three hours past her appointment time before she was interviewed. The first question given to her in the interview was, "Can you spell?"

"Yes," she said.

"Then spell 'cook.'"

The woman responded, "C-O-O-K."

The examiner then asked, "Do you know anything about numbers?"

The woman replied, "Yes, sir, some things."

The examiner said, "Please add two plus two."

The candidate replied, "Four."

"Fine," announced the candidate. "We'll be in touch." At the board meeting of examiners held the next day, the examiner reported that the woman had all the qualifications to be a fine mother. Fie said, "First I tested her on self-denial, making her arrive at five in the morning on a snowy day. Then I tested her on patience. She waited three hours without complaint. Third, I tested her on temper, asking her questions a child could answer. She never showed indignation or anger. She'll make a fine mother." And all on the board agreed.

The Test of True Greatness

When you go through deep waters and great trouble, I will be with you. When you go through rivers of difficulty, you will not drown! When you walk through the fire of oppression, you will not be burned up—the flames will not consume you. For I am the Lord your God, your Savior, the Holy One of Israel.

ISAIAH 43:2-3 TLB

College football star Mike Rohrbach, of the University of Washington, once made three trips into the end zone in a big game against Stanford University. At the close of the game, he and about a dozen other players from both teams knelt in the end zone. Thousands of fans wondered what that post-game huddle was all about. So did the sportscasters. Rohrbach, a member of the Fellowship of Christian Athletes, was happy to tell them that the players had "thanked the Lord that we got a chance to compete and see each other as friends." Win or lose, they knew the greater value of the game lay in the relationships they might develop with each other and with God.

The same spirit of prayer invaded the Washington Redskins locker room after they were defeated in a Super Bowl by the Miami Dolphins. After the team prayed together, one of the players, who had fumbled four times, reminded his fellow team members that the real success of any person or team lay not in the way they handled a victory but in the way they handled defeat. Any theology must survive tragedy and loss, or it is not good theology.91

Whether we win or lose, the Lord remains the same. That's the perspective we must always have when we pray. God does not promise we won't ever face defeat. He promises us His presence in *all things* and His power to *face all things.*

MY THOUGHTS:

_____
_____
_____
_____
_____
_____
_____
_____
_____
_____
_____
_____
_____
_____
_____
_____
_____

WHEN I FACE DEFEAT, I NEED TO LOOK TO GOD FOR . . .

A Little Help from a Friend

There is a friend that sticketh closer than a brother.
PROVERBS 18:24

MY THOUGHTS:

_____
_____
_____
_____
_____
_____
_____
_____
_____
_____
_____
_____
_____
_____
_____
_____
_____

HOW CAN I ENCOURAGE THE DEVELOPMENT OF MY CHILD'S MOST POSITIVE FRIENDSHIPS?

A mother once told this story about her young son who wouldn't go to kindergarten:

"I can't go to school!" he would cry, his big blue eyes filling up with tears. "There's a gorilla up on the corner waiting to gobble me up! You can't see him, but he's there! He hides when grown-ups come around. Do you want me to be gobbled up by a gorilla?"

By the time the first ten days of school had passed, this mother had tried everything: bribery, pleading, and threatening. She even locked him out of the house only to find him sitting under the neighbor's bushes, waiting for the time to come home.

The one day as he dawdled on the porch steps, pleading with his mother not to send him to sure death, one of his classmates, Tommy, came walking up the street and talked him into going to school. Her son met Tommy every day for the rest of the year.

This mother writes, "Wherever you are today, Tommy, know that you have my undying gratitude, though I do have one request. Your kindergarten pal has been in school for eighteen years and is still playing eeny-meeny-miney-mo with his college majors. Would you mind dropping in and cajoling this kid into graduating?"

On Earth as It is in Heaven

"Pray along these lines: 'Our Father in heaven, we honor your holy name. We ask that your kingdom will come now. May your will he done here on earth, just as it is in heaven.'"

MATTHEW 6:9-10 TLB

A number of years ago, Pat Robertson was praying and fasting when he heard the Lord ask him, "What do I desire for man?"

Startled, Robertson replied, "I don't know, Lord. You know." He was impressed to turn to the opening chapter of the Bible, where his eyes locked on the phrase, "And God said, Let us make a man in our image, after our likeness: and let them have dominion."

Suddenly, he felt he knew the Lord's purpose for the life of every person—to have dominion over all things on the earth in order to bring the kingdom of God into reality. *Out of heaven . . . to the earth!* That was God's plan!

In his book *The Secret Kingdom*, Robertson explains: "God gives man the authority to govern all that is willing to be governed," and "He grants man authority over the untamed and the rebellious . . . Implicit in the grant was a requirement that man order the planet according to God's will and for God's purposes. This was a grant of freedom, not of license."[92]

We are free today to pray anything we desire to pray. However, we are wise to pray those things that we know are according to God's will and His plan—those things that are in Heaven that God desires to see on the earth. As we pray, we can expect to see our prayers fully answered.

MY THOUGHTS:

TODAY I FEEL LED TO PRAY FOR GOD'S WILL REGARDING WHAT ISSUES AND SITUATIONS?

The Trying Twos

Patience is better than strength. Controlling your temper is better than capturing a city.

PROVERBS 16:32 NCV

MY THOUGHTS:

_____
_____
_____
_____
_____
_____
_____
_____
_____
_____
_____
_____
_____
_____
_____

INSTEAD OF USING GUILT TO CONTROL MY CHILDREN'S BEHAVIOR, WHAT TOOLS WILL I USE TO TRAIN THEM?

During a dinner party, the hosts' two young children entered the dining room totally nude and began to walk slowly on tiptoe around the table. The parents were at first so astonished, and then so embarrassed, that they pretended nothing unusual was happening. They kept the conversation going, and the guests cooperated in the charade, also pretending as if nothing extraordinary was happening in the room.

After completely encircling the table, the children tiptoed from the room. There was a moment of silence at the table as everyone exhaled and stifled their giggles. Then one of the children was overheard saying to the other in the adjacent hallway, "You see, Mommy was right. It is vanishing cream!"

While their rambunctious energy and inexhaustible curiosity can be tiring to adults, toddlers don't mean to misbehave nearly as much as they mean to make sense of the world in which they find themselves. Your discipline, patience, and encouragement are like red, yellow, and green lights governing their "tear" through the exploration process.

When your children try your patience, try to respond in such a way that delivers a verdict of "not guilty."

Answered Prayer

The eyes of the Lord are on the righteous and his ears are attentive to their prayer.

1 PETER 3:12 NIV

Years ago, a devout woman earnestly prayed that her son might be called to preach. He grew up, accepted Christ as his Savior and Lord, and subsequently began to prepare for the calling to which he seemed destined. Before his training was complete, however, he concluded that he was not called to this work. He left school and began to work for a bank. He continued in that field and became a great financier. He died rich and successful.

When her son's will was read, the mother learned that he had left his vast fortune to a theological seminary in Kentucky. By his one act, many young men have been prepared to preach the Gospel.

Centuries earlier, another mother had a similar experience. Hearing that her son desired to visit Rome, she diligently prayed that he would not go. She feared the vices of the city would overwhelm him. Even so, he went. While in Rome, he was converted to Christianity. In his *Confessions*, Augustine writes that his mother's prayer was answered not in its outward form but in its inward heart. What she had really prayed for was that he might be saved from the ways of sin, and he was.[93]

In both cases, the prayers of these mothers were not granted, but they were answered. Today, trust God to respond to you in the way that's best for you–for eternity.

MY THOUGHTS:

_____
_____
_____
_____
_____
_____
_____
_____
_____
_____
_____
_____
_____
_____
_____

GOD MAY NOT ANSWER MY PRAYERS IN THE WAY I EXPECT, BUT I CAN TRUST HIM TO . . .

A Parent's Prayer

We are labourers together with God.
1 CORINTHIANS 3:9

MY THOUGHTS:

_____
_____
_____
_____
_____
_____
_____
_____
_____
_____
_____
_____
_____
_____
_____
_____
_____
_____

**WHAT THINGS
WOULD I INCLUDE
IN MY OWN VERSION
OF "A PARENT'S
PRAYER"?**

Columnist Abigail Van Buren published "A Parent's Prayer" in her "Dear Abby" column. It read, in part:

Oh, heavenly Father, make me a better parent. Teach me to understand my children, to listen patiently to what they have to say, and to answer all their questions kindly. Keep me from interrupting them or contradicting them. Make me as courteous to them as I would have them be to me. Forbid that I should ever laugh at their mistakes, or resort to shame or ridicule when they displease me. May I never punish them for my own selfish satisfaction or to show my power.

Let me not tempt my child to lie or steal. And guide me hour by hour that I may demonstrate by all I say and do that honesty produces happiness. Reduce, I pray, the meanness in me. And when I am out of sorts, help me, O Lord, to hold my tongue. May I ever be mindful that my children are children and I should not expect of them the judgment of adults.

Let me not rob them of the opportunity to wait on themselves and to make decisions. Bless me with the bigness to give them all their reasonable requests, and the courage to deny them privileges I know will do them harm. . . . And fit me, oh Lord, to be loved and respected and imitated by my children. Amen.

Times of Refreshment

july 8

Wonderful times of refreshment will come from the presence of the Lord.

ACTS 3:20 NLT

In *The Power and Blessing*, Jack Hayford writes:

I had gone on vacation, and I needed it! I remember how delightful it was to get to the beach . . . they were great days. But about the fourth day, when everything seemed to be so relaxing, out from under pressure, I found I was feeling empty inside. As I thought about my good external feeling, I wondered about the hollowness I felt inside. Then, it occurred to me.

For four days, I hadn't read a word of Scripture; I hadn't prayed a prayer; I hadn't once sung a song of praise. It was just kind of, "Let's get away from it all." Without planning or saying as much, it was as though we were so involved with church, the Bible, and prayer that we didn't want to do anything especially "godly" for awhile . . .

But I was "called back" by the inner "hollowness" that I felt. And through that experience I learned the impracticality of trying to recover at the physical/emotional level of my life if I neglect the spiritual level.[94]

When we are weary, rest and relaxation alone will not meet our needs. As spiritually alive creatures in Christ Jesus, our true rejuvenation comes when we go to the fountain of life, Jesus himself. He gives us water that satisfies our parched souls and provides energy for our minds and bodies.

MY THOUGHTS:

_____
_____
_____
_____
_____
_____
_____
_____
_____
_____
_____
_____
_____
_____
_____
_____
_____

WITH WHAT THINGS HAVE I TRIED TO FILL THE HOLLOWNESS IN MY SOUL?

197

july 9

A Good Nights Sleep

I stretch myself out. I sleep. Then I'm up again—rested, tall and steady.
PSALM 3:5 MSG

MY THOUGHTS:

_____
_____
_____
_____
_____
_____
_____
_____
_____
_____
_____
_____
_____
_____
_____
_____
_____
_____

WHAT SITUATIONS MIGHT LOOK MUCH BETTER AFTER A GOOD NIGHT'S SLEEP?

Kais Rayes writes that he and his wife found their whole life turned upside down when their first child was born. Every night, the baby seemed to be fussy, and many nights, it seemed to the young couple that their baby cried far more than he slept. Says Rayes, "My wife would wake me up, saying, 'Get up, honey! Go see why the baby is crying!'" As a result, Rayes found himself suffering from severe sleep deprivation.

While complaining to his coworkers about his problem one day, one of his colleagues suggested a book on infant massage. He immediately went in search of the book; and that night he tried the technique, gently rubbing his baby's back, arms, head, and legs until the baby was completely relaxed and obviously had fallen into a deep sleep. Quietly tiptoeing from the darkened room so as not to disturb the rhythmic breathing of the baby, he made his way directly to his own bed in hopes of enjoying a well-deserved full night of sleep.

But . . . in the middle of the night . . . his wife awoke him in a panic. "Get up, honey!" she said as she jostled him awake. "Go see why the baby is *not* crying!"

Wait on the Lord

Wait on the Lord: be of good courage, and he shall strengthen thine heart: wait, I say, on the Lord.

PSALM 27:14

In *Three Steps Forward, Two Steps Back*, Charles Swindoll, writes:

It's awfully hard for a country that exists on frozen dinners, instant mashed potatoes, powdered orange juice, packaged cake mixes, instant-print cameras, and freeway express lanes to teach its young how to wait.

One evening I was fussing about seeds in the grapes my wife had served for supper. After crunching into another seed, I laid down the law. "No more grapes served in the Swindoll home unless they are seedless!" I announced with characteristic dogmatism.

Later, when nobody else was around to hear her reproof, Cynthia edged up to me and quietly asked: "Do you know why seeds in grapes bug you?"

"Sure," I said, "because I bite into those bitter little things, and they scatter all over my mouth!"

"No," she smiled, "it's because you're too impatient to dig them out first. The purple grapes really taste better . . . but they take a little more time."[95]

Two answers to prayer are decisive: yes and no. One answer gives us something concrete to do: if. But when God answers by saying "wait," it is perhaps the most difficult for us because we are left in suspense with little to do other than trust. Often in our impatience, we attempt to create an answer of our own. If we really want God's best, however, perhaps we should give Him all the time He needs to prepare us for it!

MY THOUGHTS:

_____
_____
_____
_____
_____
_____
_____
_____
_____
_____
_____
_____
_____
_____
_____
_____
_____
_____
_____

WHAT DOES "WAIT ON THE LORD" MEAN TO ME?

Ask for God's Wise Ideas

july 11

The wisdom that comes from God is first of all pure, then peaceful, gentle.

JAMES 3:17 NCV

MY THOUGHTS:

_____
_____
_____
_____
_____
_____
_____
_____
_____
_____
_____
_____
_____
_____

**WHAT THINGS HAVE
I NOTICED HAVE A
CALMING EFFECT ON
MY CHILD?**

A mother was at her wit's end. Her baby had screamed all day, nonstop. She knew he was in the throes of teething, but what could she do? She had tried rocking him, giving him pieces of ice, carrying him, and every other remedy suggested by her mother and friends. Nothing had worked. Finally, in great frustration, she laid her child in his crib, took a shower, washed her hair, set it, and went to sit under her hair dryer. She thought, *If I can't stop my baby's crying, at least I can stop myself from hearing his cries.* To her surprise, when she came out from under the hair dryer to get a drink of water, she found her baby asleep. The next day when he began to cry she turned on the hair dryer and within minutes, he was calm. She discovered the vacuum cleaner also had this effect, as well as the sound of the tumbling dryer. She said, "I got more housework done than I ever dreamed possible, all in an attempt to calm my child."

Sometimes tantrums are the result of over-stimulation. A child is too tired, surrounded by too many sights and sounds, feeling too many conflicting feelings . . . and yes, even receiving too much reaction from parents! In removing some of the stimulation, a child is given just what he or she needs: calm.

A Friend of God

The Lord spake unto Moses face to face, as a man speaketh unto his friend.

EXODUS 33:11

There once was a Godly man in Germany named Bengel, who was known for his intimacy with Christ. A friend of this saintly man desired to learn his secrets, so he hid himself in Bengel's room one night. He hoped to observe his friend at devotions. Within a short while, Bengel entered the room, sat down at his table, and began reading the New Testament.

Hours passed without Bengel uttering a word. He simply read page after page. Then, as the clock struck midnight, he spread out his hands and said with great joy, "Dear Jesus, we are on the same old terms!"

Then closing his Bible, he climbed into bed and was soon asleep.

Bengel had learned the secret of a deep relationship with Christ—listening to Him through the Scriptures, loving Him in his heart, and talking to Him as a friend.

The more we spend time with our Lord, the better we get to know Him. That knowing should be our greatest goal and joy in prayer. As William Cowper once wrote:

What various hindrances we meet
In coming to a mercy seat!
Yet who that knows the worth of prayer
But wishes to be often there![96]

MY THOUGHTS:

I CAN TAKE THE FOLLOWING STEPS TO DEEPEN MY FRIENDSHIP WITH GOD . . .

The Teen Years

It takes wisdom to build a house, and understanding to set it on a firm foundation.

PROVERBS 24:3 MSG

MY THOUGHTS:

_____
_____
_____
_____
_____
_____
_____
_____
_____
_____
_____
_____
_____
_____
_____
_____
_____

HOW CAN I BECOME MORE UNDERSTANDING OF MY TEENAGER'S UNIQUE NEEDS?

In her book *Murphy Must Have Been a Mother*, Teresa Bloomingdale tells about her daughter's preparing for high school. "I don't have anything to wear," the daughter complained. Mother agreed, "I know that, honey, and I told you we'd go on a shopping spree next Saturday."

"I can't buy clothes now!" the daughter said. "Why not? School starts next week," asked Mom. The daughter said, "I can't get clothes for school until I go to school and see what clothes I should get. What if I showed up in jeans and all the other girls were in skirts? I'd die!"

"Then wear a skirt," the mother suggested. "And find everyone else in jeans?" the daughter asked. When Mom suggested she call a friend and find out what she was going to wear, the daughter said, "Are you kidding? She'd think I don't have a mind of my own!"

Another friend finally called, and the two girls decided on their first-day-of-the-year outfits: blue jeans, white knit shirts, white bobby sox, and topsider shoes. The author wrote, "And these are the girls who spent eight years complaining because they had to wear look-alike uniforms!"

What a Difference Prayer Makes

The effectual fervent prayer of a righteous man availeth much.

JAMES 5:16

Christian cardiologist Dr. Randolph Byrd had a great interest in knowing if prayer had a "scientifically measurable" impact on healing. He said, "After much prayer, the idea of what to do came to me." Over a ten-month period, a computer assigned 393 patients in the coronary care unit at San Francisco General Hospital to one of two groups.

The first group was prayed for by home prayer groups. The second group was not remembered in prayer. The home prayer groups were from various Christian denominations. They were given only the first names of the patients and a brief description of each person's diagnosis and condition. They were prayed for each day.

The prayed-for patients differed from those not prayed for in these ways: They were five times less likely to require antibiotics; they were three times less likely to develop fluid in the lungs; none required an artificial airway attached to a ventilator; and fewer died.

If the technique being studied had been a new drug or procedure, it certainly would have been heralded as a breakthrough. Even Dr. William Nolan, the author of a book denouncing faith healing, said, "It sounds like this study will stand up to scrutiny . . . Maybe we doctors ought to be writing on our order sheets, 'Pray three times a day.'"[97]

MY THOUGHTS:

WHICH PEOPLE IN MY LIFE COULD BENEFIT FROM MY PRAYERS TODAY?

God Will Do It

I know whom I have believed, and am convinced that he is able to guard what I have entrusted to him for that day.

TIMOTHY 1:12 NIV

MY THOUGHTS:

_____
_____
_____
_____
_____
_____
_____
_____
_____
_____
_____
_____
_____
_____
_____
_____
_____
_____

IN WHAT AREAS IS IT MOST DIFFICULT FOR ME TO ENTRUST MY CHILD TO GOD'S CARE?

A woman was preparing to leave her child with a babysitter while she joined her husband for the weekend. He had been out of town for several weeks, and she was looking forward to their time together, even as she felt a little fear and doubt about leaving her four-year-old daughter. She watched from a window as her daughter churned down the driveway on her tricycle, making a right turn at the tree. Her "driving" over the tree roots, however, ended in the tricycle tipping over. She came running into the house with a wail and lifted her skinned knee for her mother to kiss.

"Who will kiss my knee while you're away?" her daughter asked, her chin quivering.

The mother was about to mention the babysitter when she heard herself saying, "I know! God will do it." Her daughter beamed, well satisfied with that answer, and immediately headed back to her tricycle.

The mother found her answer reviving her own faith, and she left for her weekend feeling much more positive about leaving her daughter in the Heavenly Father's hands!

A Helpful Prop

The Lord is near to all who call upon Him, to all who call upon Him sincerely and in truth.

PSALM 145:18 AMP

The story is told of an old Scotsman who was quite ill. The family called for their minister. As the pastor entered the man's room and sat down, he noticed another chair on the opposite side of the bed. The pastor said, "Well, I see I'm not your first visitor of the day."

The old man looked up, puzzled for a moment, then realized that the pastor had noticed the empty chair drawn close to his bedside. "Well, Pastor," he began, "let me tell you about that chair. Many years ago I found it difficult to pray, so one day I shared this problem with my pastor. He told me not to worry about kneeling or about placing myself in some pious posture. Instead, he suggested, 'Just sit down, put a chair opposite you, imagine Jesus sitting in it, and then talk with Him as you would a friend.'" The old Scot added, "I've been doing that ever since."

A short time later, the daughter of the old man called the minister to tell him her father had died very suddenly. She said, "I had just gone to lie down for an hour or two. He seemed to be sleeping so comfortably. When I went back, he was gone. What was odd was that his hand was on the empty chair at the side of the bed. Isn't that strange?"

The minister replied, "No, that's not so strange, I think I understand."[98]

MY THOUGHTS:

_____
_____
_____
_____
_____
_____
_____
_____
_____
_____
_____
_____
_____
_____
_____
_____
_____

WHAT STEPS CAN I TAKE TO MAKE JESUS MORE REAL TO ME AND MY CHILDREN?

Teach Kids to Persevere

Do not throw away your confidence; it will he richly rewarded.
HEBREWS 10:35 NIV

MY THOUGHTS:

_____
_____
_____
_____
_____
_____
_____
_____
_____
_____
_____
_____
_____
_____
_____
_____
_____

*WHAT ARE MY
CHILD'S DREAMS?
AND WHAT CAN I DO
TO HELP MAKE
THOSE DREAMS
COME TRUE?*

Victor Villasenor remained illiterate until adulthood because of dyslexia. Then a woman in his native country of Mexico taught him to read. Ironically, Victor decided he wanted to become a great writer, and he asked God to help him fulfill his dream.

For ten years, Victor worked hard at manual labor—digging ditches and cleaning houses. As he worked, he thought of interesting characters and plots. At night, he read voraciously, devouring more than five thousand books, memorizing favorite opening lines, and analyzing literary styles. Then he started writing: nine novels, sixty- five short stories, and ten plays. He sent them all to publishers—and all were rejected. One publisher sent a two-word response: "You're kidding." Instead of being discouraged, Victor was happy that the publisher had read his work! In 1972, after 260 rejections, Victor sold his first novel, Macho. He then published a nonfiction book and an award- winning screenplay. He is best known for his saga about his own family, *Rain of Gold*, which took twelve years to write."

Encourage your children to dream big! Then motivate them to turn those dreams into reality!

What Would You Do?

To him that knoweth to do good, and doeth it not, to him it is sin.

JAMES 4:17

MY THOUGHTS:

A few years ago, a cable-television program decided to test the compassion of the people in the city where the program originated. An actor was hired to fake a fainting spell on a busy street corner and lie "unconscious" on the ground until someone came to his aid. Out-of-the-way cameras recorded the reactions of those who passed by. Literally hundreds of people came within inches of the man—who, it should be noted, was well groomed and neatly dressed. Most passersby gave him a quick glance and kept walking. Some took a longer look, but they also kept walking. No one wanted to get involved—not even by notifying a policeman who was standing on the next corner. Eventually the actor revived himself since no one came to his aid.

A similar story is told in the Bible in Luke 10:30-37. A Jewish man was beaten and left for dead by robbers. Both a priest and a Levite saw him lying in the ditch but crossed the road to avoid him. Then a Samaritan stopped, bandaged his wounds, took him to an inn, and paid his expenses. It should be noted that the Samaritans were people greatly despised by the Jews.

We are presumptuous to pray that God will meet our needs if we are unwilling to extend ourselves to meet the needs of others.

HOW DO I RESPOND WHEN THERE IS CLEARLY SOMETHING I CAN DO? AND EXAMPLE WOULD BE . . .

Works in Progress

He shall be like a tree planted by the rivers of water, that bringeth forth his fruit in his season.

PSALM 1:3

MY THOUGHTS:

_____

_____

_____

_____

_____

_____

_____

_____

_____

_____

_____

_____

_____

_____

_____

_____

WHERE ARE EACH OF MY FAMILY MEMBERS IN THEIR PERSONAL GROWTH PROCESSES?

A vibrant old woman astounded everyone with her consistent cheerfulness, even though she seemed to have abundant troubles and few pleasures. When she was asked the secret of her upbeat personality, she said, "Well, the Bible says often, 'And it came to pass'—not 'and it came to stay!'"

One of life's greatest lessons is that we are all "works in progress." Your children won't be the same a year from now as they are today. Neither will you be the same parent!

A little girl was once asked by her Sunday school teacher, "Who made you?"

She quickly answered, "Well, God made a part of me."

The teacher asked, "What do you mean, God made a part of you?"

She replied, "Well, God made me real little, and I just grew the rest myself."

Certainly God makes himself available to help us in our growth processes, but He also expects us to grow through the decisions we make, the challenges we undertake, and the efforts we put forth. Embrace the changes that come your way. They are part of God's ongoing process for you—both as a parent and as a person.[100]

He Hears

Hear me when I call, O God of my righteousness: thou hast enlarged me when I was in distress; have mercy upon me, and hear my prayer.

PSALM 4:1

Admiral James Kelly, the navy's chief of chaplains, tells how the members of the Pueblo crew—taken captive by the North confidence Koreans—began to pray more and more frequently as the weary months of their imprisonment dragged on.

At mealtimes, the men would bow their heads slightly and thank God for the food before them. If Communist guards spotted them, however, the guards would scream, "This is not a church! This food is a gift from the Democratic People's Republic of North Korea!"

At night, the men dared not kneel beside their bunks, so they prayed as they were lying on their backs. Instead of praying to the Lord by name, they referred to Him as Commworldflt, which stood for "Commander of the world's fleets." These sailors felt they were making contact with the Supreme Commander of all things, and they stood firm in their belief that they were under His protection and care.101

Regardless of our circumstances, even when we cannot pray openly, God looks at our hearts. Whatever language we may use, whatever words are spoken, He hears us when our hearts are praying.

MY THOUGHTS:

_____
_____
_____
_____
_____
_____
_____
_____
_____
_____
_____
_____
_____
_____
_____
_____
_____
_____
_____

I NEED TO DEVELOP CONFIDENCE THAT GOD HEARS ME WHEN I PRAY ABOUT . . .

God Has the Solution

Now a word to you parents. Don't keep on scolding and nagging your children, making them angry and resentful. Rather, bring them up with the loving discipline the Lord himself approves, with suggestions and godly advice.

EPHESIANS 6:4 TLB

MY THOUGHTS:

_____
_____
_____
_____
_____
_____
_____
_____
_____
_____
_____
_____
_____
_____
_____
_____
_____
_____

WHAT PROBLEM-CAUSING CHILD IN OUR LIVES COULD USE SOME ATTENTION FROM OUR FAMILY?

A junior class in a Chicago church was disrupted every Sunday by one boy. The teacher was in turmoil. She asked herself, *Is my responsibility to this boy or to the others in the class who are disturbed during the lesson?*

Finally, she went to the Sunday school superintendent who advised her the class came first and the problem-causing boy should be told to stay at home. The teacher, however, wasn't willing to settle for that solution. She felt concerned about the boy, whom she believed to be brilliant, and she could not bring herself to tell anyone to stay away from church.

Then she had an idea. She asked the boy to come to her house the next Saturday to help prepare some of the materials for Sunday's lesson. He gladly came without embarrassment and provided real help to her. From that time on, he often came on Saturdays. He became an asset to the class and never again was a hindrance.

Not every behavior problem can be resolved so easily, but one thing is certain: God has a solution for every child. Ask the Lord to reveal the highly individualized solutions you need to reach each of your children effectively.[102]

Protected by Prayer

The end of all things is near. Therefore be clear minded and self-controlled so that you can pray.

1 PETER 4:7 NIV

When Evelyn Christenson—founder of United Prayer Ministries—arrived in El Salvador early one morning, she discovered that three hours earlier, Communist rebels had knocked out all electricity in San Salvador. As she was driven into the city, everywhere Christenson looked she saw the signs of civil war: tanks rumbling in the streets and soldiers standing with guns cocked, ready to fire. That afternoon, on a street near the university where she was speaking, a car was blown up.

As she was being driven to the airport the next day, assailants rushed a taxi ahead of her and dragged out its occupants. Her driver careened around the besieged taxi and sped away. Christenson shot up a desperate prayer: "Oh, Father, protect us! Don't let them get us!"

Immediately, she was calm and felt the Lord reassure her, "You don't have to pray that prayer. You are already protected by all that praying." Her mind turned to family, board members, and friends whom she knew were praying. Then she remembered the 1,000 prayer-clock members who were praying around the clock and the women at the previous day's meeting in Guatemala, who had formed a prayer chain to pray for her safety in El Salvador. *Yes . . . all that praying!* she thought, rejoicing.[103]

In times of danger, there's no greater source of protection than God, no more effective weapon than prayer.

MY THOUGHTS:

TODAY I FEEL LED TO OFFER A PRAYER OF PROTECTION OVER WHAT SITUATIONS?

Pray for Patience and Options

He that is slow to anger is better than the mighty; and he that ruleth his spirit than he that taketh a city.

PROVERBS 16:32

MY THOUGHTS:

_____
_____
_____
_____
_____
_____
_____
_____
_____
_____
_____
_____
_____
_____
_____

THE NEXT TIME I EXPERIENCE AN UNEXPECTED DELAY, I CAN USE THE TIME TO ACCOMPLISH . . .

The last place most people want to be is stuck on an ice-covered road in a traffic jam. Bill found himself in just this position at the base of an ice-covered hill one morning. He knew there was no hope except to turn around slowly. He maneuvered his vehicle off the pavement and onto the grassy shoulder where he thought he could gain more traction to turn his car around. *Patience, Bill*, he kept telling himself. It took him ten slow, frustrating minutes. But no sooner was he on the shoulder of the road than a car came up too quickly behind him, skid on the ice, and crashed at a ninety-degree angle into the truck immediately in front of him. He was trapped again—this time by an accident!

After checking to make certain both drivers were uninjured, Bill used his cell phone to call for a tow truck. *Why didn't I think of using my car phone earlier?* he asked himself. For the next hour, Bill made phone calls—the same calls he would have made at his desk in the office. He accomplished an entire morning's work by the side of an icy road.

When delays come your way, trust God for two things a parent needs every day: patience and options.

Spending Time with the One You Love

One thing have I desired of the Lord, that will I seek after; that I may dwell in the house of the Lord all the days of my life, to behold the beauty of the Lord, and to inquire in his temple.

PSALM 27:4

Corrie ten Boom has written the following:

If you want to hear God's voice and you are uncertain, then remain in His presence until He changes this uncertainty. Often much can happen during this waiting for the Lord. Sometimes He changes pride into humility; doubt into faith and peace; sometimes lust into purity. The Lord can and will do it.

We must also understand that sometimes the silence of the Lord is His way of letting us grow, just as a mother allows her child to fall and get up again when he is learning to walk. If at times God allows a conflict, it may be His way of training us.

Psalm 32:8 says: "I will instruct thee and teach thee in the way which thou shalt go: I will guide thee with mine eye." Could it be clearer? And Psalm 48:14 says: "For this God is our God for ever and ever: he will be our guide even unto death."

It is not at all difficult for the Lord to guide us. And asking things of God gives us a wonderful opportunity to have fellowship with Him. What a comfort it is to know that before we were born, God made His plan for us. He gave us our talents and qualities, and He most certainly will not waste them.[104]

MY THOUGHTS:

_____

_____

_____

_____

_____

_____

_____

_____

_____

_____

_____

_____

_____

WHAT THINGS CAN I REARRANGE IN MY LIFE SO THAT I HAVE MORE TIME TO SPEND WITH GOD?

july 25

Getting Quiet Inside

He leadeth me beside the still waters. He restoreth my soul.
PSALMS 23:2-3

MY THOUGHTS:

_____

I WILL TEACH MY CHILDREN HEALTHY WAYS TO REGAIN SELF-CONTROL BY . . .

Danny's world was turned upside down when his father died—his home totally changed, and his mother became ill. Although his loved ones understood the reason for his insecurity, they didn't know how to deal with his tirades. A special teacher was consulted.

The teacher spent some time with Danny, and when he went into one of his "cyclone imitations," she quietly, but firmly, took hold of his arms and looked him steadily in the eyes. He looked back in fear, expecting her to punish him. Instead she said, "Danny, when little boys act that way, I hold them like this until they get quiet inside."

He didn't struggle. After a moment he said, "You can let go now. I won't do it again."

The teacher said, "Fine," and let go.

The next day, Danny started on a rampage again, this time with one eye on his teacher. She walked slowly toward him as she had the day before, but before she reached him, he suddenly grabbed his own arms and said, "You don't have to hold me. I can hold myself." And he did.

Eventually, children must learn to discipline themselves. It helps, however, to have a patient mother who shows by example how to hold with arms of love.[105]

214

Day-to-Day Dependency

We're depending on God; he's everything we need. What's more, our hearts brim with joy since we've taken for our own his holy name.

PSALMS 33:20-21 MSG

Several men went on a mission trip to Haiti. While they were there, they met a nineteen-year-old youth who deeply loved Christ. He impressed them so greatly that they invited him to visit them in the United States and paid for his trip. When he arrived, the young Haitian felt as if he were in another world. He had never slept between sheets, had never had three meals in one day, had never used indoor plumbing, and had never tasted a hamburger.

By the end of the six-week visit, the young man had made many friends, so his hosts held a farewell dinner in his honor. Several members of the group offered warm parting remarks. Then they asked the youth if he would like to say something. "Yes," he replied, "I would. I want to thank you so much for inviting me here. I have really enjoyed this time in the United States. But I am also very glad to be going home. You have so much in America that I'm beginning to lose my grip on my day-to-day dependency on Christ."[06]

Are you truly relying on the Lord to lead you, give you wisdom, and meet your needs, or are you trusting in your own ability? His desire is that we rely completely on Him. When we do this, He can provide everything He desires to give us because we are open to receive it.

MY THOUGHTS:

IN WHAT AREAS OF MY LIFE DO I NEED TO LEARN TO DEPEND MORE ON GOD?

Random Acts of Kindness

"Let your light shine before men, that they may see your good deeds and praise your Father in heaven."

MATTHEW 5:16 NIV

MY THOUGHTS:

_____
_____
_____
_____
_____
_____
_____
_____
_____
_____
_____
_____
_____
_____
_____
_____
_____

I WILL INITIATE RANDOM ACTS OF KINDNESS IN MY HOME AND COMMUNITY BY . . .

One night while watching the news, Chuck Wall—a human relations instructor at Bakersfield College in California—heard a cliche that stuck in his mind: "Another random act of senseless violence . . ."

Wall got an idea. He assigned his students to perform an out-of-the-ordinary act of kindness and then write an essay about it. One student paid his mother's utility bills. Another bought thirty blankets from the Salvation Army and took them to homeless people who had gathered under a bridge.

For his part, Wall created a bumper sticker that read, "Today, I will commit one random act of senseless KINDNESS . . . Will You?" A bank and a union printed the bumper stickers, and some of the students sold them for a dollar each. The profits went to the county Braille center. The bumper stickers were pasted on all 113 patrol cars in the county, and the message was repeated in pulpits, schools, and professional associations.

Wall commented later, "I had no idea our community was in such need of something positive."

Every community—and every home—needs those who will give their best efforts, creative ideas, and kindness. As a mother, will you lead the way?[107]

Prayer Keeps Us from Unraveling

I had fainted, unless I had believed to see the goodness of the Lord in the land of the living.

PSALM 27:13

It was only four days until her seventeenth birthday, but this year there would be no celebration. It was the depth of the Great Depression, and her father was dying. Her that my mother prayed as the children knelt around his bed, but the girl wondered whether anyone was listening. *Is God near enough to hear our prayer? Does He take any notice of our situation?*

It rained the day of the funeral. Only her mother's friends came. The friends of her father didn't bother. The girl, who worked as a maid, had to borrow a dress for the occasion. When she returned home, a sense of desolation nearly overwhelmed her. Her mother, who had been silent for three days, went into the kitchen, picked up a broom, and began to sweep.

Years later the girl would write, "I cannot explain how that action and the soft whisk-whisk sound gave me courage to go on. My mother was now the head of the house, and we followed. We did not sit down and ask, 'What next? What will we do?' Our home was mortgaged, and my father's lawyer stole her property. She walked out of his office a penniless widow with seven children, ages eight to eighteen. Later someone asked my mother how she had stood it. Her answer was simple: 'I prayed.'"[108]

MY THOUGHTS:

_____
_____
_____
_____
_____
_____
_____
_____
_____
_____
_____
_____
_____
_____
_____
_____
_____

WHAT STEPS CAN I TAKE TO ENSURE THAT MY CHILDREN FEEL SAFE AND SECURE IN THE FACE OF TRAGEDY?

Don't Be a Hope-Stealer

A kind man benefits himself but a cruel man brings trouble on himself.
PROVERBS 11:17 NIV

MY THOUGHTS:

_____
_____
_____
_____
_____
_____
_____
_____
_____
_____
_____
_____
_____
_____
_____
_____

I CAN CONVEY HOPE AND MY UNCONDITIONAL ACCEPTANCE TO MY CHILDREN BY . . .

A couple was about to leave their home one evening to attend an elite society party when the phone rang.

"Hello, Mom," the caller said. "I'm back in the states with an early release from my army duties in Vietnam!"

"Wonderful!" the mother exclaimed. "When will you be home?"

"I'd like to bring a buddy home with me," the son replied. "Both of his legs have been amputated, one arm is gone, his face is disfigured, and one ear and one eye are missing. He's not much to look at, but he needs a home real bad."

"Sure, bring him home for a few days," she said.

"You don't understand," the young man said, "I want to bring him home to live there with you."

The mother stammered, "What would our friends think? It would be just too much for your father . . ." Before she could finish, she heard a dial tone.

Later that night when the couple returned home, they had a message to call the police department. The chief of police said, "Ma'am, we just found a young man with both legs and one arm missing. His face is badly mangled. He shot himself in the head. His identification indicates he is your son."

All of us need love and acceptance, especially those who face special challenges. Build up their hopes and support their dreams, and you will find that your own hopes as a mother will be strengthened as well.[109]

The Power of Forgiveness

Be not overcome of evil, but overcome evil with good.

ROMANS 12:21

Soon after the birth of the Solidarity movement in Poland, Father Jerzy Popieluszko preached among the striking workers in Warsaw's huge steelworks. When martial law was imposed, he made a foray into the night to spread Christmas peace to the soldiers. Then he instituted a monthly "Mass for the Homeland," dedicated to victims of the repressive Communist regime. Tens of thousands attended these services.

Father Jerzy's influence and popularity did not escape the notice of Communist officials. The secret police followed him. He received unsigned, threatening letters. On the first anniversary of imposed martial law, a pipe bomb sailed into his apartment and exploded. Then, after celebrating a special Mass and giving a homily entitled "Overcome Evil with Good," he disappeared. His body was found in the Vistula River.

Word of Father Jerzy's death came as fifty thousand people were listening, in tears, to a tape of his final sermon. In a second, people were down on their knees, crying loudly. And then ... three times they repeated after the priest, "And forgive us our trespasses as we forgive them that trespass against us." The crowd could forgive!

Father Antoni Lewek, one of the priests present, said, "It was a Christian answer to the unchristian deed of the murderers."[110]

Forgiveness gives us tremendous power in prayer. When we forgive, we are releasing those who have hurt or offended us to God, and then He is free to deal with them and to work a healing in our own hearts as well.

MY THOUGHTS:

IN WHAT AREAS OF MY LIFE CAN I OVERCOME EVIL WITH GOOD? AN EXAMPLE WOULD BE . . .

219

july 31

They that know thy name will put their trust in thee: for thou, Lord, hast not forsaken them that seek thee.

PSALM 9:10

MY THOUGHTS:

_____
_____
_____
_____
_____
_____
_____
_____
_____
_____
_____
_____
_____
_____
_____
_____
_____

TODAY I CHOOSE TO TRUST THAT GOD IS WORKING IN THE AREAS OF . . .

In *God: A Biography,* Steven Mosley tells a story about Robert Foss and his Aunt Lana, who experienced a vision that intruded her prayers. Upon reflection and research, they concluded this "picture from God" was of a quiet cove near the Quinault Indian reservation.

Since the family had clothes to deliver to the reservation, Robert and his aunt decided to deliver them immediately. On the way, they found the exact spot Aunt Lana had seen in her vision. However, nothing unusual happened when they stopped at the beach she had seen.

Upon arrival at the reservation, an old Indian grandmother said happily, "You've come! I've been expecting you." As they unloaded the clothes, she told about the trouble in her family and the lack of warm clothing for her grandchildren. One day, she had gone to a quiet place on the beach to ask for God's help. As they compared notes, they discovered her prayer had occurred on the exact day and hour the "picture" first came to Aunt Lana's mind!

Every mother has finite vision and is unable to see all that is going on backstage in God's unfolding plan. We need to keep our attention on the current assignment and then trust God daily that He is arranging all things for the eternal benefit of our lives and the lives of our children.[111]

The Jesus Prayer

The Lord is good to all: and his tender mercies are over all his works.

PSALM 145:9

Christians in the Orthodox Church, and many other mainline denominations, use a prayer called the "Jesus Prayer." It is often voiced in the rhythm of breathing. As such, it is a prayer that becomes for many a means of "praying without ceasing." The words are simple, but they cover everything we truly need: "Lord Jesus Christ, Son of God, have mercy on us."

Some Christians become critical of repetitious prayers. Jesus, however, did not preach against repetition. He preached against the use of *vain* repetition—repetition for the sake of appearing holy to others. A prayer voiced from the heart, filled with meaning to the speaker, is never a vain prayer.

The Very Reverend Kenneth R. Waldron, priest of both the Ukrainian Orthodox Church and the Anglican Church, underwent surgery. He wrote, "The last moment of consciousness before the anesthetic took over, I heard my surgeon repeating in a whisper, '*Gospodi pomiluy, Gospodi pomiluy, Gospodi pomiluy.*'" He was praying, "Lord, have mercy on us." To Reverend Waldron, it was a tremendous comfort to drift into unconsciousness, hearing those words from the lips of his surgeon.[112]

MY THOUGHTS:

_____

_____

_____

_____

_____

_____

_____

_____

_____

_____

_____

_____

_____

_____

_____

_____

_____

WHO ARE THE PEOPLE IN MY LIFE THAT PARTICULARLY NEED GOD'S MERCY TODAY? AM I WILLING TO PRAY THAT SIMPLE PRAYER FOR THEM?

Parting Words Should Always Be Loving Words

My Son! My very own Son! Today I celebrate you!
ACTS 13:32 MSG

MY THOUGHTS:

_____
_____
_____
_____
_____
_____
_____
_____
_____
_____
_____
_____
_____
_____
_____
_____
_____

IN WHAT WAYS CAN I
CELEBRATE MY
FAMILY MEMBERS
TODAY? AN
EXAMPLE WOULD BE
. . .

While preparing to speak at a convention, a woman wanted her husband to go out for sandwiches while she got ready for the event. She requested a chicken sandwich with no mayonnaise. She made sure he understood the order, even to the point of his replying, "Yep, I got it. N-o-o-o-o mayo."

When the sandwich arrived, however, she found it smothered with mayonnaise. Her husband seemed to totally have forgotten her request. She launched into a tirade of "you never listen—you only care about yourself' statements. Tension filled the air in their hotel room for a full hour before she finally asked her husband to forgive her.

Later that evening after she had spoken, a woman came to her and said, "It's lovely to see how much you and your husband love each other. Treasure one another!" She walked away with tears in her eyes.

A woman standing nearby said, "She lost her husband last month. He died of a heart attack. They had been married only two years."

The speaker thought, *How would I feel if the last thing I got to say to my husband was that he blew my sandwich order?*

What was the last thing you said to your family as they walked out of the house? Express gratitude for their lives rather than irritation at their faults.[113]

Thankful and Listening

Lead me in thy truth, and teach me: for thou art the God of my salvation; on thee do I wait all the day.

PSALM 25:5

A minister had returned to school to work on his graduate degree. As he neared the end of his studies, he began to actively search for a pastorate. He had been serving as interim minister at a small church, which had invited him to become their permanent pastor, but he felt that he could attain a better position with his graduate degree. Soon he was invited to visit a number of larger, more prestigious churches. He became anxious about why he wasn't chosen and was puzzled about what he might do to turn things around.

One day at a prayer seminar, he received new insight into the importance of both thanksgiving and listening as parts of prayer. He decided to try both. He began to spend his prayer times thanking God for His many blessings, including the church he had been pastoring. Then, as he listened for God to speak, he realized that he truly enjoyed the work he had been doing. He accepted the call to the little church and was very happy there for many years.[114]

The Lord's Prayer calls us to pray, "Thy will be done. Thy kingdom come." We may find if we pray with a thankful heart, His kingdom has already come, and His will is being done—in us!

MY THOUGHTS:

WHAT STEPS CAN I TAKE TO ENSURE THAT I AM SPENDING TIME JUST LISTENING TO GOD? WHAT THINGS CAN I THANK HIM FOR TODAY?

Concern Need Not Worry

august 4

May the Lord bless and protect you; may the Lord's face radiate with joy because of you; may he be gracious to you, show you his favor, and give you his peace.

NUMBERS 6:24-26 TLB

MY THOUGHTS:

_____
_____
_____
_____
_____
_____
_____
_____
_____
_____
_____
_____
_____
_____
_____
_____

WHAT ARE SOME FAITH-FILLED ADMONITIONS THAT I COULD SAY TO THE ONES I LOVE?

A woman once recalled a number of admonitions she had heard down through the years from her father:

· Don't walk with a spoon in your mouth. You'll trip and that spoon will go right down your throat.

· Don't race around that coffee table. You'll split your head on the corners. They should pad corners!

· Don't eat raw cookie dough. You might get salmonella poisoning.

· Did you wash your hands?

· Watch out for waiters. You don't want to get hot coffee poured on your head.

· Be sure to check the lead content of those mini-blinds you are buying.

· Watch how you use that cleaning fluid. It's poisonous.

· Watch your step when you board the train. You don't want to fall onto the tracks.

She now realized that when her elderly father comes to visit and she takes him to the station to return home, she finds herself saying as she waves good-bye, "Be careful, Dad."

Concern for one's children, spouse, and other family members is a sign of love, but worry is a sign of doubt and fear. We each must learn the difference.[115]

Love in the Way They Need It

Dear friends, since God so loved us, we also ought to love one another.

1 JOHN 4:11 NIV

J. Hudson Taylor, founder of the China Inland Mission, prepared himself for missionary service by doing Gospel work among the poor in London. One night, a man asked him to come and pray for his sick wife. He had sought a priest but had been told he would have to pay eighteen pence, which he did not have. He didn't even have money to buy a loaf of bread.

Taylor gladly went with him but was conscience-stricken. He was living on a starvation diet himself, but he did have one coin in his pocket—a half crown. He thought, *If only I had two shillings and a sixpence, instead of this half crown, I would give these poor people a shilling.* Upon arriving at the man's tenement, he was overcome at seeing the sunken cheeks of the children and the exhausted mother who lay with a tiny infant by her side.

Taylor spoke to them, trying to bring comfort and encouragement, but inside he cried, *You hypocrite! Telling these people about a kind and loving Father in Heaven, and not prepared yourself to trust Him without half a crown.* Before he could pray, he dug deep into his pocket for the half crown and gave it to the man. "And how the joy came back in full flood tide to my heart! . . . Not only was the poor woman's life saved, but my life as fully realized had been saved too."[116]

MY THOUGHTS:

HOW WOULD JESUS HAVE ME SHOW HIS LOVE TODAY? SOME EXAMPLES WOULD BE . . .

See Them Through Gods Eyes

The Lord seeth not as man seeth; for man looketh on the outward appearance, hut the Lord looketh on the heart.

1 SAMUEL 16:7

MY THOUGHTS:

_____
_____
_____
_____
_____
_____
_____
_____
_____
_____
_____
_____
_____
_____
_____
_____
_____
_____
_____

TODAY I WILL APPLAUD THE GOOD I SEE IN OTHERS BY . . .

Nikola Tesla is the scientist who invented the method of generating electricity that is called "alternating current." Many scientists regard him as an even greater genius than the more widely recognized Alexander Graham Bell.

Tesla had an unusual habit. During thunderstorms, he would sit on a black mohair couch by the window and applaud each lightning strike. It was as though one genius was recognizing and appreciating the work of another! Tesla knew better than anyone the wonder of lightning, because he had spent years researching electricity.

For thousands of years, lightning was feared and avoided. There was nothing in lightning strikes that would lead a person to conclude that a similar power might be generated and harnessed and that such a power might be used for good purposes.

Rather than applauding the workmanship of God in others, we too often are critical, unloving, and even fearful. What a difference it makes when we see others—our children, mate, friends, coworkers, and neighbors—as bearers of God's grace, love, and goodness![117]

He Will Even Help Take Away the Desire

May the God of peace . . . equip you with everything good for doing his will, and may he work in us what is pleasing to him, through Jesus Christ.

HEBREWS 13:20-21 NIV

F. B. Meyer has written:

I knelt by my bed, with the door of my room locked, and resolved that I would not sleep until I had settled the matter and surrendered everything to Jesus. It seemed as though Jesus was by my side and then I took from my pocket a large bunch of keys. From that bunch I took one tiny key, which I kept, and then held to Jesus the bunch with the one missing. "Here are the keys of my life," I said. He looked at me sadly and asked, "Are all there?" "All but one tiny one, to a small cupboard. It is so small that it cannot amount to anything." He replied, "Child, if you cannot trust Me with everything, you cannot trust Me with anything . . ."

At last I said, "Lord, I cannot give the key, but I am willing to have You come and take it." It was as I expected. I seemed to hold out my hand, and He came and opened the fingers and took the key from me. Then He went straight to that cupboard, unlocked and opened it, and saw there a thing so terrible and hideous. He said, "This must go out. You must never go that way again." And the moment He took the thing from me, He took the desire for it out of my soul, and I began to hate it. Then I yielded myself absolutely to Him and said, "From this night I want You to do as You will."[118]

MY THOUGHTS:

_____

_____

_____

_____

_____

_____

_____

_____

_____

_____

_____

_____

_____

_____

_____

_____

_____

_____

I SENSE GOD ASKING FOR THE KEY TO WHAT AREAS OF MY LIFE?

Practice Believing Impossible Things

"The things which are impossible with men are possible with God."
LUKE 18:27

MY THOUGHTS:

_____
_____
_____
_____
_____
_____
_____
_____
_____
_____
_____
_____
_____
_____
_____
_____
_____

IF I TRULY BELIEVE
THAT GOD'S WORD
IS TRUE, WHAT
THINGS CAN I BEGIN
TO BELIEVE HE WILL
DO?

In Lewis Carroll's famous book *Through the Looking Glass*, he presents the following conversation between Alice and the queen:

"I can't believe that!" said Alice.

"Can't you?" the queen said in a pitying tone. "Try again, draw a long breath, and shut your eyes."

Alice laughed. "There's no use trying," she said. "One can't believe impossible things."

"I daresay you haven't had much practice," said the queen. "When I was your age, I always did it for half an hour a day. Why, sometimes I've believed as many as six impossible things before breakfast."

One of the things we must recognize is that most of the inventions and major achievements of the past century have been rooted in what was once considered to be impossible.

Can a human being fly? Can a machine process information faster than a human can write? Can a person walk on the moon? Can a person's voice and picture be sent around the world without that person moving an inch? Can you become the mother you truly would like to be? It's not impossible![119]

Strength in Gentleness

You have also given me the shield of Your salvation; Your right hand has held me up, Your gentleness has made me great.

PSALM 18:35 NKJV

Mentor Graham was so absorbed in evaluating assignments that he failed to the people notice the youthful giant who slouched into his Illinois schoolroom one day after school. After his eyes had adjusted to the brightness of the late-afternoon sunshine, causing the husky young man to be in silhouette before him, he recognized the youth as a newcomer to the community. The lad already had a reputation for "whipping the daylights" out of all the local toughs.

Graham would have been justified in thinking, *What does he want here? Am I in danger?* Rather, he looked up and down the six-foot-four-inches of muscle and ignorance before him and offered to help the lad with his reading. When the young man left the schoolroom an hour later, he had several books under his arm—a loan from Mentor Graham with a promise of more in the future.

Few people remember Graham. He was a quiet man, simply willing to do his best for any student who came his way. His pupil, however, became far more famous. His name was Abraham Lincoln.

A kind, helpful response to others is often perceived by them as strength. And it is this gentle strength which will draw people to you.

MY THOUGHTS:

_____
_____
_____
_____
_____
_____
_____
_____
_____
_____
_____
_____
_____
_____
_____
_____
_____
_____
_____

WHO ARE THE PEOPLE IN MY LIFE THAT NEED A GENTLE TOUCH TODAY?

august 10

Do not forsake your friend.
PROVERBS 27:10 NIV

MY THOUGHTS:

_____
_____
_____
_____
_____
_____
_____
_____
_____
_____
_____
_____
_____
_____
_____
_____
_____

WHAT AREAS OF MY LIFE DO I BELIEVE ARE OUT OF BALANCE? AN EXAMPLE WOULD BE . . .

Most of us try to prove ourselves by working extra hard to get ahead. Yet despite our best efforts, the volume of work seems to increase geometrically. Not only do we find we're not moving ahead, but we're not even keeping pace! Rather than stop and regroup, we push ahead and eventually develop burnout.

That's what happened to Denise. Her job ate up her life to the point where every surface in her home was cluttered with unfinished work. Each time a friend called, Denise had to cut the call short, claiming she had "too much work to do."

Finally, Denise's friends decided enough was enough. They showed up at her door one Saturday morning and announced, "We're the cleaning crew you've been meaning to call. We're going to help you get your life back." True to their word, they brought order back into Denise's life and even concluded the day with dinner at a fine restaurant. Their fee? A promise from Denise that she would stop neglecting her friends and make time for a real life.[120]

Today, step back, regroup, and reprioritize your life.

The Pleasure of Your Presence

The Lord said to her, "Martha, dear friend, you are so upset over all these details! There is really only one thing worth being concerned about. Mary has discovered it—and I won't take it away from her!"

LUKE 10:41-42 TLB

A father and his daughter had a very close relationship, and they spent a great deal of time in each other's company. Then one day, the father noticed a change in his daughter's behavior. If he suggested they go for a walk, she excused herself from going. If he offered an ice cream treat at a nearby soda shop, she declined the offer but encouraged him to go on. If he said he was about to drive through the countryside on errands—an activity she had dearly loved—she gave some reason why she couldn't go.

The father grieved her absence, and although he searched his heart and memory for an incident which might have breached their relationship, he could find no reason for her behavior.

When his birthday came, she proudly presented him with a pair of exquisitely knitted slippers, saying, "I made these by myself, just for you." In that moment, he understood where she had been for the past three months.

He said to her, "My darling, I like these slippers very much, but next time, let me buy slippers, so I can spend with you all the hours you worked on them. I would rather have the joy of your company than anything you can make for me."[121]

So it is with our Heavenly Father. He much prefers the pleasure of our presence than any works or good deeds we might present to Him.

MY THOUGHTS:

_____
_____
_____
_____
_____
_____
_____
_____
_____
_____
_____
_____
_____
_____
_____
_____
_____
_____

WHAT ARE THE THINGS I TEND TO DO RATHER THAN SPEND TIME WITH GOD?

Always Available

I will never leave thee, nor forsake thee.
HEBREWS 13:5

MY THOUGHTS:

_____

_____

_____

_____

_____

_____

_____

_____

_____

_____

_____

_____

_____

_____

_____

_____

_____

WHAT STEPS CAN I TAKE TO ENSURE THAT MY CHILDREN KNOW I'M THERE FOR THEM?

Betty felt affirmed greatly by a statement that her son Rick made to her while he was a college student. They were discussing the fact that a neighbor boy, Steve, who always seemed to be in trouble, was now driving his third car, having wrecked the first two cars his parents had given him. Betty expressed her gratitude to Rick for being a son who had never given her or his father a problem in all his twenty-one years. She then voiced her regret that they had not been able to afford to buy him even one car.

Her son responded, "You and Dad gave me something more important, Mom. It was something Steve never had. You were parents who were always there."

Children not only need parents who are "there" for them in times of major crisis, but parents who are there to hear their successes, moments of indecision, feelings, reactions, opinions, and responses.

God is always available and accessible to us as mothers, so let's reflect those same traits to our children.[122]

The First Word of the Day

Very early in the morning, while it was still dark, Jesus got up, left the house and went off to a solitary place, where he prayed.

MARK 1:35 NIV

For several nights, a little girl threw one shoe under her bed before climbing into it at night. Her mother asked her why. "Teacher said," the girl replied, "that if we have to kneel by our beds to look for our shoes, we'll remember to say our morning prayers while we're there."

The habit of early-morning prayer has been kept by many notable Christian leaders, including the great evangelist Billy Sunday. Shortly after Billy was converted and joined the church, a Christian man put his arm on the young man's shoulder and said, "William, there are three simple rules I can give to you, and if you will hold to them, you will never write 'backslider' after your name.

"Take fifteen minutes each day to listen to God talking to you. Take fifteen minutes each day to talk to God. Take fifteen minutes each day to talk to others about God."

The young convert was deeply impressed, and he determined to make those three things the foremost disciplines of his Christian life. From that day onward, throughout his life, he spent the first minutes of every day alone with God and His Word. Before he read a letter, looked at a paper, or even read a telegram, he went first to the Bible, so the first word he received for the day would be directly from God.[123]

MY THOUGHTS:

WHAT STEPS CAN I TAKE TO ENSURE THAT I START MY DAY WITH THE LORD?

Give God Your Garbage

It is vain for you to . . . eat the bread of [anxious] toil—for He gives [blessings] to His beloved in sleep.

PSALM 127:2 AMP

MY THOUGHTS:

_____
_____
_____
_____
_____
_____
_____
_____
_____
_____
_____
_____
_____
_____
_____
_____
_____

WHAT "GARBAGE"
DO I NEED TO TURN
OVER TO GOD
TODAY?

John H. Timmerman once wrote: *In the back corner of my yard, partitioned by a rose bed and a 40-year-old lilac bush, rests a pile, 8 feet long, 4 feet wide, and 4 feet high—my compost pile. Old-fashioned chicken wire stapled to well-anchored stakes holds it in place. Into it I toss every bit of yard scrap and a heavy dose of kitchen scrap . . . a bit of lime now and then . . . and an occasional handful of fertilizer. The compost pile burns hot, never smells, and each October yields about 70 bushels of fine black dirt, dark as midnight, moist and flaky, that I spread in the garden . . . It nurtures 80 roses and a half-dozen beds of perennials and annuals.*

Each night when we go to bed, we are wise to turn the day's "garbage" over to the Lord in prayer and to trust God to transform our mistakes and errors into something useful. As we rest our bodies, we must also rest our hearts, believing that God can turn all things to good. And indeed He does. The garbage of our lives often becomes the compost for spiritual fruit.

The key is not in "sleeping on a problem" but rather in choosing to sleep in *spite* of a problem. We must trust God as the only One who truly can turn a day of disaster into a dawning of hope.[124]

A Meaningful Routine

It is good to praise the Lord ... to proclaim your love in the morning and your faithfulness at night.

PSALMS 92:1-2 NIV

Every day throughout her childhood, a young woman ended her day by sitting on the edge of her bed with her mother and reciting the Lord's Prayer. After her "Amen," her mother would add, "And dear God, bless . . . and proceed to call out the names of numerous family members and friends, even people they had read about or heard about in the news.

Years passed. Then the little girl, now a mother with two daughters of her own, went on vacation to visit her in-laws. As a treat, the girls were allowed to stay up late. By eleven o'clock all the adults were exhausted and prepared for bed. Her youngest daughter, however, refused to budge. Not wanting the evening to end, she screamed, "No, no, no," and sat down in the middle of the hallway.

Suddenly, the mother recalled her prayer times with her mother. She picked up her daughter, who protested all the way, and carried her to her bedroom for the night. Sitting on the edge of the bed with her, she began to pray, "Our Father, who art in Heaven . . ." and her daughter joined in. They finished their prayer with a long list of "God blesses." In fact, the little girl fell asleep right in the middle of one of her requests![125]

MY THOUGHTS:

_____

_____

_____

_____

_____

_____

_____

_____

_____

_____

_____

_____

_____

_____

_____

WHAT ISSUES OR SITUATIONS DO I WANT TO PRAY WITH MY CHILDREN ABOUT TONIGHT?

235

Catastrophe or Celebration

Thank [God] in everything [no matter what the circumstances may he, be thankful and give thanks].

1 THESSALONIANS 5:18 AMP

MY THOUGHTS:

_____
_____
_____
_____
_____
_____
_____
_____
_____
_____
_____
_____
_____
_____
_____

HOW DO I RESPOND WHEN I FACE WHAT SEEMS TO BE CATASTROPHE? AN EXAMPLE WOULD BE . . .

Worry is often linked to the fact that we don't know how to respond to potential, past, or current events in our lives—or what to do about potential consequences. We don't know whether the long-term effect of a situation will be good or bad.

A man in China raised horses for a living, and one day one of his prized stallions ran away. His friends gathered at his home to help him mourn his loss. But the next week, the horse returned, bringing with it seven strays. The same friends gathered again, this time to celebrate his good fortune. That afternoon, the horse kicked the owner's son and broke his back. The friends came again to express their sorrow and concern. But a month later, war broke out, and the man's son was exempt from military service. Again, the friends came together to rejoice.

Often at the time we are going through an experience, we truly can't tell a catastrophe from a cause for celebration. God asks us to trust Him with each circumstance as it arises and to walk out each day with faith. We are to expect the best, believing that God can and will work all things for both His and our eternal benefit and the eternal benefit of our children.[126]

Fervor in Prayer

Never be lacking in zeal, but keep your spiritual fervor, serving the Lord.
ROMANS 12:11 NIV

In an old book titled *Prevailing Prayer*, the author describes John Wesley's prayer life this way:

As a matter of habit and rule, John Wesley's ordinary private praying consumed two hours a day. At times he would gather his company and pray all night, or till the power of God came down. Nothing was considered too great or too small to take to the Lord. Seized with a pain in the midst of his preaching, so that he could not speak, "I know my remedy," he said, and immediately kneeled down. In a moment the pain was gone, and the voice of the Lord cried aloud to sinners. Being seized with a pain, fever and cough, so that he could scarcely speak, "I called on Jesus aloud to increase my faith. While I was speaking my pain vanished away, my fever left me, and my bodily strength returned."

Wesley moved things mightily, because he moved God mightily. He became the prince of evangelists, because he was the prince of prayers. He stirred the world with the fire of his zeal, because he had stirred Heaven by the fire of his prayers. His pleas had access to men's consciences, because they had access to God.

MY THOUGHTS:

WHAT STEPS CAN I TAKE TO INCREASE MY SPIRITUAL FERVOR?

Set Aside the Contest of Wills

august 18

Peacemakers who sow in peace raise a harvest of righteousness.
JAMES 3:18 NIV

MY THOUGHTS:

_____
_____
_____
_____
_____
_____
_____
_____
_____
_____
_____
_____
_____
_____
_____
_____

WHAT ARE SOME STRATEGIES I CAN EMPLOY TO PEACEFULLY PERSUADE MY CHILD?

An extreme example of an adult acting like a child is portrayed in the movie Mommie Dearest based upon a book by Christina Crawford. In one scene, the mother insists that her daughter finish eating a piece of steak on her plate. The daughter refuses, insisting that the meat is raw.

Long after the rest of the family has left the table, the daughter is forced by her mother to remain there. The mother is determined to win this battle of wills. The daughter falls asleep at the table, only to find the piece of steak on her breakfast plate the next morning. The battle continues for several meals, the piece of meat appearing on each plate put before the child until finally the mother gives in and disposes of the offensive, rotting meat.

What lesson does the daughter learn in this? Sadly, the only lesson seems to be that adults can be as stubborn as children.

Are you in a contest of wills with your child today? Is eternity at stake? Is evil truly afoot? Or are you simply engaged in a battle to save face or a contest to determine who is more powerful? Those who seek peace—and use peaceful means to reach it—are generally the winners in the long run.

"You'll Take Care of Me, Won't You?"

I will say of the Lord, He is my refuge and my fortress: my God; in him will I trust . . . He shall give his angels charge over thee, to keep thee in all thy ways.

PSALM 91:2,11

A sensitive, timid boy was accustomed to lying down to sleep in his bed and then listening to the voices of his parents in their lighted sitting room across the hallway. To him, it seemed that his parents never slept, for he left them awake when he was put to bed at night, and he found them awake when he left his bed in the morning. This thought brought him comfort since he often imagined monsters in the darkness of his room.

Just to make certain his strong father was standing guard, however, he had a habit, night after night, of calling out to his father, "Are you there, Papa?"

The answer would come back cheerily, "Yes, son, I'm here."

"You'll take care of me tonight, Papa?" was the next question.

"Yes, I'll take care of you, son," was the comforting response. "Go to sleep now. Good night." Assured of his father's care, the little boy would fall asleep.

The routine meant little to the father but much to the son. Years later, himself a father and grandfather, he still calls out to his Heavenly Father each night, "Father, You'll take care of me tonight, won't You?"

And the Father always answers back, "He that keepeth thee will not slumber" (Psalm 121:3).[127]

MY THOUGHTS:

_____
_____
_____
_____
_____
_____
_____
_____
_____
_____
_____
_____
_____
_____
_____
_____
_____

TONIGHT I WILL ASSURE MY CHILDREN THAT GOD IS WATCHING OVER THEM BY . . .

239

Tea Time

august 20

"'Just as you did it to one of the least of these who are members of my family, you did it to me.'"

MATTHEW 25:40 NRSV

MY THOUGHTS:

_____
_____
_____
_____
_____
_____
_____
_____
_____
_____
_____
_____
_____
_____
_____
_____
_____
_____

MY CHILDREN KNOW THEY CAN TALK TO ME WHEN . . .

As Lisa's two daughters entered their teen years and began to walk straight to their rooms after arriving home from school each day, she became concerned about her ability to communicate with them. Her solution? She implemented "tea time."

Each day, she prepared a pot of hot tea—or a big pitcher of iced tea—and put out small sandwiches, fruit, and sweets on a tray which she decorated with fresh flowers and pretty dishes and napkins. Lisa would sit down with her own cup of tea so that when her daughters arrived home, both tea and Mom might be available. At first, her daughters ignored the tray of goodies. Then gradually, they began to stop by to say "hi" and pick up a sandwich or cookie. Soon, however, they began to stop and have tea and conversation with Mom. For her part, Lisa chose primarily to listen and pour tea. The more willing she was to listen, the more her daughters shared their feelings and experiences about their day. Lisa concluded, "I want my daughters to know there is a time each day when they know where to find me and when they know I'll listen."

Do your children know when you have time for them?

Prayer for Friends

Pray for each other so that you can live together whole and healed.
JAMES 5:16 MSG

Consider these three prayers for friends:

Dear God, Lover of us all, do not let me go down into the grave with old broken friendships unresolved. Give to us and to all with whom we have shared our lives and deepest selves along the way, the courage not only to express anger when we feel let down, but Your more generous love which always seeks to reconcile and so to build a more enduring love between those we have held dear as friends.—Kathy Keay

Let us pray for our friends, that they may lead happy and useful lives. Let us pray for any friends with whom we have quarreled, that we may have the chance to be reconciled. Let us pray for those who are living in new surroundings and lack friends. Let us pray for those who have lost their friends by the way they live. Let us pray for those who befriend the friendless. God, our Father, make us true and loyal friends. Grant that all our friends may lead us nearer to You.—Caryl Micklem

Send down the dew of Thy heavenly grace upon us, that we may have joy in each other that passeth not away; and, having lived together in love here ... may live for ever together with them, being made one in Thee, in Thy glorious kingdom hereafter.—John Austin[128]

MY THOUGHTS:

_____
_____
_____
_____
_____
_____
_____
_____
_____
_____
_____
_____
_____
_____
_____
_____
_____

FOR WHOM AND FOR WHAT DO I FEEL LED TO PRAY TODAY?

241

Respond with Joy and Delight

august 22

Satisfy us in the morning with your unfailing love, that we may sing for joy and he glad all our days.

PSALM 90:14 NIV

MY THOUGHTS:

_____
_____
_____
_____
_____
_____
_____
_____
_____
_____
_____
_____
_____
_____
_____

WHAT ARE THE THINGS THAT KEEP ME FROM SEEING GOD IN EVERYTHING?

Each day, a man routinely walked to and from his office along Lake Michigan—a beautiful way to combine his commute to work with exercise. He enjoyed the walk on most days but was frustrated by the automated sprinkler systems along the walkway. Specifically, he found it annoying that the sprinklers sprayed water beyond the lawns onto the sidewalks.

One day as he swerved to avoid the sweep of a sprinkler, he noticed a woman jogging past him. She headed straight for the sprinkler, and when she reached it, she simply stopped in her tracks, her Walkman still clamped to her ears, and let it soak her completely. The executive found himself chuckling inside at the obvious joy she took in being sprayed by the sprinkler. He noticed that several others also were smiling, obviously enjoying the freedom she seemed to experience. Reflecting on this as he continued his walk, the executive concluded the jogger was someone who was more glad about life than she was mad, sad, or afraid. He found himself interested in wanting to know why.

Today, respond to everything you experience with joy and delight. A joyful response to life is one of the greatest witnesses a mother can have![129]

You Deserve a Break Today

"Be ye therefore merciful, as your Father also is merciful."

LUKE 6:36

During her senior year of high school, Lynn became ill with bronchitis and missed individuals two weeks of school. She returned to school to discover she had nine tests to make up in one week! When she got to the last test, she drew a total blank. She admitted to her teacher, "I can't do this. I don't know any of these answers."

He went over to her, and looking at her paper, he said, "You know the answer to that! We just talked about it in class yesterday. You answered a question I asked about that."

In spite of several hints, she just could not remember. She said, "You're just gonna have to give me an F. I can't do it. I feel too bad." He reached down with his red pencil, and as she watched, certain he was going to put an F on the paper, he wrote a big, bold A at the top of the page.

"What are you doing?" she asked.

He said, "If you had been here and you felt good and you'd had time to study, that's what you would have earned. So that's what you are going to get."

Lynn reflected later, "I realized there are people who will give you a break once in a while. It was empowering. It was like he was saying, 'I know who you are, not just what you do.' That's an amazing gift to give somebody. That's the kind of teacher I want to be."[30]

We should always take into consideration the whole of who a person is and not just the mistake or blunder he or she may have made most recently.

MY THOUGHTS:

_____
_____
_____
_____
_____
_____
_____
_____
_____
_____
_____
_____
_____
_____
_____
_____

WHAT INDIVIDUALS DO I KNOW WHO NEED A BREAK TODAY? HOW CAN I HELP?

Choose to Laugh and Have Fun

august 24

They shall walk in the light of your presence. They rejoice all day long.
PSALMS 89:15-16 TLB

MY THOUGHTS:

_____
_____
_____
_____
_____
_____
_____
_____
_____
_____
_____
_____
_____
_____
_____
_____

WE CAN INCREASE THE LAUGHTER IN OUR HOME BY . . .

Dr. Fry has called laughter a stationary jogger. He has said, "There is hardly a system in the body a hearty laugh doesn't stimulate."

Norman Cousins, former editor of *Saturday Review*, believed that his recovery from a deadly form of spinal arthritis was due to massive doses of vitamin C and a tremendous amount of laughter every day. More than seventy years ago, Bernard MacFadden wrote that laughter is a form of exercise. He and his followers derived so much benefit from laughter exercise that he called it his Laugh Cure.[131]

Laughter has long been regarded as a sign of mental health. In the movie *Patch Adams*, Dr. Hunter Adams, while still a medical student, gives a long list of laughter's benefits to a supervising physician, including a greater release of endorphins and other hormones to the brain, relaxed muscle systems, increased circulation, and lower blood pressure.

Choosing to have fun and laugh heartily at life's foibles may be one of the best choices a mother can make for health and genuine quality of life. It certainly is worth a try since laughter has no known negative side effects!

Do It Today

The soul of the sluggard desireth, and hath nothing: but the soul of the diligent shall be made fat.

PROVERBS 13:4

Colonel Rahl, the Hessian commander at Trenton, was in the midst of a game of cards when a courier brought a message to him.

Rahl casually put the letter in his pocket and did not read it until the game was finished. The message was that Washington was crossing the Delaware River. He quickly moved to rally his men, but he was too late. He died just before his regiment was taken captive. Because of a few moments of delay, he lost honor, liberty, and life![132]

There is an old saying, "Tomorrow is the devil's motto." The world's history has proved it to be true.

Many a success has been thwarted because of half-finished plans and un-executed resolutions.

In evaluating your immediate future, as well as your ultimate goals, ask yourself these questions:

· What am I *truly* doing (or planning to do) with my life? Are my actions helping me to attain my goals? What are my motivations?

· Is it what God requires of me? Given the talents, traits, experiences, and abilities He has given me, does it seem likely that this is what God has prepared for me to do and desires that I accomplish for His sake?

If your answer to this last question is no, then reevaluate the first question. If your answer is yes, then do what you know to do with as much energy and enthusiasm as possible!

MY THOUGHTS:

WHAT THINGS HAVE I BEEN PUTTING OFF THAT NEED TO BE DONE TODAY?

A Wise Answer

The value of wisdom is far above rubies; nothing can be compared with it.

PROVERBS 8:11 TLB

MY THOUGHTS:

_____
_____
_____
_____
_____
_____
_____
_____
_____
_____
_____
_____
_____
_____
_____
_____

WHAT STEPS CAN I TAKE TO PREPARE FOR THE INEVITABLE QUESTIONS MY CHILDREN WILL ASK?

In *The Hiding Place*, Corrie ten Boom tells about a lesson she learned from her father one day while they were riding a train. She asked her father, "What is sex sin?"

Her father looked at her for a moment, then stood up, lifted his traveling case from the rack over their heads, and set it on the floor of the train car. "Will you carry it off the train, Corrie?" he asked.

Corrie stood up and began to tug at the case, which was filled with watches and spare parts he had purchased that morning. "It's too heavy," she said.

"Yes," he said, "and it would be a pretty poor father who would ask his little girl to carry such a load. It's the same way, Corrie, with knowledge. Some knowledge is too heavy for children. When you are older and stronger, you can bear it. For now you must trust me to carry it for you."

There are many issues and questions which children are too young to carry. Wisdom is knowing what knowledge is necessary and when and how it should be learned and applied. A good parent is wise not to teach everything he or she knows and not to bother learning what is unimportant to teach.[133]

Face Your Fears

Fear thou not; for I am with thee: be not dismayed; for I am thy God: I will strengthen thee; yea, I will help thee; yea, I will uphold thee with the right hand of my righteousness.

ISAIAH 41:10

E leanor Roosevelt is often described as a woman of great strength, courage, and conviction. She stated that early in her life, however, she was afraid of everything. She once wrote the following:

I can remember vividly an occasion when I was living in my grandmother's house on Thirty-seventh Street in New York City. One of my aunts was ill and asked for some ice, which was kept in the icebox out-of-doors in the back yard.

I was so frightened that I shook. But I could not refuse to go. If I did that, she would never again ask me to help her and I could not bear not to be asked.

I had to go down alone from the third floor in the dark, creeping through the big house, which was so hostile and unfamiliar at night, in which unknown terrors seemed to lurk. Down to the basement, shutting a door behind me that cut me off from the house and safety. Out in the blackness of the back yard.

I suffered agonies of fear that night. But I learned that I could face the dark and it never again held such horror for me.[134]

If you want to accomplish anything of merit or lasting value in life, you will have to face down your fears—including the fear of failure.

MY THOUGHTS:

_____
_____
_____
_____
_____
_____
_____
_____
_____
_____
_____
_____
_____
_____
_____
_____

WHAT FEARS DO I SENSE GOD WANTS TO HELP ME OVERCOME?

august 28

Parenting Requires Discipline

Study to shew thyself approved unto God, a workman that needeth not to be ashamed, rightly dividing the word of truth.

2 TIMOTHY 2:15

MY THOUGHTS:

_____
_____
_____
_____
_____
_____
_____
_____
_____
_____
_____
_____
_____
_____
_____
_____

IN WHAT AREAS OF MY LIFE DO I NEED TO DO MORE STUDYING?

Several years ago, well-known author and pastor Bill Hybels played on a park district football team. He was assigned to play defensive middle linebacker, which was fine him since his favorite professional athlete was Mike Singletary, all-pro middle linebacker for the Chicago Bears.

Hybels writes in Honest to God:

I crouched low and stared intently at the quarterback, readying myself to explode into the middle of the action in typical Singletary style. The battle raged . . . and reality struck with a vengeance. Using a simple head fake, the quarterback sent me in the opposite direction of the play, and the offense gained fifteen yards. So went the rest of the game. By the fourth quarter, I came to a brilliant conclusion: If I wanted to play football like Mike Singletary, I would have to do more than try to mimic his on-the-field actions. I would have to get behind the scenes, and practice like he practiced. I would have to lift weights and run laps like he did. I would have to memorize plays and study films as he did. If I wanted his success on the field, I would have to pursue his disciplines off the field.[135]

No parent can be an at-home "star" without backstage homework. The same is true in the Christian life.

Our Lives Teach Others What Christ is Like

A good name is rather to be chosen than great riches.

PROVERBS 22:1

John Selwyn, who became the bishop of the South Pacific, was renowned for his boxing skill during his university days. On one occasion after he had become bishop, he had to utter grave words of warning and rebuke to a professed convert. The man clenched his fist and violently struck the bishop on the face.

In response, Selwyn simply folded his arms and looked into the man's face. With his powerful arm and massive fist, he could easily have knocked the man down, but instead he waited calmly for another blow. It was too much for his assailant. Ashamed, he fled into the jungle.

Years later, the bishop became seriously ill, so he returned home. One day the man who had struck him came to his successor to confess Christ in baptism. Convinced of the genuineness of his conversion, the new bishop asked what "new name" he desired to take as a Christian. "Call me John Selwyn," the man replied, "for it was he who taught me what Jesus Christ is like."[136]

Do others call you a Christian, or is that only what you call yourself? If not the name of Christ, what name do your friends give you behind your back?

MY THOUGHTS:

WHAT NAME WOULD MY CHILDREN CALL ME? AM I SATISFIED WITH THAT?

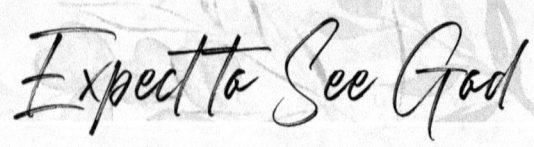

Expect to See God

august 30

Open thou mine eyes, that I may behold wondrous things out of thy law.

PSALM 119:18

MY THOUGHTS:

There is an old legend that once upon a time, God decided to become visible to a king and a peasant. He sent an angel to tell His plans.

"O king," the angel said, "God has deigned to be revealed to you in whatever manner you wish. In what form do you want God to appear to you?"

The king royally proclaimed, "How else would I wish to see God, except in majesty and power? Show God to us in His full glory of power." God granted his wish. A bolt of lightning struck and instantly vaporized the king and his court.

The angel then said to the peasant, "God has deigned to reveal himself to you in whatever manner you wish. In what form do you want to see God?"

The peasant thought for a while and then said, "I am a poor man and am not worthy to see God face to face. If it is God's will to reveal himself to me, let it be in those things I know—the earth I plow, the water I drink, and the food I eat. Let me see His presence in the faces of my family, neighbors, and—if God deems it good—even in my own reflection." God granted his wish, and he lived a long and happy life.[137]

IN WHAT WAYS AM I EXPECTING TO SEE GOD?

You Have a Built-In Audience

Everyone should be quick to listen, slow to speak and slow to become angry, for man's anger does not bring about the righteous life that God desires.

JAMES 1:19-20 NIV

Sundays were very important to Peggy, a working single mother. Worshiping God refreshed her spirit and her mind. Fellowship with other church members gave her support and encouragement. However, the hassle of prodding a slow-moving teenage daughter to get ready for church often took its toll on her patience.

Running late one Sunday morning, Peggy got stuck on the freeway behind an elderly couple moving well below the speed limit. Her frustration mounted with each passing mile. "Why do people so old even get on the freeway? Why can't they speed up? They're making me late to church!" she yelled, her daughter being her only audience.

Finally, an opening in the next lane allowed her to slip past the older couple. She looked over at them as she passed, ready to give them an angry glare and discovered that the driver of the car was her beloved pastor![138]

How many times are we quick to judge, even quick to respond in anger, only to discover that it is our own motives and attitudes that are in need of judgment!

MY THOUGHTS:

_____

_____

_____

_____

_____

_____

_____

_____

_____

_____

_____

_____

_____

_____

_____

_____

WHAT POOR ATTITUDES DO I POSSESS THAT I WOULD NOT TOLERATE IN MY CHILDREN?

Telling the Truth is Cool

You have preserved me because I was honest; you have admitted me forever to your presence.

PSALM 41:12 TLB

MY THOUGHTS:

_____
_____
_____
_____
_____
_____
_____
_____
_____
_____
_____
_____
_____
_____

WHAT KIND OF EXAMPLE AM I SETTING FOR MY CHILDREN REGARDING TELLING THE TRUTH?

A high-school student announced to his mother one day, "I won't be going to school this morning."

"Are you sick?" the mother asked.

"No, but it's senior skip day, and everybody will be at home."

She replied, "Everybody may skip, but you'd better be there." She knew that the assistant principal made it a priority to call about each child that didn't show up at school.

Sure enough, the assistant principal called her that evening, asking, "Is John sick?"

"No," the mother said, "I told him to be in school, and he disobeyed me."

The next day her son walked out of the house angry, mumbling at his long "grounding" sentence. She expected him to return home in that same mood. To her surprise, he entered the house and said, "Thank you."

"For what?" she asked.

He said, "The principal said he called parents for fourteen hours and you were the only one who told him the truth. I think it's cool to have the only mom brave enough to tell the truth."

It takes courage to tell the truth. Kids need to learn that lesson as much as mothers need to remember it.[139]

A Positive Way to Confront

Reckless words pierce like a sword, but the tongue of the wise brings healing.

PROVERBS 12:18 NIV

Dianne Hales has offered these guidelines for tactfully confronting someone make my about undesirable behavior:

1. *Do no harm.* Before blurting out any sordid truth, gauge whether or not your friend is ready to hear it. Ask yourself what you hope to accomplish by getting involved. Says one family counselor, "It's always a good idea to knock before entering another person's psyche."

2. *Be sensitive, not superior.* Choose the time and place wisely. Never set another person up for embarrassment. Sandwich your comments between compliments.

3. *Keep your emotions in check.* Think twice before popping off in anger.

4. *"Seed" the unconscious.* Depersonalize the issue. Describe a parallel situation as a mirror for the person. Express your concerns using "I" statements, not accusatory "you" statements.

5. *Be brief.* Get to the point quickly, then say no more. Give the person time to recover and respond.[140]

Always ask yourself, Do I want to bash or help the person? If your motive truly is to help, you'll find a way to speak the truth with love.

MY THOUGHTS:

_____
_____
_____
_____
_____
_____
_____
_____
_____
_____
_____
_____
_____
_____
_____
_____
_____
_____
_____
_____

HOW CAN I MAKE MY CONFRONTATIONAL STYLE MORE POSITIVE? AN EXAMPLE WOULD BE . . .

Mothers Can Shape Attitudes

Your attitude should be the kind that was shown us by Jesus Christ.
PHILIPPIANS 2:5 TLB

MY THOUGHTS:

_____

_____

_____

_____

_____

_____

_____

_____

_____

_____

_____

_____

_____

_____

_____

*WHAT ATTITUDES
DO I EXPECT FROM
MYSELF AND MY
CHILDREN TODAY?
ARE MY
EXPECTATIONS
REASONABLE?*

Lou Holtz, famous head football coach at Notre Dame, is a man known for winning—winning seasons, a lifetime winning record, and a winning attitude. Holtz admits, however, that he didn't always have a winning attitude. Holtz's first job as a head coach was at the College of William and Mary. Upon reviewing the schedule his team faced, Holtz concluded that he didn't think his team could even be competitive. He was right. Week after week, his team lost.

By the second year, Holtz felt he could field a competitive team, but he didn't believe the team could beat its powerhouse opponents. Again, the team did as expected—it never lost a game by more than six points, but it consistently lost to the "big" schools when winning mattered most to fans and recruits.

Finally, Holtz realized what was happening. He concluded that confidence was the one factor that was making the difference. When the team played expecting to lose, it did. He made a life-changing decision: expect the best from yourself and others, and then you won't be surprised when you get it.[141]

Struck to the Heart

He it is who gave himself for us that he might redeem us from all iniquity and purify for himself a people of his own who are zealous for good deeds.

TITUS 2:14 NRSV

Kidnapped by pirates as a teenager, Patrick was taken from his well-to-do home in Roman Britain in 405 AD, transported to Ireland, sold to a farmer, and given responsibility for the man's sheep. Patrick had grown up in a Christian home; however, his faith did not become real to him until one day, while tending sheep in the barren hills of Ireland, he encountered the Great Shepherd and committed his life to Him.

Patrick eventually escaped from slavery and returned to Britain, where he became a priest. Then in a dream, he heard an Irish voice pleading with him, "Holy boy, we are asking you to come home and walk among us again." To return to the land of his servitude? It was an unlikely mission, but Patrick now saw himself as a slave to Christ. The Lord gave him a compassion for the Irish. He later wrote, "I was struck to the heart."

Patrick returned to Ireland to take the Gospel to those enslaved by superstition and Druid worship. He baptized thousands of converts, discipled new believers, trained church leaders, ordained pastors, disciplined unrepentant church members, commissioned evangelists, and started scores of churches.[142]

To some, Patrick was a fanatic. To those to whom he brought the message of Christ, he was and remains Saint Patrick.

MY THOUGHTS:

_____

WHAT ISSUES OR CALLINGS STRIKE ME IN THE HEART? WHY?

Don't Do for Them What They Can Do for Themselves

Commit everything you do to the Lord. Trust him to help you do it, and he will.

PSALM 37:5 TLB

MY THOUGHTS:

_____
_____
_____
_____
_____
_____
_____
_____
_____
_____
_____
_____
_____
_____
_____

WHAT DOES GOD WANT MY CHILDREN TO DO FOR THEMSELVES? AN EXAMPLE WOULD BE . . .

At age sixty, Mary's mother developed severe pelvic pain. Exploratory surgery revealed osteoporosis, and Mary was told her mother would spend the rest of her life in a wheelchair.

Mary began to take over the chores of cleaning and cooking for her parents. One day her mother said to her, "Unless you are just coming for a cup of tea and a chat, stop coming over here. I want you to stop cleaning my house, bringing me flowers, and cooking."

Mary asked, "Why don't you want me to help you? It's one way I can give back to you."

Her mother replied, "I want to let go of everything that looks like a reward for being sick. I want to heal. I'm going to put all of my energy into getting well and strong." Within six months, the doctors were amazed that her mother's pelvic bone was regenerating itself. A few months later, she was walking again, and at age seventy-five, she went skydiving!

Mary discovered that doing all she could to please her mother was not actually what was best for her mother. Before doing everything for our children, we should ask God what He desires for them and then line up our parenting efforts accordingly. Sometimes less immediate help yields longterm results.[143]

Get Your Mind Off Yourself and Onto God

If thou faint in the day of adversity, thy strength is small.

PROVERBS 24:10

As a passenger on the *SS Constitution,* Norman Vincent Peale once found himself skirting the edge of a hurricane. He has written, "The ship was bucking like a demented horse. I was lying on my bed in my cabin, thinking pale green thoughts, when the door opened and in came a cheery fellow who had a cabin down the corridor . . . He said, 'Let's go up and look at the storm.'"

When Peale protested and asked the man to leave, the man took out a booklet and read him a passage about the importance of taking authority over weaknesses and fears. Peale wasn't all that impressed but asked, "Who wrote it?"

The man replied, "You did."

Shamed into going up on deck, Peale writes, "Mountainous waves came racing at us like avalanches, the wind ripping the spray off their crests like smoke. Great streamers of spume lashed our faces and soaked our clothes. I could taste the salt on my lips. The deck heaved, the gale shrieked in our ears, but the ship was more than equal to it . . . I was lost in admiration . . . of nature's power and fury, and the courage and ingenuity of the puny creature called man who had built this ship and could drive it through the teeth of such a storm." His seasickness completely disappeared.[144]

Get your mind off yourself and onto God. He not only calms stormy seas but gives us courage to ride the waves.

MY THOUGHTS:

_____
_____
_____
_____
_____
_____
_____
_____
_____
_____
_____
_____
_____
_____
_____
_____

TODAY I WILL GET MY MIND OFF MY PROBLEMS AND ONTO GOD BY . . .

257

Teamwork

Two are better than one; because they have a good reward for their labour. For if they fall, the one will lift up his fellow.

ECCLESIASTES 4:9-10

MY THOUGHTS:

_____
_____
_____
_____
_____
_____
_____
_____
_____
_____
_____
_____
_____
_____
_____
_____

WHAT SITUATIONS COULD OUR FAMILY TACKLE AS A TEAM AND BE MORE EFFECTIVE?

CBS newsman Charles Osgood once told a story of two women who lived in the same convalescent center. Each had suffered a debilitating stroke. Ruth's stroke damage was all on her right side, while Margaret's damage was on her left side.

Both of the women had once been accomplished pianists, but their strokes had forced them to face the fact that they might never play again. Then the convalescent center director asked the two women to try playing the center's piano together, Ruth taking the left-hand part and Margaret the right. They did . . . and the music they made together was beautiful. A friendship developed, and both women felt a renewal of meaning and joy in their lives.[145]

As Christians, we are called to work together with other believers—sharing our skills with others, and in turn receiving other people's gifts in our own areas of lack. In this way, the entire body of Christ is made strong and effective as a whole, and the specific needs of each individual are met. What one family member cannot do alone, perhaps we as a family can accomplish together.

A Present Friend

Your own friend and your father's friend, forsake them not;. . . Better is a neighbor who is near [in spirit] than a brother who is far off [in heart].

PROVERBS 27:10 AMP

Friendship is something we often take for granted. Then, if a friend moves away or dies, we are reminded that friendship must be consistently nurtured, for it thrives on frequent encounters, meaningful exchanges, and shared secrets.

I would rather have the sunshine
Of your pleasant smile today,
Than to have on some tomorrow
A belated, grand banquet.
I would rather have the pleasure
Of your happy presence now,
Than to wait until tomorrow
For some stilted pledge or vow.
I would rather walk with you awhile
Today in some friendly mode,
Than to wait until tomorrow comes
To drive along the road.
I'd rather be the present friend
In every gentle way,
So let us make the most of it
While it is called today.[146]

E. J. MORGAN

Today, take time to be a "present friend" who expresses friendship in a "gentle way."

MY THOUGHTS:

_____
_____
_____
_____
_____
_____
_____
_____
_____
_____
_____
_____
_____
_____
_____

TO WHOM SHOULD I TAKE TIME TO BE A "PRESENT FRIEND" TODAY? HOW WILL I APPROACH THAT PERSON?

259

Struggle and Pressure Aren't All Bad

september 9

When the way is rough, your patience has a chance to grow. So let it grow, and don't try to squirm out of your problems. For when your patience is finally in full bloom, then you will be ready for anything, strong in character, full and complete.
JAMES 1:3-4 TLB

MY THOUGHTS:

_____
_____
_____
_____
_____
_____
_____
_____
_____
_____
_____
_____
_____
_____
_____
_____

WITH WHAT ATTITUDES DO I USUALLY CONFRONT STRESS AND STRUGGLE?

A man once found the cocoon of an what emperor moth and took it home to watch the moth emerge. One day a small opening appeared, and for several hours the moth struggled but couldn't seem to force its body past a certain point. Deciding that something was wrong, the man cut the remaining bit of cocoon with scissors. The moth then emerged easily—its body large and swollen, its wings small and shriveled.

The man continued to watch, expecting that in a few hours the wings would spread out into their large natural beauty. That didn't happen. The moth spent its entire life dragging around a swollen body and shriveled wings—it never did fly.

The man consulted a biologist to discover what had happened to the moth. He learned that the constricting cocoon and struggle are both normal and necessary. The struggle actually causes fluid from the moth's body to move into its wings, reducing the size of the body and making the wings strong and larger.[147]

The struggle and pressure you are under today is not without value in your life. Trust God to use it as a means of developing your endurance, building your patience, and perhaps even forcing you to reevaluate your priorities. And as you learn, you can pass this same lesson on to your kids.

Taking Back the Land

Take possession of the land and settle in it, because I have given it to you to occupy.

NUMBERS 33:53 NLT

Years ago, Austin—an inner-city neighborhood in Chicago—was a solid, stable community. But like many urban centers in America after the 1960s, the area experienced "white flight." Property values plunged. Large corporations like Sunbeam and Shell Oil and many small businesses moved out—as did a number of churches.

Today, Austin's streets are rife with crack and cocaine. The generals of the local gangs carry submachine guns, make twenty- thousand-dollar drug deals, and routinely kill each other.

Not all of Austin is caught in this mire, however. The Rock of Our Salvation Church and Circle Urban Ministries offer many services to the community: a health clinic, legal clinic, individual and family counseling, food for the hungry, shelters for the homeless, low-rent housing, high-school equivalency education, job training, job placement, and worship opportunities. The leaders of the church and outreach ministries are Raleigh Washington, who is black, and Glen Kehrein, who is white.

In recent years, Circle Urban Ministries has been buying up former crack dens and vacant lots and renovating them into housing. Glen has said, "We're . . . taking back the turf, block by block. We can't buy it all. But we can buy enough so Christians can move in and by their presence preserve the rest of it."[48]

Faith is intended for action.

MY THOUGHTS:

_____
_____
_____
_____
_____
_____
_____
_____
_____
_____
_____
_____
_____
_____
_____
_____
_____
_____

WHAT THINGS COULD I GET INVOLVED IN THAT WOULD REALLY MAKE A DIFFERENCE?

His Will is Best

Help me to do your will, for you are my God. Lead me in good paths, for your Spirit is good.

PSALM 143:10 TLB

MY THOUGHTS:

_____
_____
_____
_____
_____
_____
_____
_____
_____
_____
_____
_____
_____
_____
_____
_____

WHAT DREAMS AM I INSTILLING IN MY CHILDREN? AN EXAMPLE WOULD BE . . .

When he was in eighth grade, all Chuck Swindoll wanted for Christmas was a new basketball. His father, who worked in a machine shop, had made him an iron hoop for a basket. Chuck practiced until he could sink nine out of ten free throws, and he worked hard on a two-hand set throw.

Then one November evening, his old tattered basketball burst. With six weeks to go before Christmas, he dropped numerous hints and did his chores with renewed energy, even volunteering to wax the kitchen floor! Sure enough, a brightly wrapped box appeared under the Christmas tree— the right shape, the right sound when shaken, and with Chuck's name written on it. He could hardly wait. On Christmas Day, he tore at the wrapping only to discover a world globe inside. It had no bounce to it.

Disappointed at the time, Chuck has reflected back on this experience: "My mother's vision eclipsed my fantasy and became my reality. I still enjoy watching basketball, but what really excites me is the idea of sharing our Savior with people in places like Singapore and Moscow, Delhi and Montreal."[149]

Build Them Up

Let's agree to use all our energy in getting along with each other. Help others with encouraging words; don't drag them down by finding fault.

ROMANS 14:19 MSG

A man once watched his six-year-old son as he built a model airplane. The boy was using a super adhesive glue, and in less than three minutes, his right index finger was bonded to a shiny blue wing of his DC-10. He tried desperately to free it. He tugged it, pulled it, and waved it frantically, but it wouldn't budge. The father soon located a solvent that dissolved the glue, and the crisis was over.

Some time later, this same father visited a new family in the neighborhood. The mother of the family introduced her three children to him: "This is Pete. He's the clumsy one of the lot. That's Kathy coming in with mud on her shoes. She's the sloppy one. As always, Mike's last. He'll be late for his own funeral, I promise you."

The father noted, "This woman did a thorough job of gluing her children to their faults and mistakes."[150]

Many people feel glued to false guilt and negative self-esteem. Don't contribute to this gluing process in your children or those you love. Rather, be one who bears the solvent of the Gospel, with the message of God's free gift of unconditional love, forgiveness, and spiritual freedom for all who will turn to Him.

MY THOUGHTS:

IN WHAT WAYS AM I CONVEYING GOD'S UNCONDITIONAL LOVE TO MY FAMILY?

september 13

Lasting Value

The children of Your servants will continue, And their descendants will be established before You.

PSALM 102:28 NKJV

MY THOUGHTS:

_____
_____
_____
_____
_____
_____
_____
_____
_____
_____
_____
_____
_____
_____
_____
_____
_____
_____

WHEN I THINK ABOUT THE FACT THAT I'M ACTUALLY SCULPTING A HUMAN LIFE, I . . .

Those who visit Mount Rushmore in South Dakota generally come away with a much greater appreciation for all that was involved in the tremendous undertaking to sculpt the faces of America's most beloved presidents—Washington, Lincoln, Jefferson, and Theodore Roosevelt—into the side of a cliff.

For fourteen years, the sculptor, Gutzon Borglum, worked on the mountain. His other well-known works—the head of Lincoln for the Capitol Rotunda in Washington, D.C., and the twelve apostles for the Cathedral of Saint John the Divine in New York City—are grand but certainly not on the scale of Mount Rushmore. Borglum could be certain of one thing as he hung on scaffolding month after month, year after year: Mount Rushmore wasn't going anywhere. His work there would remain long after his lifetime.

Mothering is much like sculpting. The end products may take years to produce, and the "works in progress" may seem unimpressive at times. However, when those children become adults and begin to put the lessons of their childhood to good use, they become blessings to everyone around them.

Don't think about instructing and disciplining today; instead, focus on the fact that you are sculpting lives![15]

Money

Command those who are rich in this present world not to be arrogant nor to put their hope in wealth, which is so uncertain, but to put their hope in God, who richly provides us with everything for our enjoyment.

1 TIMOTHY 6:17 NIV

In the aftermath of the sinking of the ill-fated *Titanic*, reports noted that eleven millionaires had been among the hundreds on board who went to a watery grave in April 1912. Their combined wealth totaled nearly $200,000,000. Yet if these millionaires could have sent a message to the living about the most important things in life, not one would have mentioned money.

Newspapers also reported that Major A. H. Peuchen of Toronto, who was a survivor of the tragedy, had left more than $300,000 in money, jewelry, and securities in his cabin. He started back for the box when evacuation efforts began, but then he thought an instant and quickly turned away. Later he said, "The money seemed a mockery at that time. I picked up three oranges instead."

Money is intended to serve us not to rule us. Marguerite Jackson, an Indianapolis widow, was ruled by her wealth. She lived in constant fear that her money would be stolen. When she died, more than $5,000,000 dollars was found in her home. The money, one report concluded, "had brought Mrs. Jackson nothing but a life of private terror."[152]

We can decide how we regard money today. We can view it as a tool or a crutch, a prison or a key.

MY THOUGHTS:

WHAT ARE MY
ATTITUDES ABOUT
MONEY? AN
EXAMPLE WOULD BE
. . .

september 15

What Do You See?

I pray that the eyes of your heart may be enlightened.
EPHESIANS 1:18 NASB

MY THOUGHTS:

_____
_____
_____
_____
_____
_____
_____
_____
_____
_____
_____
_____
_____
_____
_____

WHAT THINGS CAN I LOOK FOR TODAY THAT BRING ME JOY?

Barbara Johnson was having a rotten day. She had overslept and was late for work. Everything at the office had been done in a frenzy. By the time she reached the bus stop for her trip home, her stomach was in a knot. As usual, the bus was late and over filled—she had to stand in the aisle.

A few moments after the bus pulled away, she heard a deep voice from the front of the bus say, "Beautiful day, isn't it?" She couldn't see the man, but she could hear him as he commented on the spring scenery. He called attention to each passing landmark: the church, the park, the cemetery, the firehouse. All the passengers began gazing out the windows, taking in the sight of spring foliage and late-afternoon sunshine. His enthusiasm was so contagious that even Barbara found herself smiling.

When the bus reached her stop, she maneuvered toward the door, glad to finally get a look at the "guide" who had brought a smile to her face. What she saw was a plump man with a black beard, wearing dark glasses and carrying a thin, white cane.

What we "see" as mothers has more to do with inner vision than physical eyesight. Choose to see those things that bring happiness to your heart.[153]

Jesus Loves Me

We know the love that God has for us, and we trust that love. God is love.

1 JOHN 4:16 NCV

Many people are familiar with the following childhood chorus:

> Jesus loves me, this I know,
> For the Bible tells me so.
> Little ones to Him belong,
> They are weak, but He is strong.

But are you familiar with the verses that C. D. Frey has written for this tune?

> Jesus loves me, this I know,
> Though my hair is white as snow;
> Though my sight is growing dim,
> Still He bids me trust in Him.
> Though my steps are, oh, so slow,
> With my hands in His I'll go
> On through life, let come what may,
> He'll be there to lead the way.
> When the nights are dark and long,
> In my heart He puts a song,
> Telling me in words so clear,
> "Have no fear for I am near."
> When my work on earth is done
> And life's victories have been won
> He will take me home above
> To the fullness of His love.[154]

The fact is, no matter what your age, Jesus still loves you!

MY THOUGHTS:

_____
_____
_____
_____
_____
_____
_____
_____
_____
_____
_____
_____
_____
_____
_____
_____
_____
_____

IF I KNEW IN THE DEPTHS OF MY BEING THAT JESUS REALLY LOVES ME, I WOULD . . .

Yielding Brings Joy

The meek also shall increase their joy in the Lord.
ISAIAH 29:19

MY THOUGHTS:

_____
_____
_____
_____
_____
_____
_____
_____
_____
_____
_____
_____
_____
_____
_____
_____
_____
_____

Jockeys who consistently ride into the winner's circle are in complete control of their horses during a race. The winning horse is referred to as the "meekest on the track." Why? Because a winning horse responds quickly to the jockey's commands and is totally submitted to its rider. Self-willed and factious horses frequently are left at the gate. And even though they may run faster than the others, they make mistakes and rarely finish with the leaders.

This understanding of meekness on the horse track is related to an ancient definition of meekness: "yielding the will to the bit and the bridle."

If we willingly yield our lives to God—to the "bit and the bridle" of His will—then we are in the best position to win life's race. Jesus said, "Blessed are the meek: for they shall inherit the earth" (Matthew 5:5). Mothers who make themselves *available* to God are those who are used by God.[155]

I SENSE THAT GOD WANTS TO DEVELOP MEEKNESS IN ME THROUGH WHAT SITUATIONS?

The Apology

"If you are offering your gift at the altar and there remember that your brother has something against you, leave your gift there in front of the altar. First go and be reconciled to your brother."

MATTHEW 5:23-24 NIV

Laura Ingalls Wilder writes in *Little House in the Ozarks* about an old dog, Shep, who was learning to sit up and shake hands:

Try as he would, he could not seem to get the knack of keeping his balance in the upright position . . . After a particularly disheartening session one day, we saw him out on the back porch alone and not knowing that he was observed. He was practicing his lesson without a teacher. We watched while he tried and failed several times, then finally got the trick of it and sat up with his paw extended. The next time we said, 'How do you do, Shep?' he had his lesson perfectly.

As he grew older, Shep's eyesight became poor, and he didn't always recognize friends. Wilder writes, "Once he made a mistake and barked savagely at an old friend whom he really regarded as one of the family, though he had not seen him for some time. Later, as we all sat in the yard, Shep seemed uneasy . . . At last he walked deliberately to the visitor, sat up, and held out his paw. It was so plainly an apology that our friend said, 'That's all right, Shep, old fellow! Shake and forget it!' Shep shook hands and walked away perfectly satisfied.[156]

Kindness is a universal language understood by all.

MY THOUGHTS:

_____
_____
_____
_____
_____
_____
_____
_____
_____
_____
_____
_____
_____
_____
_____

TO WHOM DO I NEED TO APOLOGIZE TODAY? HOW WILL I DO IT?

269

God Has a Plan for Everyone

I know the plans I have for you, says the Lord. They are plans for good.
JEREMIAH 29:11 TLB

MY THOUGHTS:

_____
_____
_____
_____
_____
_____
_____
_____
_____
_____
_____
_____
_____
_____
_____
_____
_____

I CAN HELP BLAZE GOD'S TRAIL IN MY CHILD'S LIFE BY . . .

During the summers of his childhood, Cleve Francis walked with his mother to her work as a maid at the "big house" in town. The seven-mile round trip was a long, hot journey, but Cleve enjoyed those times because it gave him a chance to talk with his mother.

One day when he was twelve, he asked her, "Mama, why am I black?"

His mother responded without hesitation, "God is a good God. He made the heavens and the earth. He made the great mountains, rivers, and oceans. He made all living creatures, and He made you. He gave you a beautiful black color. God makes no mistakes, Cleve. You were put here on this earth for a purpose, and you must find it."

Joy filled the young boy's heart at the knowledge that he was just whom God wanted! He was proud to be one of God's chosen creatures, and he eagerly sought out God's plan for his life. Cleve found his purpose as a physician and an entertainer, and he won respect in both fields.

Helping children appreciate their unique gifts and talents and then helping them discover their purpose in using those talents is the challenge of every mother. Today, ask God to help you trail blaze His path in the lives of those you parent.[157]

Trees and Roots

Blessed is the man who trusts in the Lord, whose confidence is in him. He will be like a tree planted by the water that sends out its roots by the stream. It does not fear when heat comes; its leaves are always green. It has no worries in a year of drought and never fails to bear fruit.

JEREMIAH 17:7-8 NIV

Consider these facts about trees and roots:

· Forestry experts have estimated that the root spread of many trees is equal to the our family's spread of their branches.

· In general, as much as one-tenth of a tree is concealed in its roots.

· The combined length of the roots of a large oak tree would total several hundred miles.

· The giant saguaro tree of the southwest desert spreads its roots as much as forty or fifty feet underground laterally from the trunk.

· Hair-like as some tree roots are, an entire system of them can still exert tremendous pressure. For example, the roots of a birch tree, though considered a less sturdy tree than many others, can lift a boulder weighing twenty tons.

· A tree's root system serves two functions: to anchor the tree and to collect moisture, without which the tree could not thrive.[158]

A tree's roots adapt to strengthen it against whatever may try to attack it. If it is wind, the roots grow thick and deep. If it is drought, the roots grow toward water.

Our roots have a direct affect on our branches and, therefore, our fruit. Roots grow under the surface, out of sight. It is the inward matters of life, our thoughts and motives, that enable us to produce strength on the outside.

MY THOUGHTS:

_____
_____
_____
_____
_____
_____
_____
_____
_____
_____
_____
_____
_____
_____
_____
_____
_____
_____

WHAT IS THE STATE OF OUR FAMILY'S "ROOT SYSTEM"?

271

Determination Makes the Difference

september 21

After a while we will reap a harvest of blessing if we don't get discouraged and give up.

GALATIANS 6:9 TLB

MY THOUGHTS:

_____
_____
_____
_____
_____
_____
_____
_____
_____
_____
_____
_____
_____
_____
_____

WHICH OF MY CHILD'S ACTIVITIES CAN HELP DEVELOP DETERMINATION? HOW CAN I ENCOURAGE THAT PROCESS?

The literary world did not offer immediate stardom to Agatha Christie, one of the foremost mystery writers of all time. Her first novel, in which she introduced master sleuth Hercule Poirot, was a failure. So were her next four books. It was only with her sixth book that she gained widespread recognition.

What many people don't know about Agatha Christie is that she was determined to be more than a mystery writer. In addition to her detective novels, she wrote numerous short stories, plus six novels, under the pseudonym Mary Westmacott. Her play, The *Mousetrap*, debuted in London in 1952, and set a record for its continuous run of more than three decades. She set herself the personal goal of "producing a book every year, and possibly a few short stories." She more than met her goals. Friends and publishers remember her as a woman who approached her work in a "straightforward fashion, with no illusions." In good times and bad and regardless of personal tragedies, she kept writing—sixty-six mysteries in all.

A person rarely is born a genius. Genius usually is cultivated by people who refuse to take their hands off the plow of their own talent and by parents and teachers who inspire them to plow their own unique fields.[159]

Doing What's Right

Cling tightly to your faith in Christ and always keep your conscience clear, doing what you know is right.

1 TIMOTHY 1:19 TLB

In *Dakota*, Kathleen Norris writes the following:

A Benedictine sister from the Philippines once told me what her community did when some sisters took to the streets in the popular revolt against the Marcos regime. Some did not think it proper for nuns to demonstrate in public, let alone risk arrest. In a group meeting that began and ended with prayer, the sisters who wished to continue demonstrating explained that this was for them a religious obligation; those who disapproved also had their say. Everyone spoke; everyone heard and gave counsel.

It was eventually decided that the nuns who were demonstrating should continue to do so; those who wished to express solidarity but were unable to march would prepare food and provide medical assistance to the demonstrators, and those who disapproved would pray for everyone. The sisters laughed and said, "If one of the conservative sisters was praying that we young, crazy ones would come to our senses and stay off the streets, that was O.K. We were still a community"[60]

God calls some to action, others to support, and still others to pray. Each will be doing what is "right" in His eyes if they obey His call!

MY THOUGHTS:

_____

_____

_____

_____

_____

_____

_____

_____

_____

_____

_____

_____

_____

_____

_____

_____

HOW DO I HANDLE SITUATIONS IN WHICH MY CONSCIENCE IS PRICKED? AN EXAMPLE WOULD BE . . .

Time Management

There is a time therefor every purpose and for every work.
ECCLESIASTES 3:17

MY THOUGHTS:

_____
_____
_____
_____
_____
_____
_____
_____
_____
_____
_____
_____
_____
_____
_____
_____
_____

WHAT ARE THE "BIG
ROCKS" IN MY LIFE?

A time-management expert set a one-gallon mason jar on a table in front of the class he was teaching. He carefully placed a dozen fist-sized rocks into the jar. "Is the jar full?" he asked.

The class responded with one voice, "Yes."

Then he said, "Really?" He reached under the table and pulled out a bucket of gravel. He dumped some of it into the jar, and the pieces worked their way into the spaces between the large rocks. "Is the jar full?" he asked.

Some responded, "Probably not."

The teacher then brought out a bucket of sand. He dumped sand into the jar, allowing it to settle in the spaces between rocks and gravel. "Now is the jar full?"

The class responded, "No!"

"Good!" said the teacher as he poured water into the jar, filling it to the brim. "Now," he said, "what is the point of this illustration?"

One student quickly responded, "No matter how full your schedule, you can always fit in something else."

"No," the teacher replied. "The truth of the illustration is this: If you don't put the big rocks in first, you'll never get them in at all."[161]

When you make God your most important priority, everything else will fall into place.

Great Works

"Truly, truly, I say to you, he who believes in Me, the works that I do, he will also do; and greater works than these he will do; because I go to the Father."

JOHN 14:12 NASB

G ladys Aylward saw herself as a simple woman who just did what God called her to do. Yet, her life was so remarkable that both a book, *The Small Woman*, and a movie, *The Inn of Sixth Happiness*, were produced about the great things God accomplished through her.

A British citizen, Aylward left her home in 1920, and sailed for China. There she bought orphans who were being systematically discarded—children who had been displaced by the political upheavals of the time and left to starve or wander on their own until placed in government warehouses. Gladys gave these children a home.

When the Japanese invaded China, she was forced to flee the mainland with one hundred children. She ended up on the island of Formosa (present-day Taiwan) with her charges. There she continued to devote her life to raising children who knew no other mother.

Gladys explains her amazing work for God like this: "I did not choose this. I was led into it by God. I am not really more interested in children than I am in other people, but God through His Holy Spirit gave me to understand that this is what He wanted me to do, so I did."

MY THOUGHTS:

WHAT DO I BELIEVE IS GOD'S OVERALL PLAN FOR MY LIFE?

The Fruit of a Joyful Heart

"Out of the abundance of the heart the mouth speaketh."
MATTHEW 12:34

MY THOUGHTS:

_____
_____
_____
_____
_____
_____
_____
_____
_____
_____
_____
_____
_____
_____
_____
_____
_____

*WHAT STEPS CAN I
TAKE TO BRING
SUNSHINE INTO MY
WORLD TODAY?*

Early one morning in the locker room, Ruth overheard a cheerful voice say, "I really appreciate the book you picked up for me last week. I'm glad you suggested it." Then the voice went on to greet another person, "Good morning! Have you ever seen such a gorgeous day? I spied a pair of meadowlarks this morning."

Ruth imagined that only a wealthy woman with little to do but read and watch birds could be that cheerful. As she rounded the comer, she came face to face with a woman in a yellow housekeeping uniform—the cleaning lady—who put in long hard days with mops, brooms, and buckets. Yet she radiated sunshine!

After her laps in the pool, Ruth sank down into the warm, foamy whirlpool. Her two companions were deep in conversation—one intent on describing his woes with arthritic knees, a heart problem, sleepless nights, and pain-filled days. The water was too hot for him, he complained, and the whirlpool jets weren't strong enough. His heavy diamond ring flashed in the light as he wiped his face with a monogrammed towel. Ruth made a comparison to the cleaning woman and wondered what had made this man such a complainer when he had so much for which to be thankful.[162]

Listen to Your Heart

I will write my laws in their minds so that they will know what I want them to do without my even telling them, and these laws will be in their hearts so that they will want to obey them, and I will be their God and they shall be my people.

HEBREWS 8:10 TLB

In *First Things First*, Stephen R. Covey tells about a talk he gave to a large group of college students on the subject of the "new morality." He could tell as he talked that the students disagreed with his assertion that there are principles in this world that should be respected and adhered to, no matter who you are or how much you believe in personal freedom.

One student presented a case and said there was no right or wrong in the situation; it was a matter of interpretation. "Not so," said Covey. "Anytime you violate a fundamental principle, there's a price to be paid." By the look on the students' faces, however, Covey knew they considered him to be out of touch with present-day reality.

"Let's try an experiment," Covey suggested. "I believe that each of you knows in your heart what the truth is. Sit quietly for one minute, listen to your heart, and ask yourself what the truth is concerning this situation."

At the end of the minute, Covey again asked the young man what he thought. He admitted that his heart had told him the exact opposite of what he had been saying. Another young man admitted that he wasn't so sure of himself anymore either.[163]

There comes a time when we each need to stop listening to the crowd and pay attention to the still, small voice that speaks inside of us.

MY THOUGHTS:

_____
_____
_____
_____
_____
_____
_____
_____
_____
_____
_____
_____
_____
_____
_____
_____
_____
_____

WHAT IS MY HEART SAYING TO ME TODAY?

Quick to Forgive

Love . . . takes no account of the evil done to it [it pays no attention to a suffered wrong.]

1 CORINTHIANS 13:5 AMP

MY THOUGHTS:

_____
_____
_____
_____
_____
_____
_____
_____
_____
_____
_____
_____
_____
_____

WHAT STEPS CAN I TAKE TO HELP CULTIVATE A FORGIVING SPIRIT IN MY CHILDREN?

After supper two little brothers were playing until bedtime. Bobby accidentally hit Joe with a stick, and Joe began to wail. Accusations were exchanged until their exasperated mother finally sent both boys to bed.

As she tucked them in, she said, "Now, Joe, before you go to sleep, you need to forgive your brother for the mistake he made."

Joe thought for a few moments and then replied, "Well, OK. I'll forgive him tonight, but if I don't die before I wake up, he'd better look out in the morning."[164]

Holding a grudge or blowing a mistake out of proportion drives a wedge between two people, and if allowed to remain, that wedge can destroy a relationship. Be quick to recognize that some mistakes are not worth mentioning and some errors are not matters of eternal importance.

Those who are quick to forgive others tend to be those who are forgiven quickly. And we all must admit it's nice to be on the forgiven side of a mistake, whether we're a mother or a child.

Blessed Contentment

Don't be obsessed with getting more material things. Be relaxed with what you have.

HEBREWS 13:5 MSG

Several years ago, a newspaper cartoon was drawn of two fields divided by a fence. Both were about the same size, and each had plenty of lush green grass.

Each field had a mule whose head stuck through the wire fence, eating grass from the other's pasture. Each thought the neighboring field seemed somewhat more desirable—even though it was harder to reach.

In the process, their heads became caught in the fence. They panicked and brayed uncontrollably at being unable to free themselves. The cartoonist wisely described the situation with the caption: "DISCONTENT."

Like the mules, when we focus on what we don't have, we become blinded to the blessings which surround us. There is nothing wrong with desiring something, but to think life is easier in someone else's pasture may not be true. Besides, no matter whose pasture we are in, we will always have to deal with the attitudes of our own heart.

If there is something you desire in life, perhaps a home, a better car, or even your own business, look to Jesus to help you bring it to pass. And while He is working on it, remember to find pleasure in what He's already given you!

MY THOUGHTS:

WHAT ARE A FEW THINGS FOR WHICH I'VE NEGLECTED TO BE THANKFUL LATELY?

279

God Honors Integrity

The grass may be greener on the other side, but it still has to be mowed. Teach believers with your life: by word, by demeanor, by love, by faith, by integrity.

1 TIMOTHY 4:12 MSG

MY THOUGHTS:

_____
_____
_____
_____
_____
_____
_____
_____
_____
_____
_____
_____
_____
_____
_____
_____
_____

IN WHAT WAYS CAN I REWARD MY CHILDREN WHEN THEY DO THE RIGHT THING?

In 1994, golfer David Love III called a one-stroke penalty on himself during the second round of the Western Open. He had moved his marker to get it out of another player's putting line. A couple of holes later, he couldn't remember if he had moved his ball back to its original spot. Since he was unsure, he gave himself an extra stroke.

As it turned out, that one stroke caused him to miss the cut, and he was eliminated from the tournament. If he had made the cut and then finished dead last, he would have at least earned $2,000 for the week. When the year was over, Love was $590 short in winnings to automatically qualify for the Masters Tournament. Love began 1995 needing to win a tournament to get into the event.

Someone asked Love if it would bother him if he missed the Masters for calling a penalty on himself. Love answered quickly, "How would I feel if I won the Masters and wondered for the rest of my life if I cheated to get in?"

Fortunately, the story has a happy ending. The week before the 1995 Masters, Love qualified by winning a tournament in New Orleans. He then went on to finish second in the Master's, earning $237,600.[165]

There are times when it seems costly to preserve your character. However, it is always more costly to abandon it.

A Self-Portrait

Many women have done excellently, but you surpass them all.
PROVERBS 31:29 NRSV

Someone once asked Al Jolson, a popular musical comedy star of the 1920s, what he did to warm up a cold audience. Jolson answered, "Whenever I go out before an audience and don't get the response I feel that I ought to get . . . I don't go back behind the scenes and say to myself, That audience is dead from the neck up—it's a bunch of wooden nutmegs.' No, instead I say to myself, 'Look here, Al, what is wrong with you tonight? The audience is all right, but you're all wrong, Al.'"

Many a performer has blamed a poor showing on an audience. Al Jolson took a different approach. He tried to give the best performance of his career to his coldest, most unresponsive audiences; and the result was that before an evening was over, he had them applauding and begging for more.

You'll always be able to find excuses for mediocrity. In fact, a person intent on justifying a bad performance usually has excuses lined up before the final curtain falls. Choose instead to put your full energy into your performance. Your extra effort will turn an average performance into something outstanding.

Ah! The joy of a job well done—that is true satisfaction!

MY THOUGHTS:

IN WHAT WAYS CAN I TEACH MY CHILDREN TO DO THEIR BEST?

Joy—Responsibility and Privilege

Let everyone who trusts you be happy; let them sing glad songs forever.

PSALM 5:11 NCV

MY THOUGHTS:

_____
_____
_____
_____
_____
_____
_____
_____
_____
_____
_____
_____
_____
_____
_____
_____

WHAT STEPS CAN I TAKE TO ENSURE THAT I SMILE MORE?

George Mueller would not preach until his heart was "happy in the grace of God."

Jan Ruybroeck would not write while his feelings were low; he would retire to a quiet place and wait on God until he felt joy in his heart.

It was the happy laughter and joy of a group of Moravian Christians that convinced John Wesley of the reality of their faith and helped bring him to a point of genuine spiritual conversion.

Joy is both the responsibility and the privilege of every Christian. As Henry Evansen wrote:

· It costs nothing, but creates much.

· It enriches those who receive it without impoverishing those who give it.

· It happens in a flash, and the memory of it sometimes lasts forever.

· None are so rich that they can get along without it, and none so poor but are richer for its benefits.

It fosters good will in a business, creates happiness in a home, and is the countersign of friends. It is rest to the weary, daylight to the discouraged, sunshine to the sad, and nature's best antidote for trouble. What is it? A smile![166]

What Might They Say About You?

"Do not judge, or you too will be judged. For in the same way you judge others, you will be judged."

MATTHEW 7:1-2 NIV

According to one of Aesop's fables, when Jupiter made man, he gave him two wallets—one for his neighbor's faults, the other for his own. He then threw the wallets over man's shoulders so that one hung in front and the other in back. The one in front was for his neighbor's faults, and the one in back contained his own. While the neighbor's faults were always under his nose, it took considerable effort for him to see his own. Aesop concluded: "This custom, which began early, is not quite unknown at the present day." Indeed not.

We often tend to look at our neighbor's errors through a microscope and at our own through the wrong end of a telescope. We have two sets of weights and measures: one for home use, the other for foreign.

The story is told of a family who was on its way home from church. The father was criticizing the sermon, the mother was finding fault with the choir, and the sister was running down the organist. They all quieted down in a hurry, however, when the youngest member of the family piped up from the backseat, "I thought it was a pretty good show for a dime."[167]

Before you say anything about another person today, ask yourself, *What might that person say about me?*

MY THOUGHTS:

WHAT THINGS HAVE I BEEN SAYING ABOUT OTHERS? DO I NEED TO IMPROVE IN THIS AREA?

Make the Best of It

I have learned to he content whatever the circumstances.
PHILIPPIANS 4:11 NIV

MY THOUGHTS:

_____
_____
_____
_____
_____
_____
_____
_____
_____
_____
_____
_____
_____
_____

*WHAT ARE THE MAIN
COPING SKILLS THAT
ARE EXERCISED IN
OUR FAMILY? AN
EXAMPLE WOULD BE
. . .*

In 1992, Hurricane Andrew completely destroyed the home of one Florida couple. Devastated at the loss of all their personal belongings, the couple retreated to their vacation home on the island of Kauai to recuperate and wait out the rebuilding of their Florida home. Shortly after their arrival, a hurricane struck the Hawaiian Islands, demolishing their vacation home!

The couple acknowledged their frustration and grief in the wake of this second tragedy, but it also forced them to take a hard look at their lives. They had survived two disasters! They still had their health and human abilities. They still had faith in God and their love for one another. These were their greatest assets! They also faced the fact that no matter where they might rebuild, their home would be vulnerable to some type of natural disaster. The point was to rebuild—not to remain in ruins—and to do it with optimism and not fear.

Hard times, crises, and troubles come to all of us. It's not the nature of the crisis, but how we choose to respond to it that matters most. Those who live in contentment will have the faith and inner peace required to weather any storm.[168]

The "One-Note" Musician

Whatever your hand finds to do, do it with your might.

ECCLESIASTES 9:10 NKJV

A series of illustrations in a popular magazine once depicted the life story of a "one-note musician." From frame to frame, the tale revealed how the woman followed her daily routine of eating and sleeping until the time came for the evening concert. She carefully inspected her music on the stand and tuned her instrument. As the concert began, the conductor skillfully cued first one group of musicians and then another until finally, the crucial moment arrived. It was time for the one note to be played!

The conductor turned to the violinist and signaled her to sound her note. She did, and then the moment was over. The orchestra played on, and the "one-note" woman sat quietly through the rest of the concert—not with a sense of disappointment that she had played only one note but with a sense of contentment and peace of mind that she had played her one note in tune, on time, and with great gusto.

Sometimes "one-note" people are criticized for being limited or narrow in their perspective by those whose lifestyles require the wearing of many "hats." But a job well done by others is valued by God, so it certainly deserves our recognition and respect.

MY THOUGHTS:

_____
_____
_____
_____
_____
_____
_____
_____
_____
_____
_____
_____
_____
_____
_____
_____
_____
_____
_____
_____

WHEN I FEEL FRUSTRATED IN MY "ONE-NOTE" ROLE AS MOTHER, I WILL REALIZE . . .

Encouragement Can Make the Difference

He will not break the bruised reed, nor quench the dimly burning flame. He will encourage the fainthearted, those tempted to despair.

ISAIAH 42:3 TLB

MY THOUGHTS:

_____

_____

_____

_____

_____

_____

_____

_____

_____

_____

_____

_____

_____

_____

_____

_____

_____

_____

_____

WHAT DO I BELIEVE MY CHILDREN CAN DO? AND WHAT ARE THEY DOING RIGHT?

Kicked out of her house as a teenager, Kim ended up living with friends who were negative about life. She was intelligent but also angry and antagonistic. Her teachers discovered that although she had a hard time dealing with people, she had relevant suggestions to make and could often see problems others couldn't see. One of her teachers said to her privately, "You have a great ability to see a problem and offer a workable solution."

She shrugged and said, "You're just saying that—you don't really believe it."

The teacher replied, "No, Kim, you don't really believe it. One day you will have to decide what you're going to believe about yourself. It's up to you."

About four months after Kim graduated, she called to tell this teacher that she had a job at the phone company. She said, "The person who interviewed me asked why they should hire me. I couldn't think of anything, so I said my teacher said I was good at solving problems. They hired me as a trouble-shooter. Now I believe you."[169]

Two of the most valuable things a mother can ever tell her child are: "Here's what I believe you can do . . ." and "Here's what you are doing that's right . . ."

He Walks with You

Even when walking through the dark valley of death I will not be afraid, for you are close beside me, guarding, guiding all the way.

PSALM 23:4 TLB

On February 11, 1861, President-elect Lincoln left his home in Springfield to begin his rail journey to Washington, where he was to be inaugurated a month later. Lincoln had a premonition it would be the last time he would see Springfield. Standing on the rear platform of his railroad car, he bid the townspeople farewell. He closed his remarks with these words: "Today I leave you. I go to assume a task more difficult than that which devolved upon General Washington. The great God which guided him must help me. Without that assistance I shall surely fail; with it, I cannot fail."

The same is true for us, regardless of the tasks we face. Without God's assistance, we cannot succeed. We may get the dishes washed, the laundry folded, and the beds made. We may get our work done without accident or incident. We may find what we need at the market and manage to keep a schedule. But without God's help, our lives would be a confused mess.

Does God care about what happens in our day? Absolutely! When we become overwhelmed and the smallest of tasks seem like mountains, He helps us to "gather ourselves." Step by step He shows us the way, and our strength is renewed to go on.

MY THOUGHTS:

THROUGH WHAT SITUATION DO I NEED GOD TO SHOW ME THE WAY?

october 7

Good Deeds Live On

Day by day the Lord observes the good deeds done by godly men, and gives them eternal rewards.

PSALM 37:18 TLB

MY THOUGHTS:

_____
_____
_____
_____
_____
_____
_____
_____
_____
_____
_____
_____
_____
_____
_____
_____
_____
_____

WHAT STEPS CAN I
TAKE TO ENSURE
THAT I SET A GOOD
EXAMPLE FOR MY
CHILDREN IN
REGARD TO DOING
GOOD DEEDS?

As a child of English settlers in Africa, Peter often went on rounds with his mother, a doctor, to vaccinate children in rural areas. Even though she was authorized to vaccinate only Rhodesians, she was generous in vaccinating the Ndau people from Mozambique who were nomads in the region.

As an adult, Peter returned to the area as a reporter. He was kidnapped, labeled a spy, and taken to the rebel base camp. The longer he listened to the rebel leader speak, the more he understood. The leader was speaking Ndau! He recalled some of what he had learned as a child and spoke back in the language. The leader was shocked. "Where did you learn this?" he demanded. When Peter told him, he asked, "What is your family name?"

Peter said, "Godwin."

The leader asked again, "Was your mother the doctor?"

Peter replied, "Yes."

The leader smiled broadly. "She vaccinated me when I was a child. Look now! I grew up strong!" Peter immediately went from hostage status to honored guest. He considers a photo of his final day with the rebels to be a testament to the permanence of good deeds. Truly, the good we do to others has an eternal seed in it![170]

A Poor Response

Do not forsake wisdom, and she will protect you . . . When you walk, your steps will not be hampered; when you run, you will not stumble.

PROVERBS 4:6,12 NIV

In 1269, Kublai Khan sent a request from Peking to Rome for "a hundred wise men of the Christian religion . . . And so I shall be baptized, and when I shall be baptized all my barons and great men will be baptized, and their subjects baptized, and so there will be more Christians here than there are in your parts."

At the time Khan wrote, the Mongols were wavering in their choice of religion. Khan had been introduced to Christian concepts and was ready and willing to turn the tide of his people strongly in support of Christianity.

Pope Gregory X answered Khan's request by sending only two Dominican friars. They traveled as far as Armenia but could endure no longer and returned home.

And so passed the greatest missionary opportunity in the history of the Church. The fate of all Asia may very well have been different had Gregory fulfilled Khan's request. The greatest mass religious movement the world has ever seen might have happened but didn't, all for want of one hundred Christian servants willing to answer a call.[171]

When others ask for your help, be sure to weigh your answer. Eternity may lie in the balance.

MY THOUGHTS:

HOW DO I RESPOND WHEN THERE IS A GENUINE REQUEST FOR HELP? AN EXAMPLE WOULD BE . . .

Resist the Temptation

Keep me from lying and being dishonest.
PROVERBS 30:8 NCV

MY THOUGHTS:

_____
_____
_____
_____
_____
_____
_____
_____
_____
_____
_____
_____
_____
_____
_____

WHAT STEPS AM I TAKING TO TEACH MY CHILDREN THE IMPORTANCE OF HONESTY?

A five-year-old boy was looking forward to visiting a planetarium while the family was on vacation. When the family arrived at the site, however, they learned that children under age six were not admitted. The mother said, "Let's pretend you had a birthday. If the ticket man asks how old you are, I want you to say, 'I'm six.'"

The mother rehearsed this dialog with her son until he sounded convincing. As it turned out, she was able to buy tickets without her son ever being asked his age. When the planetarium show ended, the family moved on to the nearby museum. There, a large sign read, "Children under 5 admitted free." To avoid the admission fee, the mother had to convince her son to forget his pretend birthday.

As the family walked up to the last destination of the day, the aquarium, the mother came face to face with what she had been doing to her son. He looked up at her with a worried look on his face and asked, "Mommy, how old am I now?"

What we say to our children today affects how they will act as adults tomorrow. If something is wrong for an adult to do, then it is wrong for a child to do.[172]

Recovering From Bad Choices

If we are unfaithful, he remains faithful, for he cannot deny himself.

2 TIMOTHY 2:13 NLT

When Cathy met Jim at a softball game, she thought he was the man for her—everything she was looking for! After several months of dating, she was still as sold on him as ever, except it bothered her that he found so many excuses for drinking alcohol. "I got a raise!" "My friend is getting married!" "My sister is graduating from college!"

Despite her friends' warnings and her own misgivings, Cathy married Jim. Before long, however, the marriage was destroyed by his drinking. When the divorce was final, Cathy felt destroyed. By ignoring the Holy Spirit's warning and her friends' wise counsel, she had made one of the biggest mistakes a Christian could make. "I wanted to have my way instead of God's," she told her pastor. "I thought I knew what was best for me."

"We all think that sometimes," her pastor said. "We forget that the One who created us knows us better than we know ourselves. But remember, Cathy, He never gives up on us! When we admit our mistakes, He always forgives us and gives us another chance."

Recovering from the bad choices we've made can be heart wrenching and difficult, but God is always right there, ready to make us whole and give us a brand new life.

MY THOUGHTS:

_____
_____
_____
_____
_____
_____
_____
_____
_____
_____
_____
_____
_____
_____
_____
_____
_____
_____

HOW AM I TRAINING MY CHILDREN TO MAKE GOOD CHOICES? AN EXAMPLE WOULD BE . . .

See Past Limitations

He who is kind and merciful to the needy honors Him.
PROVERBS 14:31 AMP

MY THOUGHTS:

_____
_____
_____
_____
_____
_____
_____
_____
_____
_____
_____
_____
_____
_____
_____
_____
_____
_____

WHAT LESSONS AM I
TEACHING MY
CHILDREN ABOUT
THOSE WITH
PHYSICAL
LIMITATIONS?

Many people admire and recite the love poetry of Elizabeth Barrett Browning, but few know the motivation for her writing.

Elizabeth grew up as one of eleven about children under the absolute rule of an oppressive and dictatorial father. She was a sad and sickly teenager who became a sad and sickly adult. She did not meet Robert Browning until she was forty years old.

Robert saw Elizabeth as a beautiful, talented woman waiting to blossom. He loved her with all his heart and was willing to endure brutal confrontations with her father to win her hand in marriage.

After they married, Elizabeth explored her talents and emerged as a woman in love. She bore Browning a healthy child when she was forty-three, and it was then that she wrote "How Do I Love Thee?" as part of her _Sonnets from the Portuguese_.

When you see past physical shortcomings and take the time to value and encourage others, they, too, will rise above physical limitations to meet their full potential.

The Right Use of Strength

Learn to do good, to be fair, and to help the poor, the fatherless, and widows.

ISAIAH 1:17 TLB

During World War II, a chief petty officer was killed. His ship had visited a hundred ports, and at most of them, he had purchased something for his children—a grass skirt, a model outrigger canoe, a drum, a war club, a bolt of batik cloth, a flowered lei. He had looked forward to bringing the gifts home to his family for Christmas.

After he was killed, his commanding officer sent the presents to his wife in Texas. When his sea bag arrived, however, his widow discovered that all the souvenirs were missing. They had been stolen en route. The publisher of the Fort Worth Star Telegram heard of this tragedy and wrote Admiral Chester W Nimitz about it. It was almost Christmas. Couldn't something be done?

At the time, Nimitz was responsible for all naval and military operations over millions of square miles in the Pacific. However, he managed to take a few minutes to issue an order to the admiral in charge of Fleet Recreation. Planes attached to Fleet Recreation were ordered to fly to every port in the Pacific, where officers and men were to scour the island bases in search of replacement souvenirs. The navy plane then winged its way to Texas with a cargo of Christmas love from a war hero.[173]

Great authority is always accompanied by great responsibility—the responsibility to do the right thing.

MY THOUGHTS:

IN WHAT WAYS CAN I USE MY STRENGTH TO DO GOOD TO THOSE WHO ARE LESS FORTUNATE?

He Knows How You Feel

We do not have a high priest who is unable to sympathize with our weaknesses, but we have one who has been tempted in every way, just as we are—yet was without sin.

HEBREWS 4:15 NIV

MY THOUGHTS:

TODAY I NEED TO POUR OUT MY HEART TO GOD REGARDING . . .

When Christian singer Sheila Walsh gave birth to her son, Christian, she was on top of the world . . . until the physicians gave her a bad report. Her son had jaundice, which was the result of his early arrival and a premature liver not yet able to function normally. A blood test showed something suspicious, and before Walsh knew what was happening, her son was in pediatric intensive care.

She found an empty room at the hospital and knelt down to pray. It was then that she had an inner understanding about who God really is—not a God who sends trouble to test or judge people but a loving Father who carries our cares when times are tough. She writes in *Bring Back the Joy,* "I suddenly remembered that God had been there before me. He had watched his boy kneeling in a garden, blood flowing down his face. I knelt down broken and afraid; and when I left that room I was still afraid, but I was leaning on the Lord."

At times, keeping a "stiff upper lip" may be necessary to reassure our children, but with God, we never need to pretend to be brave. Bring your shattered hopes and stinging fears to Him so that He can heal you completely.[174]

The Truth Will Come Out

The night is far spent, the day is at hand: let us therefore cast off the works of darkness, and let us put on the armour of light.

ROMANS 13:12

A man and his girlfriend once went into a fast-food restaurant and ordered a bag of chicken to go. Moments earlier, the manager had placed the day's cash in a bag and set it at the side of the serving counter. When the clerk reached for the couple's order, he mistakenly picked up the bag of money. They paid for their chicken, got in their car, and drove to a park for a picnic. When they opened the bag, they found that there were no drumsticks, only greenbacks!

After briefly discussing their find, the couple decided the right thing to do was to return the money. When they arrived at the restaurant, the manager was ecstatic. "I can't believe it!" he said. "I'm calling the paper. They'll take your picture and run the story for sure. You've got to be the two most honest people in this city."

The young man hurriedly replied, "No, please don't call the paper! You see I'm a married man, but this woman is not my wife."[175]

Many people await the secret cloak of night's darkness before they commit their evil deeds, when in fact, they have already created darkness in their own souls. The light of the truth will illuminate any situation and expose it for what it is.

MY THOUGHTS:

WHAT AREAS OF MY LIFE NEED TO BE BROUGHT OUT INTO THE LIGHT?

295

God Sees and Rewards

As in water face reflects face, So the heart of man reflects man.
PROVERBS 27:19 NASB

MY THOUGHTS:

In a book about the village of Akenfield in England, the author tells of old farmers who could look at a field where ten people had plowed and tell you the name of the man who had done each furrow.

Likewise, there are those who frequent the Indian markets in South America who can tell by looking at a piece of rope who made it.

The difference in furrows was not a factor in whether a field produced more or fewer beans per acre. The difference in rope was not a factor in the usefulness of the rope. But in each case, the work was a reflection of the character of the worker. It was a statement about the diligence with which the person approached his or her work and the amount of pride that person took in producing quality.

It was in this same spirit of endowing work with character that the great artisans of the Middle Ages often carved the backs of their art, knowing that God alone would see them—but caring greatly that He did![176]

No other person may ever see all the messes you clean up, all the boo-boos you kiss, or many of the small sacrifices you make every day for your children. Your children are probably not aware of all you do to take make their lives meaningful and whole. But God—a parent himself—sees. Keep giving your best to your children as if God himself were right there in your laundry room.

KNOWING THAT GOD SEES AND APPRECIATES ALL THE UNSEEN THINGS I DO MAKES ME . . .

Be a Bridge Builder

Don't quarrel with anyone. Be at peace with everyone, just as much as possible.

ROMANS 12:18 TLB

In *Learning to Forgive*, Doris Donnelly writes:

Some years ago I met a family very proficient in the use of scissors . . . the friends of each family member were under constant scrutiny to determine whether they measured up to the standards imposed by mother and father. One slip . . . resulted in ostracism from the narrow circle of "friends." . . . Anyone who did not respond immediately with profuse gratitude was eliminated from the list for the next time. Snip.

Eventually I, too, was scissored out of their lives. I never knew for sure why, but I knew enough to recognize that once I was snipped away there was no hope of my being sewn into their lives again.

Last year the mother of the family died. The father and daughters, expecting large crowds to gather to say their final farewells, enlisted the assistance of the local police to handle traffic . . . Telegrams were sent . . . phone calls were made . . . local motels were alerted . . . yet in the end, only the husband, the daughters, their husbands, and a grandchild or two attended the services.[177]

Cutting imperfect people out of our lives is a prescription for loneliness. Who would remain to be our friends? Are there any people you could sew back into the fabric of your life? Why not give them a call?

MY THOUGHTS:

WHAT STEPS AM I TAKING TO TEACH MY CHILDREN THE IMPORTANCE OF MAINTAINING RELATIONSHIPS?

Don't Always Believe the "Experts"

"With God all things are possible."
MATTHEW 19:26

MY THOUGHTS:

_____
_____
_____
_____
_____
_____
_____
_____
_____
_____
_____
_____
_____
_____
_____
_____
_____
_____

WHAT STEPS CAN I TAKE TO ENCOURAGE CREATIVE THINKING IN MY CHILDREN?

We can be grateful to God that somebody refused to believe these "expert" opinions:

- "Computers in the future may weigh no more than 1.5 tons"—*Popular Mechanics*, 1949.
- "I think there is a world market for maybe five computers"—Thomas Watson, IBM chairman, 1943.
- "This 'telephone' has too many shortcomings to be seriously considered as a means of communication. The device is inherently of no value to us"—Western Union internal memo, 1876.
- "Heavier-than-air flying machines are impossible"—Lord Kelvin, Royal Society president, 1895.
- "Drill for oil? You mean drill into the ground to try and find oil? You're crazy!"—drillers whom Edwin L. Drake tried to hire to drill for oil in 1859.
- "Man will never reach the moon regardless of all future scientific advances"—Dr. Lee DeForest, inventor of the vacuum tube and father of television.
- "Everything that can be invented has been invented"—Charles H. Duell, commissioner, United States Office of Patents, 1899.

Don't be too quick to dismiss your child's or another person's idea or suggestion. It just may have life-changing merit![178]

A Terrible Shame

Fire goes out for lack of fuel, and tensions disappear when gossip stops.

PROVERBS 26:20 TLB

First, somebody told it,
Then the room couldn't hold it,
So the busy tongues rolled it
Till they got it outside.
Then the crowd came across it,
And never once lost it,
But tossed it and tossed it,
Till it grew long and wide.
This lie brought forth others,
Dark sisters and brothers,
And fathers and mothers—
A terrible crew.
And while headlong they hurried,
The people they flurried,
And troubled and worried,
As lies always do.
And so evil-bodied,
This monster lay goaded,
Till at last it exploded
In smoke and in shame.
Then from mud and from mire
The pieces flew higher,
And hit the sad victim
And killed a good name.[179]

There is never a good end to lies or gossip.

MY THOUGHTS:

_____
_____
_____
_____
_____
_____
_____
_____
_____
_____
_____
_____
_____
_____
_____
_____

WHAT IS MY RESPONSE TO GOSSIP WHEN I HEAR IT? AN EXAMPLE WOULD BE . . .

Words Can Make Them Blossom

Your words have put stumbling people on their feet, put fresh hope in people about to collapse.

JOB 4:4 MSG

MY THOUGHTS:

_____
_____
_____
_____
_____
_____
_____
_____
_____
_____
_____
_____
_____
_____

FOR WHAT PURPOSES ARE MY WORDS BEING USED? AN EXAMPLE WOULD BE . . .

Mary Ann Bird writes in *The Whisper Test*:

I grew up knowing I was different, and I hated it. I was born with a cleft palate, and when I started school my class-mates made it clear to me how I looked to others: a little girl with a misshapen lip, crooked nose, lopsided teeth, and garbled speech. When school-mates asked, "What happened to your lip?" I'd tell them I'd fallen and cut it on a piece of glass . . .

There was, however, a teacher in the second grade that we all adored—Mrs. Leonard by name. She was short, round, happy—a sparkling lady. Annually we had a hearing test . . . Mrs. Leonard gave the test to everyone in the class, and finally it was my turn. I knew from past years that as we stood against the door and covered one ear, the teacher sitting at her desk would whisper something, and we would have to repeat it back—things like "The sky is blue" or "Do you have new shoes?" I waited there for those words that God must have put into her mouth, those seven words that changed my life. Mrs. Leonard said, in her whisper, "I wish you were my little girl."

There is no known benefit from angry words fired to destroy, wound, or reject. In contrast, the benefit from words spoken to heal and restore can be eternal.[180]

God Knows What He's Doing

october 20

Trust in the Lord with all your heart, and do not rely on your own insight.

PROVERBS 3:5 NRSV

For weeks, eight-year-old Susie had been looking forward to a particular Saturday fishing trip with her dad. But when the day finally arrived, it was raining heavily.

Susie wandered around the house all morning, grumbling as she peered out the can't see windows, "Seems like the Lord would know it would have been better to have the rain yesterday than today." Her father tried to explain how important the rain was to the farmers and gardeners. But Susie only replied, "It just isn't fair."

Around three o'clock, the rain stopped. There was still time for fishing, so father and daughter quickly loaded their gear and headed for the lake. Because of the rainstorm, the fish were really biting. Within a couple of hours, they returned with a full stringer of fish.

At the family's "fish dinner" that night, Susie was asked to say grace. She concluded her prayer by saying, "And, Lord, if I sounded grumpy earlier today, it was because I couldn't see far enough ahead."[181]

When we seek God's advice in our lives, it is important to realize He alone can see what's coming!

MY THOUGHTS:

WHAT STEPS CAN I TAKE TO DEVELOP MY TRUST IN GOD WHEN I CAN'T SEE FAR ENOUGH AHEAD?

Encourage Creative Thinking

The plans of the diligent lead to profit.
PROVERBS 21:5 NIV

MY THOUGHTS:

_____
_____
_____
_____
_____
_____
_____
_____
_____
_____
_____
_____
_____
_____

IN WHAT WAYS CAN I HELP MY CHILDREN DEVELOP AND USE THEIR IMAGINATIONS?

There once was a nice young man who worked as a railroad express clerk in Minnesota. He went to work every day and enjoyed his job—an average man in an average role. One day, he received a large watches addressed to a local jeweler. The jeweler, however, did not want the watches. The clerk contacted the distributor who had sent the watches only to discover that he didn't want them back because the return postage was too expensive.

What was he to do with a box of watches? An idea dawned on the young clerk. He drew pictures of the watches, added descriptions about each one, and put together a little catalog, which he then sent to other clerks on the rail line. In just a few weeks, they bought all the watches at what was nearly a 100 percent profit to him! His effort was so successful that he used the money to order more watches and enlarged his catalog.

The clerk's name? Sears. His catalog? Sears, Roebuck, and Company.

One of the greatest challenges any parent will ever face is not in getting their children to make better grades but in getting them to work hard enough and to think creatively enough to prepare for the future God has planned for them.[182]

A Clear Conscience

I do my best always to have a clear conscience toward God and all people.

ACTS 24:16 NRSV

Kelley was surprised to find a hair dryer tucked into a corner of an old suitcase. For years she had used the case to store bits of fabric from her sewing projects. Now, while piecing together a quilt, she had unearthed it. *Where did this come from?* she asked herself.

After several days of trying to remember, she recalled having used it while visiting friends nearly a decade before. She had made several visits to the family and apparently had placed the borrowed hair dryer into her case inadvertently. To complicate matters, the family had asked about its whereabouts, and she had replied she didn't have a clue!

Embarrassed, she thought, *How can I tell my friends after all these years that I have this?* However, her conscience wouldn't let the matter rest. She finally sent the hair dryer back to the family with an apology and an explanation. With many laughs, all was quickly forgiven.

A healthy conscience is one of our greatest gifts from God. It serves to keep our lives on track and thus maintain peace in our hearts.

MY THOUGHTS:

HOW DO I TEND TO HANDLE MYSELF WHEN I MAKE A MISTAKE?

A Good Example

Brethren, join in following my example, and observe those who walk according to the pattern you have in us.

PHILIPPIANS 3:17 NASB

MY THOUGHTS:

_____
_____
_____
_____
_____
_____
_____
_____
_____
_____
_____
_____
_____
_____
_____
_____

WHAT STEPS CAN I TAKE TO TEACH MY CHILDREN TO DEAL CONSTRUCTIVELY WITH CONFLICTS?

A girl once went with her mother to a jewelry store after Christmas to exchange an expensive gift she had received for an item of the same type that was cheaper and more appropriate for her daily needs. She found an ideal replacement, and the clerk prepared a statement for the amount of cash refund to which she was entitled.

When the mother looked over the receipt, she found the owner had miscalculated. She called attention to the error. He denied the mistake, but she continued to quietly but assertively say, "I wish you would check your figures again. I believe you'll find the amount is different than what you calculated." She was polite but firm, and in the end he saw his error, made the correction, and apologized.

As the girl and her mother stepped outside the shop, she said to her mother, "I'm so glad you stood up for me. I also saw the error, but I didn't know what to do. I probably would have gone my way, frustrated and angry at being ripped off. You showed me that I could be firm without being insulting and without anybody feeling bad in the end."

When errors are corrected and everybody walks away feeling good about it—that's good parenting![183]

The Great Exchange

He hath made him to he sin for us, who knew no sin; that we might he made the righteousness of God in him.

2 CORINTHIANS 5:21

A saleswoman passed a particular comer each day on her way to work. For more than aspects o f a week, she observed a young girl trying to sell a floppy-eared puppy The saleswoman finally said to the girl, "Honey, if you really want to sell this dog, then I suggest you clean him up, brush his coat, raise your price, and make people think they're getting something big." At noon, the saleswoman noticed the girl had taken her advice. The puppy was groomed and sitting under a big sign: "TREMENDOUS Puppy for Sale—$5,000."

The saleswoman smiled and gulped, determined to tell the girl later that she may have overpriced the puppy. To her surprise, on the way home she saw the puppy was gone! Flabbergasted, the woman sought out the girl to ask if she had really sold the dog for $5,000.

The girl replied, "I sure did, and I want to thank you for all your help."

The saleswoman stuttered, "How in the world did you do it?"

The girl answered, "It was easy. I just took two $2,500 cats in exchange!"

Two thousand years ago, there was another great exchange. On a cross outside Jerusalem, Jesus Christ gave His life in exchange for ours. What value did He see in us? We were His prized creation, stolen for a season by our own will but now repurchased as His beloved possession.

MY THOUGHTS:

_____
_____
_____
_____
_____
_____
_____
_____
_____
_____
_____
_____
_____
_____
_____
_____
_____

WHAT ASPECTS OF THIS GREAT EXCHANGE WITH JESUS AM I MOST THANKFUL FOR? WHY?

Your Weaknesses Put You in Good Company

october 25

I am glad to boast about my weaknesses, so that the power of Christ may work through me.

2 CORINTHIANS 12:9 NLT

MY THOUGHTS:

_____
_____
_____
_____
_____
_____
_____
_____
_____
_____
_____
_____
_____
_____
_____
_____

WHAT STEPS CAN I TAKE TO TEACH MY CHILDREN THAT GOD USES ANYONE WHO IS WILLING?

Many people question why God would choose to use them. But the next time you are tempted to worry about your faults, consider the following:

- Moses stuttered.
- Timothy had stomach problems.
- Jacob was a liar.
- David had an affair.
- Abraham was too old.
- John was self-righteous.
- Naomi was a poor widow.
- Paul was a murderer.
- Jonah ran from God.
- Miriam was a gossip.
- Gideon doubted—and so did Thomas.
- Jeremiah was depressed and suicidal.
- Elijah was burned out.
- Martha was a worrywart.

God doesn't look at our faults, finances, or failings. He only looks at our willingness. If you are willing today to be used by God in the lives of your children and others in your world, get ready. You're just the right candidate for a job God has in mind!

Dig Down Deep

May your roots go down deep into the soil of God's marvelous love.

EPHESIANS 3:17 NLT

Many people see abundant spring rains as a great blessing to farmers, especially if the rains come after the plants have sprouted and are several inches tall. What they don't realize is that even a short drought can have a devastating effect on a crop of seedlings that have received too much rain.

Why? Because during frequent rains, the young plants are not required to push their roots deeper into the soil in search of water. If a drought occurs later, plants with shallow root systems will quickly die.

We often receive abundance into our lives—rich fellowship, great teaching, and thorough "soakings" of spiritual blessings. Yet, when stress or tragedy enters our lives, we may find ourselves thinking God has abandoned us or is unfaithful. The fact is that we have allowed the easiness of our lives to keep us from pushing our spiritual roots deeper. We have allowed others to spoon-feed us, rather than develop our own deep, personal relationship with God through prayer and study of His Word.

Only the deeply rooted are able to endure hard times without wilting. The best advice is to enjoy the "rain" while seeking to grow even closer to Him.

MY THOUGHTS:

WHAT THINGS CAN WAS AS A FAMILY DO TO GROW DEEP SPIRITUAL ROOTS?

Others Are Affected

The Lord is known by his justice.
PSALM 9:16 NIV

MY THOUGHTS:

_____
_____
_____
_____
_____
_____
_____
_____
_____
_____
_____
_____
_____
_____
_____

*WHAT STEPS CAN I
TAKE TO ENSURE
THAT MY CHILDREN
KNOW WHAT
BEHAVIORS ARE
ACCEPTABLE?*

On a recent flight, two small children who were not happy about being on an airplane, disrupted everyone else's peace. Their cries and complaints filled the cabin as they climbed all over the seats and ran up and down the aisle. The parents did everything they could to calm the children down, but nothing worked. Finally, they just gave up and let the children run wild. It was obvious from the behavior of the little boy and his sister that they were not used to being disciplined.

Eventually, a flight attendant stopped next to them and said with a big smile, "What is all this squawking up here?" After charming the fussy three-year-old and his older sister for a few minutes, the flight attendant bent down and whispered seriously, "I must remind you that this is a non-squawking flight."

The little ones became unbelievably quiet and remained that way during the entire flight, much to the relief of the rest of the passengers.

Your children's behavior affects everyone around them. Teach them to respect others by making every day a non-squawking journey.[184]

An Issue of Character

Lord, who may abide in Your tabernacle? Who may dwell in Your holy hill?... He who swears to his own hurt and does not change.

PSALMS 15:1,4 NKJV

Mel was a hard worker, always eager to do extra jobs to bring in more money. During the week, he worked as a carpenter. As a side business, he made himself available to mow large fields with his tractor.

One day, he agreed to mow a field of wild mustard and weeds for a neighbor, quoting a price of one hundred dollars. Other jobs, however, grabbed Mel's attention, and he kept putting off this job. When he finally arrived to mow the field, he informed his neighbor that the price would be two hundred dollars since the weeds had grown larger and would require two passes.

Mel had his neighbor in a sure bind, since a deadline set by the fire department for mowing weedy fields was upon him. When the neighbor questioned the morality of breaking his original agreement, Mel just shrugged his shoulders. He was secretly pleased that he had manipulated the situation to his benefit.

Mel and his neighbor lived in an area where few secrets stayed secrets. Many others who had planned on hiring Mel saw his character for what it was. In the short term, he made an extra hundred dollars. In the long term, he lost far more: thousands of dollars of referral work and his good reputation.[185]

MY THOUGHTS:

_____

_____

_____

_____

_____

_____

_____

_____

_____

_____

_____

_____

_____

_____

_____

WHAT STEPS AM I TAKING TO TEACH MY CHILDREN ABOUT KEEPING THEIR WORD?

Develop Trust in Your Relationships

Personality has the power to open doors, but character keeps them open. It is good for me to draw near to God: I have put my trust in the Lord God.

PSALM 73:28

MY THOUGHTS:

_____
_____
_____
_____
_____
_____
_____
_____
_____
_____
_____
_____
_____
_____
_____
_____
_____
_____

WHAT STEPS CAN I TAKE TO ENSURE THAT OUR FAMILY DEVELOPS THIS KIND OF TRUSTING RELATIONSHIPS WITH GOD AND EACH OTHER?

A crew of botanists was searching in the Alps for rare flowers. A very fine specimen was spotted on a small ledge of rock that could only be reached with a lifeline. The job was far too dangerous for the inexperienced botanists, so they called in a local shepherd boy who was familiar with the region. They offered him several gold coins to climb down the rope and recover the rare flower.

Although the boy desperately wanted the coins, he feared that the task was too risky. Several times he peered over the edge of the cliff, but he couldn't see any safe way of getting to the flower. Besides, he would have to place his belief in the hands of the strangers who would be holding his lifeline. Then the boy had an idea. He left the group for a few moments and finally returned, holding the hand of a much older man. The shepherd boy then ran eagerly to the brink of the cliff and said to the botanists, "You can tie the rope under my arms now. I'll go into the canyon as long as you let my father hold the rope."

This boy shared a trusting relationship with his father and was willing to put his life into his father's hands. In the same way that your children trust in you, put your trust in your Heavenly Father today.[186]

They Will Know Us by Our Love

By this shall all men know that ye are my disciples, if ye have love one to another.

JOHN 13:35

Before the colonialists imposed national boundaries, the kings of Laos and Vietnam had already reached an agreement about who was Laotian and who was Vietnamese. Those who ate short-grain rice, built their houses on stilts, and decorated their homes with Indian-style serpents were considered Laotians. Those who ate long-grain rice, built their houses on the ground, and decorated their homes with Chinese-style dragons were Vietnamese. The kings taxed the people accordingly and had little use for "boundaries" apart from this designation.

The kings knew it was not the exact locations of people's homes that determined their culture or loyalty. Instead, people belonged to the kingdom whose values they shared.

So it is with Christians. Regardless of our culture or nationality, we belong to God's kingdom. We live according to the values, standards, and commandments He has established. When we pray, "Thy kingdom come, Thy will be done," we are asking that the Heavenly law of love become established in our lives here on earth. We are His people, regardless of our address.

MY THOUGHTS:

WHAT ARE SOME OF THE WAYS OUR FAMILY REFLECTS GOD'S VALUES TO THE WORLD?

311

Communication Skills

october 31

"He that hath ears to hear, let him hear."
MATTHEW 11:15

MY THOUGHTS:

_____
_____
_____
_____
_____
_____
_____
_____
_____
_____
_____
_____
_____
_____
_____

HOW DO MY CHILDREN AND I RATE AT COMMUNICATING ON THE SAME WAVELENGTH? AN EXAMPLE WOULD BE . . .

There was once a family of children who wanted a hamster as a pet. They talked their mother into getting one as long as they agreed to take care of it. It would be their responsibility to feed and water the hamster, as well as keep the cage clean. Two months later when Mother was having to care for the hamster, she decided to find a new home for him. She broke the news to the children when they returned home from school that afternoon. They took it quite well; however, they did offer some comments.

One of the children said, "He's been around here a long time. We'll miss him."

Mom agreed, saying, "Yes, but he's too much work for one person, and since I'm that one person, I say he goes."

Another child remarked, "Well, maybe if he wouldn't eat so much and wouldn't be so messy, we could keep him."

Mom was firm. "It's time to take Danny to his new home now," she insisted. "Go and get his cage."

With one voice and in tearful outrage, the children shouted, "Danny? We thought you said 'Daddy'!"

When you communicate with your children, make sure you're on the same wavelength![187]

Our First Response—Pray

Don't worry about anything; instead, pray about everything; tell God your needs, and don't forget to thank him for his answers.

PHILIPPIANS 4:6 TLB

Why pray? We pray because prayer opens up the floodgates of God's infinite grace and power to flow toward the person in need. God can act without prayer, but He chooses to operate within the boundaries of human will and invitation. He allows us to participate in His work on earth with each prayer.

Leonard Ravenhill once said about prayer, "One might estimate the weight of the world, tell the size of the celestial city, count the stars of heaven, measure the speed of lightning, and tell the time of the rising and the setting of the sun—but you cannot estimate prayer power. Prayer is as vast as God because He is behind it. Prayer is as mighty as God because He has committed Himself to answer it."

A sign in a cotton factory read: "If your threads get tangled, send for the foreman." One day a new worker got her threads tangled. The more she tried to disentangle them, the worse the situation grew. Finally, she sent for the foreman. He asked, "Why didn't you send for me earlier?"

She replied, "I was doing my best."

He answered, "No, your best would have been to send for me."

When we face a tough situation, our first response should be to ask for God's help. He longs to be our Helper and to be fully involved in our lives.

MY THOUGHTS:

_____
_____
_____
_____
_____
_____
_____
_____
_____
_____
_____
_____
_____
_____
_____
_____
_____
_____

HOW DO MY CHILDREN AND I TYPICALLY RESPOND WHEN DIFFICULTIES ARISE? AN EXAMPLE WOULD BE . . .

313

Rescue Me

The Lord replies, "I will arise and defend the oppressed, the poor, the needy. I will rescue them as they have longed for me to do."

PSALM 12:5 TLB

MY THOUGHTS:

_____
_____
_____
_____
_____
_____
_____
_____
_____
_____
_____
_____
_____
_____
_____
_____
_____

FROM WHAT ISSUES OR SITUATIONS DO I NEED GOD TO RESCUE ME OR MY CHILDREN?

Can the Lord speak through a pop song? Fontella Bass thinks so. She was at the lowest ebb in her life during 1990. It had been twenty-five years since her rhythm-and-blues single had hit number one on the charts. She had no career to speak of, and she was broke, tired, and cold. The only heat in her house came from a gas stove in the kitchen. She had also strayed far from the church where she started singing gospel songs as a child.

Fontella says, "I said a long prayer. I said, 'I need to see a sign to continue on.'" No sooner had she prayed than she heard her hit song, "Rescue Me," on a television commercial! To her, it was as if "the Lord had stepped right into my world!"

Fontella was unaware American Express had been using her song as part of a commercial, and officials had been unable to locate her to pay royalties. No only did she receive back-royalties, but new opportunities began to open for her to sing.

She released a new album entitled *No Ways Tired*, but the best news is that she renewed her relationship with God. "For so many years I tried doing it on my own, and it didn't work," she says. "Then I took it out of my hands and turned it over to Him, and now everything's happening."[188]

Bits and Pieces

november 3

My son, give me thine heart.
PROVERBS 23:26

So many things of beauty begin as "bits and pieces"—not unlike our lives, which often seem like jigsaw puzzles with a multitude of scattered pieces.

Or the artist's collage.

Or a stained glass window.

Or a mosaic floor.

If tragedies and pain strike us, we need to allow the Master Craftsman to put us back together according to His design, rather than trying to find all the pieces and gluing ourselves together without Him.

In *The Dark Night of the Soul*, Georgia Harkness writes, "The Christian faith imparts meaning to life. A living faith that is centered in God as revealed in Christ takes our chaotic, disorganized selves, with their crude jumble of pleasures and pains, and knits them together into a steadiness and joy that can endure anything with God."[189]

Trust God today to turn your brokenness into something of beauty and value.

MY THOUGHTS:

_____
_____
_____
_____
_____
_____
_____
_____
_____
_____
_____
_____
_____
_____
_____
_____

WHAT "BITS AND PIECES" CAN I GIVE TO GOD TODAY?

A Tribute to a Mother

Encourage and rebuke with all authority.
TITUS 2:15 NIV

MY THOUGHTS:

_____
_____
_____
_____
_____
_____
_____
_____
_____
_____
_____
_____
_____
_____
_____
_____
_____
_____

HOW CAN I MAKE MY DISCIPLINARY STYLE MORE POSITIVE AND CONSTRUCTIVE?

Thomas Edison wrote the following tribute to his mother:

I did not have my mother long, but she cast over me a good influence that lasted all my life. The good effects of her early training I can never lose. If it had not been for her appreciation and her faith in me at a critical time in my experience, I would never likely have become an inventor. I was always a careless boy, and with a mother of different mental caliber, I would have turned out badly. But her firmness, her sweetness, her goodness were potent powers to keep me on the right path. My mother was the making of me. The memory of her will always be a blessing to me.

Mothers, reassure your children that you discipline them for the things they do and not for the people they are. Tell them of your love for them, and show them how important they are in your eyes. Encourage, praise, and respect their efforts. Make a memory for your children that will be a blessing to them just as Thomas Edison's mother made for him.[190]

First Things First

"Seek first the kingdom of God and His righteousness, and all these things shall he added to you."

MATTHEW 6:33 NKJV

A pastor's wife was amazed when she heard a person say, "One hour is only 4 percent of a day." She had not thought about time in this way. Sensing the need for more prayer time in her life, she thought surely she could give God at least 4 percent of her time. She determined to try it.

Rather than try to fit prayer into her schedule, she decided to "fix" a prayer time and then "fit" the rest of the day around it. At the time, her children were old enough to travel to school alone. By 8:30 each morning, a hush fell over her home. She knew her best hour for prayer would be between 8:30 and 9:30am. To guarantee she was uninterrupted, she made it known in the parish that, except for emergencies, she would be grateful if people didn't call her before 9:30 in the morning.

To her surprise, no one in the church was offended. Instead they responded very positively. Several other women began to follow her example by setting aside the same hour to pray every day!

When we seek God's plan first, all our plans with other people will have a way of falling into place.

MY THOUGHTS:

IN WHAT WAYS CAN GIVING GOD THE FIRST PART OF MY DAY IMPROVE MY QUALITY OF LIFE?

A Persistent Mother

november 6

"Our Father in heaven, . . . Give us today our daily bread."
MATTHEW 6:9, 11 NIV

MY THOUGHTS:

_____

_____

_____

_____

_____

_____

_____

_____

_____

_____

_____

_____

_____

_____

_____

_____

_____

_____

**WHAT ARE THE
POSITIVE THINGS
THAT BEING A
MOTHER MOTIVATES
ME TO DO?**

Raymond Dunn Jr. was born in 1975, in the state of New York. The Associated Press reported that at his birth he suffered a skull fracture and oxygen deprivation that caused severe retardation. The family discovered further impairments as Raymond grew. His twisted body suffered up to twenty seizures per day, and he was blind, mute, and immobile. He had severe allergies that limited him to only one food: a meat-based formula made by Gerber Foods.

Gerber stopped making the formula that Raymond lived on in 1985. His mother searched the country to buy what stores had in stock, amassing cases and cases, but her supply ran out in 1990. In desperation, she appealed to Gerber for help. Raymond would starve to death without this particular food.

The Gerber employees listened. In an unparalleled action, volunteers donated hundreds of hours to bring out old equipment, set up production lines, obtain special approval from the USDA, and produce the formula—all for one special boy.

Raymond, known as the Gerber Boy, died in January 1995 from his physical problems. But during his brief lifetime, he called forth a wonderful essence called compassion.[191]

Getting the Last Word

If you have been trapped by what you said, ensnared by the words of your mouth, then do this, my son, to free yourself, since you have fallen into your neighbor's hands: Go and humble yourself; press your plea with your neighbor!

PROVERBS 6:2-3 NIV

In 1755, a twenty-three-year-old colonel was in the midst of running for a seat in the Virginia assembly when he made an insulting remark as part of a campaign speech. The remark was addressed to a hot-tempered man named Payne, who responded by knocking the colonel down with a hickory stick. Soldiers rushed to the colonel's assistance, and it appeared that a full-blown flight would ensue. But the would-be politician got up, dusted himself off, called off the soldiers, and left the scene.

The next morning the colonel wrote Payne, requesting his presence at a local tavern. Payne obliged but wondered what demands the colonel might make—perhaps another verbal confrontation or even a duel. To Payne's surprise, the colonel met him with an apology, asking forgiveness for his derogatory remarks and offering a handshake.

The move may have been viewed by others as politically expedient, but Colonel George Washington considered it personally imperative if he was to enjoy internal peace as he continued with his campaign.

The moment we feel like demanding forgiveness from others may be the moment when we are to forgive.

MY THOUGHTS:

IS THERE ANYONE TO WHOM I NEED TO SPEAK A WORD OF APOLOGY? HOW WILL I APPROACH THAT PERSON?

Invest in the Creativity of Your Child

Direct my footsteps according to your word.
PSALM 119:133 NIV

MY THOUGHTS:

_____
_____
_____
_____
_____
_____
_____
_____
_____
_____
_____
_____
_____
_____
_____

WHAT ARE SOME THINGS I CAN DO TO CREATE AN ATMOSPHERE OF CREATIVITY IN MY HOME?

The 3M Company is unique among many large corporations. To encourage creativity, the company allows its researchers to spend 15 percent of their time on any project that interests them.

Several years ago, Art Fry, a scientist in 3M's commercial office, took advantage of this creative time and came up with an idea for one of 3M's best-selling products. It all started when he vowed to find a solution to a small irritation he faced every Sunday morning. As a member of his church choir, he routinely marked pages in the hymnal with small bits of paper, but the little pieces were always falling out on the floor.

Then Fry had an idea. He remembered an adhesive developed by a coworker that everyone thought was a failure because it did not stick well. "I coated the adhesive on a paper sample," Fry recalls, "and I found that it was not only a good bookmark, but it was great for writing notes. It will stay in place as long as you want it to, and then you can remove it without damage."

The resulting product was called Post-it! It has become one of 3M's most successful office products.

Make a major investment in the creative processes of your child. One day he or she might invent something to benefit us all.[192]

Respect Must Be Earned

A ruler who lacks understanding is . . . a great oppressor.
PROVERBS 28:16 AMP

Irving Bluestein, a seventy-eight-year-old retired salesman in California, still remembers the good teachers he had in school.

There was Miss Candy, who said, "An make to earn empty wagon makes the most noise." She taught Bluestein that a person who talks a lot often has the least to say.

Mr. Spangler and Mr. Glazer were very fair but also very strict. Mr. Spangler, a baseball and football coach, never allowed students to con their way to good grades.

Mr. Lester was an English teacher who later went to Hollywood to be an advisor for a movie, then wrote a story that was made into a movie. Bluestein recalls that he had a habit of chewing on pretzels and had a good sense of humor.

What made each of these teachers truly memorable to Bluestein, however, was this: "They got your respect without bullying you."[193]

The respect of others can never be dictated, legislated, demanded, or required. It should never be taken for granted. Respect from others can only be earned—through expressions of love, honesty, fairness, and high moral values.

MY THOUGHTS:

_____
_____
_____
_____
_____
_____
_____
_____
_____
_____
_____
_____
_____
_____
_____
_____
_____

WHAT ADJUSTMENTS DO I NEED TO MAKE TO EARN OR MAINTAIN THE RESPECT OF MY CHILDREN?

Positive Kids in a Negative World

Keep thy heart with all diligence; for out of it are the issues of life. Put away from thee a froward mouth, and perverse lips put far from thee.

PROVERBS 4:23-24

MY THOUGHTS:

_____
_____
_____
_____
_____
_____
_____
_____
_____
_____
_____
_____
_____
_____
_____

WHAT SUBSTITUTIONS CAN WE MAKE TO CREATE A MORE POSITIVE ATMOSPHERE IN OUR HOME?

In an interview published in *People Weekly*, gospel singer CeCe Winans talked candidly about raising her children. She had grown up in a Christian home and was not even allowed to wear makeup until she was eighteen. One result was that she wasn't about to embrace pop rock professionally or personally.

"I don't listen to secular music at home," said Winans, who lives in Nashville with her husband and manager, Alvin Love, and their kids, Alvin III and Ashley. "Very seldom do you find a mainstream artist who does only clean music. It's hard for me to wonder whether my children are going to listen to just the clean songs, so it's better to eliminate that music altogether."

CeCe made it clear that parents are responsible for the atmosphere that surrounds their children in the home. She understood her responsibilities and eliminated those things that she felt were detrimental to her children's spiritual growth.

Parents have many difficult decisions to make in the raising of their children. Often that means they have to give up something for themselves to substitute positive influences and reinforce the values of faith, hope, and love in the home.[194]

Sharing Abundance

"Give, and you will receive. You will be given much. Pressed down, shaken together, and running over, it will spill into your lap. The way you give to others is the way God will give to you."

LUKE 6:38 NCV

There was a wealthy noble-woman who had grown tired of life. She had everything one could wish for except happiness and contentment. She said, "I am weary of life. I will go to the river and there end my life."

As she walked along, she felt a little hand tugging at her skirts. Looking down, she saw a frail, hungry-looking little boy who pleaded, "There are six of us. We are dying for want of food!" The noblewoman thought, *Why should I not relieve this wretched family? I have the means, and it seems I will have no more use for riches when I am gone.*

Following the little boy, she entered a scene of misery, sickness, and want. She opened her purse and emptied its contents. The family members were beside themselves with joy and gratitude. Even more taken with their need, the noblewoman said, "I'll return tomorrow, and I will share with you more of the good things which God has given to me in abundance!"

She left that scene of want and wretchedness, rejoicing that the child had found her. For the first time in her life, she understood the reason for her wealth. Never again did she think of ending her life, which was now filled with meaning and purpose.

MY THOUGHTS:

WHAT OF OUR ABUNDANCE COULD WE SHARE TO BENEFIT OTHERS? AN EXAMPLE WOULD BE . . .

All Children Are Winner

I have loved thee with an everlasting love: therefore with lovingkindness have I drawn thee.

JEREMIAH 31:3

MY THOUGHTS:

_____
_____
_____
_____
_____
_____
_____
_____
_____
_____
_____
_____
_____
_____
_____
_____

I CAN HELP MY CHILDREN SEE THEMSELVES AS WINNERS IN GOD'S EYES BY . . .

Cathy Rigby was a member of the United States Women's Gymnastics Team in the 1972 Olympics at Munich, and she had only one goal in mind—to win a gold medal. She had trained hard over a long period of time and knew she was ready to compete.

On the day she was scheduled to perform, she prayed for strength and the control to get through her routine without making mistakes. She was tense with determination not to let herself or the American team down.

She performed well, but when it was finished and the winners were announced, her name was not among them. Cathy was crushed by her defeat. Afterward she joined her parents in the stands all set for a good cry. As she sat down, she could barely manage to say, "I'm sorry. I did my best."

"You know that, and I know that," her mother said, "and I'm sure God knows that too." Then Cathy recalls, her mother said ten words that she has never forgotten: "Doing your best is more important than being the best."

Help your kids understand that whether they win or lose, you still love them. In God's eyes, all of His children are winners![195]

Faithful in the Small Things

"'Thou hast been faithful over a few things, I will make thee ruler over many things: enter thou into the joy of thy lord.'"

MATTHEW 25:21

In speaking to a group of ministers, Fred Craddock noted the importance of being faithful in the little things of life. He said:

To give my life for Christ appears glorious. To pour myself out of others . . . to pay the ultimate price of martyrdom—I'll do it. I'm ready, Lord, to go out in a blaze of glory.

We think giving our all to the Lord is like taking a $1,000 bill and laying it on the table—"Here's my life, Lord. I'm giving it all."

But the reality for most of us is that He sends us to the bank and has us cash in the $1,000 for quarters. We go through life putting out 25 cents here and 50 cents there. Listen to the neighbor kid's troubles instead of saying, "Get lost." Go to a committee meeting. Give a cup of water to a shaky old man in a nursing home.

Usually giving our life to Christ isn't glorious. It's done in all those little acts of love, 25 cents at a time. It would be easy to go out in a flash of glory; it's harder to live the Christian life little by little over the long haul.[196]

Ask the Lord to show you how you can spend your life well.

MY THOUGHTS:

_____
_____
_____
_____
_____
_____
_____
_____
_____
_____
_____
_____
_____
_____
_____
_____

I BELIEVE GOD IS LEADING ME TO SPEND TODAY DOING WHAT THINGS?

Allow Room for Difference

We're Christ's representatives. God uses us to persuade men and women to drop their differences and enter into God's work of making things right between them.

2 CORINTHIANS 5:20 MSG

MY THOUGHTS:

_____

_____

_____

_____

_____

_____

_____

_____

_____

_____

_____

_____

_____

_____

_____

_____

HOW DO I FEEL ABOUT MY CHILDREN DEVELOPING THEIR OWN VIEWS?

In an article in *Focus on the Family* magazine, one father described a Thanksgiving that he would never forget. During a family gathering, an older cousin introduced his innocent seventh-grade son to contemporary Christian music.

Overnight his son wasn't satisfied with the children's tunes he'd grown up with and sang in church. The music had to be louder, more rhythmic, and intense. The man and his wife were upset that this cousin had dragged their son away from the "refined" musical taste they had carefully instilled.

It took a week of late-night debate between husband and wife before they finally admitted that their son was growing up. He had stumbled into one of the issues that almost all teenagers use to exhibit their individuality and rattle their parents' cages. The parents reluctantly decided to judge their son's songs by the lyrics rather than the beat. As the teenage years went along, music turned out to be a blessing in their home rather than a source of anxiety.

Allow your child the freedom to grow in ways that may not be the same as yours.[197]

Grief Turned to Joy

Everlasting joy shall be upon their head: they shall obtain gladness and joy; and sorrow and mourning shall flee away.

ISAIAH 51:11

In a matter of seconds, Vickie's life was shattered. A trapeze artist, she lost control of the fly bar one day and careened headfirst into the net. She broke her neck between the fifth and sixth cervical vertebrae and became paralyzed, a quadriplegic.

Three years after the accident, she had fallen into deep despair and self-pity and was determined to take her life. Her attempt failed, and she ended up in a psychiatric hospital. On the fourth anniversary of her fall, she and her husband separated. Bitterness set in.

One day a Christian home health aide was assigned to her. Mae Lynne introduced Vickie to Jesus Christ and the Bible. Vickie began to learn to "stand firm" in her faith and to "walk" in obedience to God.

A minister faithfully taught her for two years. Then Vickie began a ministry of encouragement by writing a dozen letters each week to prison inmates and others with disabilities. She now says, "Quadriplegics aren't supposed to have this much joy, are they?"

Vickie still uses a wheelchair, becomes dizzy at times, has occasional respiratory problems, and needs an attendant's care. However, she has deep inner strength because of her relationship with Jesus. Now others describe her as "a fountain of smiles."

MY THOUGHTS:

_____
_____
_____
_____
_____
_____
_____
_____
_____
_____
_____
_____
_____
_____
_____
_____
_____
_____

WHAT SITUATIONS DO MY CHILDREN OR I NEED TO SEE FROM A MORE POSITIVE PERSPECTIVE?

A Lasting Legacy

Be ye followers of me, even as I also am of Christ.
1 CORINTHIANS 11:1

MY THOUGHTS:

_____
_____
_____
_____
_____
_____
_____
_____
_____
_____
_____
_____
_____
_____
_____
_____
_____
_____

WHAT KIND OF SPIRITUAL LEGACY AM I LEAVING FOR MY CHILDREN TO FOLLOW? AN EXAMPLE WOULD BE . . .

Abraham Lincoln's indebtedness to and regard for the Bible is beyond dispute. He read the Bible in his boyhood, and its influence upon him increased over the years. When he addressed the pubic, he quoted from the Bible more than any other book. Lincoln's literary style was also influenced by the Bible, especially the writings of the prophets of Israel. The style of his deeply moving second inaugural speech is strongly reminiscent of the book of Isaiah.

Lincoln not only spoke and wrote in the style of the Bible but obviously thought in terms of Biblical ideas and convictions, to an extent that has very likely been unparalleled among modern statesmen.

Moreover, Lincoln was a man of prayer who did so without apology or self-consciousness. He did not hesitate to request the prayers of others or to acknowledge that he himself prayed often. He regarded prayer as a necessity. He routinely spoke of seeking divine guidance, as though it were an entirely natural and reasonable thing to do.

Lincoln is often heralded as the greatest American president. His spirituality was undoubtedly the greatest reason for the decisions that led to his success.[198]

Never curtail your pursuit of God. It is the most important thing you can do to leave a lasting legacy of accomplishment and purpose.

Talk Yourself Through It

Come now, and let us reason together, saith the Lord.

ISAIAH 1:18

A man noticed a woman in the grocery store with a three-year-old girl in her basket. As they passed the cookie section, the little girl asked for cookies, and her mother told her no. The little girl started to whine and fuss, and the mother said quietly, "Now, Monica, don't be upset. We just have half the aisles left to go through. It won't be long."

Soon they came to the candy aisle, where the little girl began to shout for candy. When told she couldn't have any, she began to scream. The mother said, "There, there, Monica, don't cry—only two more aisles to go, and then we'll be checking out."

When they got to the checkout stand, the little girl immediately clamored for gum. She burst into a terrible tantrum upon discovering there'd be no gum purchased. The mother patiently said, "Monica, we'll be through this checkout stand in five minutes, and then you can go home and have a nice nap."

The man followed them out to the parking lot and stopped the woman to commend her. "I couldn't help noticing how patient you were with little Monica," he said.

At that time the mother said, *"I'm Monica. My little girl's name is Tammy."*

Sometimes the only way to make it through the day is to talk yourself through it![199]

MY THOUGHTS:

_____

_____

_____

_____

_____

_____

_____

_____

_____

_____

_____

_____

_____

_____

_____

WHAT SITUATIONS WOULD BE MORE MANAGEABLE IF I WOULD TALK MYSELF THROUGH THEM?

Housecleaning

God demonstrates His own love toward us, in that while we were still sinners, Christ died for us.

ROMANS 5:8 NKJV

MY THOUGHTS:

_____
_____
_____
_____
_____
_____
_____
_____
_____
_____
_____
_____
_____
_____
_____

WHAT WOULD I CONSIDER TO BE THE "JUNK ROOM" OF MY LIFE?

At a crucial transition time, a Christian woman cried out to the Lord, despairing over the lack of spiritual power and fruitfulness she was experiencing in her life. Suddenly she sensed Jesus standing beside her, asking, "May I have the keys to your life?"

The experience was so realistic, the woman reached into her pocket and took out a ring of keys. "Are all the keys here?" the Lord asked.

"Yes, except the key to one small room in my life."

"If you cannot trust Me in all rooms of your life, I cannot accept any of the keys."

The woman was so overwhelmed at the thought of the Lord moving out of her life altogether, she cried, "Lord . . . take the keys to all the rooms of my life!"

Many of us have rooms we hope no one will ever see. We intend to clean them out someday, but "someday" never seems to come. When we invite Jesus into these rooms, He will help us clean them. With Him, we have the courage to throw away all the "junk" and fill the rooms with His love, peace, and joy.

All You Need is Love

What a man desires is unfailing love.
PROVERBS 19:22 NIV

K arl Menninger once said, "Love cures people—both the ones who give it and the ones who receive it." He organized the work of the Menninger Clinic around love. "From the top psychiatrist down to the electricians and caregivers," Menninger said, "all contacts with patients must manifest love." And it was "love unlimited." The result was that hospitalization time was cut in half.

One of the patients at the clinic was a woman who sat in her rocking chair for three years and never said a word to anyone. Her doctor called a nurse and said, "Mary, I'm giving you Mrs. Brown as your patient. All I'm asking you to do is to love her till she gets well." The nurse tried it. She got a rocking chair of the same kind as Mrs. Brown's; sat beside her; and loved her morning, noon, and night. On the third day, Mrs. Brown spoke. Within a week, she was out of her shell—and healthy.

Research projects have been done to ascertain the bonding that develops between a mother and her child in the first months after childbirth. Studies have shown that babies deprived of touch and their mothers' voices develop at a slower rate than those held and spoken to. God did not mean for us to grow up in a vacuum. Hug the members of your family daily—both children and adults. We all need love![200]

MY THOUGHTS:

WHAT CAN I DO TO SHOW MY LOVE TO EACH MEMBER OF MY FAMILY TODAY?

He Doesn't Remember

I, even I, am He Who blots out and cancels your transgressions, for My own sake, and I will not remember your sins.

ISAIAH 43:25 AMP

MY THOUGHTS:

_____
_____
_____
_____
_____
_____
_____
_____
_____
_____
_____
_____
_____
_____
_____

HOW CAN WE DEVELOP A "FORGIVE AND FORGET" POLICY IN OUR HOME?

A much-loved minister of God once carried a secret burden of long-past sin buried deep in his heart. He had committed the sin many years before, during his seminary training. No one knew what he had done, but they did know he had repented. Even so, he had suffered years of remorse over the incident without any sense of God's forgiveness.

A woman in his church deeply loved God and claimed to have visions in which Jesus Christ spoke to her. The minister, skeptical of her claims, asked of her, "The next time you speak to the Lord, would you please ask Him what sin your minister committed while he was in seminary." The woman agreed.

When she came to the church a few days later, the minister asked, "Did He visit you?"

She said, "Yes."

"And did you ask Him what sin I committed in seminary?"

"Yes, I asked Him," she replied.

"Well, what did He say?"

"He said, 'I don't remember.'"

The Necessary Skills

God gave them knowledge and skill in all learning and wisdom.

DANIEL 1:17

A ten-year-old boy decided to study judo despite the fact that he had lost his left arm in a devastating car accident. He began lessons with an old Japanese judo master. The boy couldn't understand why the master had taught him only one move.

"Sensei," the boy finally said, "shouldn't I be learning more moves?"

"This is the only move you know, but this is the only move you'll ever know," the sensei replied.

Several months later, the boy went to his first tournament. He deftly used his one move to win the first three matches and was now in the finals.

This time his opponent was more experienced, but he made a critical mistake: he dropped his guard. Instantly, the boy used his move to pin him, and in doing so, he won the match and the tournament.

On the way home, the little boy asked, "Sensei, how did I win the tournament with only one move?"

"You won for two reasons," the sensei answered. "First, you've almost mastered one of the most difficult throws in all of judo. Second, the only known defense for that move is for your opponent to grip your left arm."[201]

Are you teaching your children the skills they'll need to succeed in life?

MY THOUGHTS:

WHAT ARE THE MOST IMPORTANT LIFE SKILLS THAT MY CHILDREN NEED TO LEARN FROM ME?

333

Words Are Powerful

Set a watch, O Lord, before my mouth; keep the door of my lips.
PSALM 141:3

MY THOUGHTS:

_____
_____
_____
_____
_____
_____
_____
_____
_____
_____
_____
_____
_____
_____
_____
_____
_____

WHAT NEGATIVE WORDS DO I NEED TO REPLACE WITH MORE POSITIVE ONES?

A heart doctor was amazed at the great improvement one of his patients had made. When he had seen the woman a few months earlier, she was seriously ill in the hospital, needing an oxygen mask. He asked the woman what had happened.

The woman said, "I was sure the end was near and that you and your staff had given up hope. However, Thursday morning when you entered with your troops, something happened that changed everything. You listened to my heart; you seemed pleased by the finding, and you announced to all those standing about my bed that I had a 'wholesome gallop.' I knew that the doctors, in talking to me, might try to soften things. But I knew they wouldn't kid each other. So when I overheard you tell your colleagues I had a wholesome gallop, I figured I still had a lot of kick to my heart and could not be dying. My spirits were for the first time lifted, and I knew I would live and recover."

The heart doctor never told the woman that a third-sound gallop is a poor sign that denotes the heart muscle is straining and usually failing!

Just a few words can be enough to make a difference in a person's life. How important it is to choose our words wisely!

Let Them Go

"There is hope for your future," declares the Lord. "Your children will return to their own land."

JEREMIAH 31:17 NIV

Bill Cosby writes in Fatherhood, "Some authority on parenting once said, 'Hold them very close and then let them go.'" This is the hardest truth for parents to learn: that their children are continually growing away from them. It is, however, a part of the evolution of life. Your children grow to adulthood, establish homes of their own, have your grandchildren, and the cycle of life continues.

Mr. Cosby went on to tell this story about his daughter: "You have to remember that rejection, like one I received on a certain day when I called my daughter at college, means no lessening of her love. Someone in her dorm picked up the phone and I asked to speak to my daughter. The person left and returned about a minute later to say, 'She says she's sleeping right now.'"

A child's rejection hurts, but it doesn't mean that your child loves you any less. Be glad that you have done a good job in preparing him or her to be independent. Use the first rejection to prepare yourself for the many more to come. It's just another stage in your child's growth and development ... as well as yours!

MY THOUGHTS:

_____
_____
_____
_____
_____
_____
_____
_____
_____
_____
_____
_____
_____
_____
_____
_____

WHAT STEPS CAN I TAKE NOW TO ENSURE THAT I CAN MOVE SMOOTHLY THROUGH THE LETTING-GO PROCESS?

Do What Works

Let us run with perseverance the race marked out for us.
HEBREWS 12:1 NIV

MY THOUGHTS:

_____
_____
_____
_____
_____
_____
_____
_____
_____
_____
_____
_____
_____
_____
_____
_____
_____

WHAT POSITIVE LIFE SKILLS WORKS FOR ME? AN EXAMPLE WOULD BE . . .

W. Clement Stone, the insurance mogul, recalls the following:

Selling newspapers on Chicago's tough South Side wasn't easy, especially with the older kids taking over the busy corners, yelling louder, and threatening me with clenched fists. The memory of those dim days is still with me, for it's the first time I can recall turning a disadvantage into an advantage... Hoelle's Restaurant was near the corner where I tried to work...

It was a busy and prosperous place that presented a frightening aspect to a child of six. I was nervous, but I walked in hurriedly and made a lucky sale at the first table. Then diners at the second and third tables bought papers. When I started for the fourth ... Mr. Hoelle pushed me out the front door. But I had sold three papers. So when Mr. Hoelle wasn't looking, I walked back in and called at the fourth table.

Apparently, the jovial customer liked my gumption; he paid for the paper and gave me an extra dime before Mr. Hoelle pushed me out once again. But I had already sold four papers and got a "bonus" dime besides. I walked into the restaurant and started selling again. There was a lot of laughter. The customers were enjoying the show. One whispered loudly, "Let him be," as Mr. Hoelle came toward me. About five minutes later, I had sold all my papers.[202]

Find out what works for you, and stick with it!

Teach Them How to Think

Let me give you understanding . . . Let me show you common sense!

PROVERBS 8:4 TLB

A mother and father helped their oldest son pack his belongings and prepare for his first year of college. The parents had provided him with every conceivable that he might need to begin living independently. They also gave him his first checkbook with the funds deposited into the account to pay his beginning college expenses. Two months later, bank overdrafts on the son's account began arriving at the parents' home.

"How are things at school?" Dad asked in a phone call to his son.

"Just great, Dad," his son replied.

"John," his dad responded, "you've written over $500 in checks when there was only $10 left in your checking account. You are extensively overdrawn."

"But that can't be," argued John, "I still have several checks left in my checkbook."

Parents often assume that their children have learned a necessary skill at school, when the reality is, they haven't. They may have been exposed to the information at some point but did not receive any practical experience to make it a part of their lives. Make it a point to teach your children things like how to balance a checkbook, do the laundry, and comparison shop for groceries. They'll thank you for it later![203]

MY THOUGHTS:

WHAT PRACTICAL SKILLS DO I NEED TO TEACH MY CHILDREN?

Look Up

I will lift up mine eyes unto the hills, from whence cometh my help. My help cometh from the Lord, which made heaven and earth.

PSALMS 121:1-2

MY THOUGHTS:

_____
_____
_____
_____
_____
_____
_____
_____
_____
_____
_____
_____
_____
_____
_____
_____

HOW CAN I LEARN TO MORE "SELF-FORGETFUL" AND FIND MY JOY IN THE HAPPINESS OF HOSE AROUND ME RATHER THAN IN MYSELF?

The story of Helen Keller is well known. She was deaf and blind from a childhood disease, and her teacher, Anne Sullivan, opened the world to her through the other senses of taste, touch, and smell. In her autobiography, Helen Keller wrote:

Fate—silent, pitiless—bars the way. Fain would I question his imperious decree; for my heart is undisciplined and passionate, but my tongue will not utter the bitter, futile words that rise to my lips, and they fall back into my heart like unshed tears. Silence sits immense upon my soul. Then comes hope with a smile and whispers, "There is joy in self-forgetfulness." So I try to make the light in other people's eyes my sun, the music in others' ears my symphony, the smile on others' lips my happiness.

How sad it is when we search only within ourselves for a reason to be happy! The happiness in those around us is reason enough to have joy, regardless of our situation or handicap.

If we look to Jesus, all will be well with us—inside and out.

The Joy in Giving

Do not put out the Spirit's fire.
1 THESSALONIANS 5:19 NIV

Many years ago, a man named David received a new car as a gift from his prosperous brother. One evening as he was leaving work, he noticed a poor child eyeing his shiny new car.

"Is this your car?" the boy asked.

David nodded and said, "My brother gave it to me for Christmas."

The boy said, "It didn't cost you anything? Boy, I wish . . ." David expected the boy to wish that he had a generous brother, but what the boy said astonished him. He said, "I wish I could be a brother like that."

He asked the young boy if he'd like a ride home. The little boy hopped in quickly, and David smiled, thinking that the boy was anxious to show off to his neighbors and family. Again he was wrong. When the two pulled up in front of the boy's house, the boy asked him to wait a minute. He then ran up the steps and soon returned carrying his crippled brother. David was moved deeply when he heard him say, "There it is, Buddy, just like I told you upstairs. His brother gave it to him. Someday I'm gonna give you one just like it."

This child found his happiness in the joy of giving. Where could one find a better place to look?[204]

MY THOUGHTS:

_____
_____
_____
_____
_____
_____
_____
_____
_____
_____
_____
_____
_____
_____
_____
_____
_____
_____

WHAT STEPS CAN I TAKE TO TEACH MY CHILDREN THE JOY OF GIVING?

Knowing When to Leave

Withdraw thy foot from thy neighbour's house; lest he be weary of thee, and so hate thee.

PROVERBS 25:17

MY THOUGHTS:

_____
_____
_____
_____
_____
_____
_____
_____
_____
_____
_____
_____
_____
_____
_____
_____

WHAT STEPS CAN I TAKE TO ENSURE THAT MY CHILDREN GAIN A SENSE OF RESPECT AND CONSIDERATION FOR OTHERS?

It has been said that fish and houseguests have one thing in common—after three days they both begin to stink. Depending on the circumstances, a stay may not require that much time before it "goes bad." Generally speaking, the more displaced your hosts have made themselves on your account, the shorter your stay should be. Be certain before you visit with relatives or friends that you both know when you will arrive and when you will depart. The old entertainer's rule of thumb, "Leave them wanting more" is good advice for a houseguest.

The same goes for shorter visits—better to leave earlier than later. When your hosts begin to yawn or gather up the dishes, take the hint!

George Washington visited the home of friends one evening, and when the hour came for him to leave, he said good-bye to the adults, then paused at the entrance where a little girl opened the door to let him out. Washington bowed to her and said, "I am sorry, my little dear, to give you so much trouble."

She replied, "I wish, sir, it was to let you in." Now that's a welcome guest!

Moved with Compassion

Jesus, moved with compassion, put forth his hand, and touched him.

MARK 1:41

A young girl remembers her grandpa as an old man confined to his chair most of the time due to severe arthritis. His Bible always seemed to be cradled on his frail legs.

One time everyone was in the kitchen compassion except the little girl and Grandpa. Grandpa's lunch was brought to him on a tray because it was too difficult for him to eat at the table. The little girl's mother called for her to come and eat. She started to obey, but something made her stop. There sat Grandpa all alone. Her heart was moved with compassion. She went to his chair, put her arms around him, and said, "I love you, Grandpa."

Then her grandpa did something she neither expected nor understood at the time: he cried. That small act of kindness meant the world to him.

Regardless of age, we all need a human touch. It creates a connection with others so that we don't feel so alone. We never know how much our random acts of kindness mean to others. Give someone an unexpected hug today![205]

MY THOUGHTS:

_____
_____
_____
_____
_____
_____
_____
_____
_____
_____
_____
_____
_____
_____
_____
_____

WHAT STEPS CAN I TAKE TO FAN THE FLAME OF COMPASSION WITHIN MY CHILDREN?

Who Can Measure the Value?

"Those who try to hold on to their lives will give up true life. Those who give up their lives for me will hold on to true life."

MATTHEW 10:39 NCV

MY THOUGHTS:

_____
_____
_____
_____
_____
_____
_____
_____
_____
_____
_____
_____
_____
_____
_____
_____
_____
_____

WHAT ARE SOME OF THE BLESSINGS I'VE RECEIVED SINCE BECOMING GOD'S CHILD?

While serving in India, a devout English judge befriended a young Indian man. Having been raised in a prominent Indian family, he had been cast out after he converted to Christianity. The judge took the boy into his household where he happily worked as a house boy.

It was the custom of the household to have a devotional time every evening. One night the judge read aloud the words of Jesus: "Every one that hath forsaken houses, or brethren, or sisters, or father, or mother, or wife, or children, or lands, for my name's sake, shall receive an hundredfold" (Matthew 19:29).

The judge turned to the lad and said, "Nobody here has done this except you, Norbudur. Will you tell us, is it true what Jesus has said?"

The young Indian man read the verse aloud for himself and then turned to the family and said, "No, there is an error."

Startled the judge responded, "There is?"

The youth replied, "It says He gives an hundredfold. I know He gives a thousandfold."

With eternal life, intimacy with the Father, and all the riches of Heaven, who can truly measure the value of what it means when Jesus Christ comes into a person's life?

Guard the Treasure of Your Family

"Lord, let our eyes be opened."
MATTHEW 20:33 NRSV

E ach morning, the mother walked her frightened kindergartner to her classroom. They faced the same routine every day, going through the same reassuring gestures. The mother wasn't alone in this ritual. In the beginning, there were many teary-eyed children, but they soon grew braver until the group was reduced to two: her daughter, Sarah, and a little boy named Danny.

Danny was brought to class by his father—a man with a square jaw, designer suits, and a perfect smile that would cut through any heart in a flash. Sarah's mother found herself walking with him to their cars every day. From the beginning, she was aware of his attentiveness toward her. He was likable, handsome, and wooing.

She began to feel uneasy but persuaded herself they were not doing anything wrong. Each time they spoke, her feelings of guilt weakened. She enjoyed his friendship, the new attention, and the secret feelings. She told herself again and again, "This is only a friendship."

Then one morning she realized she enjoyed his attention far too much for this to remain a safe situation. She changed the time she brought Sarah to school and thanked God for opening her eyes in time.

Keep your family safe by using wisdom when developing relationships with others.[206]

MY THOUGHTS:

WHAT SAFEGUARDS CAN I SET IN PLACE TO PROTECT MY FAMILY AND OUR RELATIONSHIPS?

343

A Different Anthem

Only a fool would say to himself, "There is no God."
PSALM 53:1 TLB

MY THOUGHTS:

_____
_____
_____
_____
_____
_____
_____
_____
_____
_____
_____
_____
_____
_____
_____
_____
_____
_____

**WHAT IS THE
ANTHEM OF OUR
HOUSEHOLD?**

Lyman Abbot once paraphrased the Lord's Prayer to reflect the philosophy of those without God:

*Our brethren who art on earth,
hallowed be our name.
Our kingdom come,
our will be done on earth,
for there is no heaven.
We must get this day our daily bread;
we neither forgive nor are forgiven.
We fear not temptation,
for we deliver ourselves from evil.
For ours is the kingdom and the power,
and there is no glory and no forever.*[207]

Most people would agree upon reading this "humanist's prayer"—*how empty, how shallow, how self-serving.* Yet humanism is the philosophy by which millions of Americans live their lives every day. They enjoy a standard of living that is far beyond that experienced by people elsewhere in the world, yet they rarely pause to thank the Source of that abundance —the One who gives them life, breath, and all other blessings.

Isn't it time to pray a different anthem?

*Praise God from whom all blessings flow,
Praise Him all creatures here below.
Praise Him above ye heavenly host.
Praise Father, Son, and Holy Ghost!*

Doing the Right Thing Matters

Righteousness exalteth a nation: but sin is a reproach to any people.

PROVERBS 14:34

Most people know of the Great Depression that occurred during the 1930s, but few today know about the financial depression that occurred in the first half of the 1800s. Governments went into financial panic. Pennsylvania, one of the wealthier states at the time, rejected its debts . . . in effect declaring itself bankrupt. Illinois felt that with such a move made by its wealthy neighbor, it might be justified in doing likewise.

When Stephen Douglas heard of the proposal for bankruptcy, he strongly opposed it. Although ill at the time, he insisted that he be carried to the state legislature on a stretcher. Lying on his back, he made this historic resolution: "That Illinois be honest." The motion touched the hearts of every member of the state house, and the resolution was adopted with eagerness. The action by Illinois kept the practice of repudiation from spreading among the states. Many historians credit this move as a key reason why Illinois is one of the most prosperous states today.

Choosing the right direction sometimes means choosing the unpopular direction with the greatest amount of discomfort. Teach your children that there is no substitute for the rewards that can come at the end of such a journey.

MY THOUGHTS:

_____
_____
_____
_____
_____
_____
_____
_____
_____
_____
_____
_____
_____
_____
_____
_____
_____
_____

HOW CAN I INSTILL IN MY CHILDREN THE CONVICTION TO TAKE RIGHTEOUS STANDS?

Faith, Not Sight

december 4

Morality is always higher than law.We walk by faith, not by sight.
2 CORINTHIANS 5:7

MY THOUGHTS:

_____
_____
_____
_____
_____
_____
_____
_____
_____
_____
_____
_____
_____
_____
_____
_____

I NEED TO WALK BY
FAITH I REGARD TO
GOD'S PROMISES TO
. . .

Sometimes I'm sad. I know not why
My heart is sore distressed;
It seems the burdens of this world
Have settled on my heart.
And yet I know . . . I know that God
Who doeth all things right
Will lead me thus to understand
To walk by FAITH . . . not SIGHT.
And though I may not see the way
He's planned for me to go . . .
That way seems dark to me just now
But oh, I'm sure He knows!
Today He guides my feeble step
Tomorrow's in His right . . .
He has asked me to never fear . . .
But walk by FAITH . . . not SIGHT.
Some day the mists will roll away,
The sun will shine again.
I'll see the beauty in the flowers.
I'll hear the bird's refrain.
And then I'll know my Father's hand
Has led the way to light
Because I placed my hand in His
And walked by FAITH . . . not SIGHT.

RUTH A. MORGAN[208]

Set the Example as a Worshipper

Give unto the Lord the glory due unto his name; worship the Lord in the beauty of holiness.

PSALM 29:2

The great missionary Dr. Albert Schweitzer tells us in his memoirs that the most important thing his parents did for him when he was a child was to take him to the worship services of their church.

"From the service in which I joined as a child," he wrote, "I have taken with me into life a feeling for what is solemn and a need for quiet and self-recollection without which I cannot realize the meaning of my life. I cannot therefore support the opinion of those who would not let the children take part in grown-up people's services until they to some extent understood them. The important thing is not that they shall understand but that they shall feel something of what is serious and solemn. The fact that the child sees his parents full of devotion and has to feel something of devotion himself, that is what gives the service its meaning to him."

G. Raymond Campbell also advises parents not to worry about their children's behavior in church. He says that a four-year- old whose parents have a genuine feeling of reverence and worship will be better behaved than some adults who squirm and twist, whisper, and feel no sense of reverence in the presence of God. Children are much more influenced by your behavior than your words. Model for them your trust in a loving God.[209]

MY THOUGHTS:

_____
_____
_____
_____
_____
_____
_____
_____
_____
_____
_____
_____
_____
_____
_____
_____
_____

IN WHAT WAYS DO I MODEL MY LOVE FOR GOD TO MY CHILDREN?

A Goal for God

Christ is the power of God and the wisdom of God to those people God has called.

1 CORINTHIANS 1:24 NCV

MY THOUGHTS:

_____
_____
_____
_____
_____
_____
_____
_____
_____
_____
_____
_____
_____
_____
_____
_____

WHAT IS MY "GOAL FOR GOD," AND HOW CAN I BEGIN TO ACCOMPLISH IT?

In 1969, after deciding that he was "tired of preaching to nice people," the Reverend Stan E George retired from the pulpit. He decided to reach out and share the Gospel with bikers and hippies, the kind of people who never went to church. Over the next eighteen years, he motorcycled over miles for the Lord.

During that time, he built a national "Christian Motorcyclist Club" that had members. At age eighty-two, he made a cross-country trip, riding his trusty motorcycle from San Clemente, California, to Halifax, Nova Scotia.

As George traveled by motorcycle, he used a number of techniques to draw interest to his message, including magic tricks, jokes, and tales of his odd adventures. He was committed to doing whatever it took so that his listeners would never be bored.[210]

Is there something you believe God is asking you to do today? Don't let your age, your social standing, your present career, your race, or your limitations stand in your way. Find a method for accomplishing your goals that you enjoy doing and that allows you to pursue your "goal for God." Then, rev up your engine, and go for it!

A Prayer for Family

I will see them, and I will listen to the prayers prayed in this place.

2 CHRONICLES 7:15 NCV

The following famous prayer, written by Robert Louis Stevenson, embodies what we all desire for our children and extended families. In it he expresses thanksgiving for even the simplest of life's pleasures and firmly leaves its trials and tribulations at the feet of God:

Lord, behold our family here assembled. We thank Thee for this place in which we dwell; for the love that unites us; for the peace accorded us this day; for the hope with which we expect the morrow; for the health, the work, the food, and the bright skies that make our lives delightful; for our friends in all parts of the earth, and our friendly helpers in the foreign isle . . .

Give us courage, gaiety, and the quiet mind. Spare to us our friends, soften to us our enemies. Bless us, if it may be, in all our innocent endeavors. If it may not, give us the strength to encounter that which is to come, that we be brave in peril, constant in tribulation, temperate in wrath, and in all changes of fortune and down to the gates of death, loyal and loving one to another. Amen.[211]

MY THOUGHTS:

WHAT IS MY PRAYER FOR MY FAMILY TODAY?

Something Good

december 8

Let no corrupt communication proceed out of your mouth, but that which is good to the use of edifying, that it may minister grace unto the hearers.

EPHESIANS 4:29

MY THOUGHTS:

_____
_____
_____
_____
_____
_____
_____
_____
_____
_____
_____
_____
_____
_____
_____

WHAT INDIVIDUALS CAN I SAY SOMETHING GOOD ABOUT TODAY?

Wouldn't this world be better,
If folks whom we meet would say,
"I know something good about you,"
And treat you just that way?

Wouldn't it be splendid,
If each handshake, good and true,
Carried with it this assurance:
"I know something good about you?"

Wouldn't life be happier,
If the good that's in us all,
Were the only thing about us
That people would recall?

Wouldn't our days be sweeter,
If we praised the good we see?
For there is a lot of goodness,
In the worst of you and me.

Wouldn't it be fine to practice,
This way of thinking too;
You know something good about me,
I know something good about you?[212]

Since we can never know or tell the full story about any other human being, why not just skip to the good highlights?

Care Enough to Discipline

december 9

Discipline your son, and he will give you peace; he will bring delight to your soul.

PROVERBS 29:17 NIV

A local minister was visiting a group home when one small boy decided to test his limits by stomping on the flower bed. The minister said, "Michael, if you stomp on those flowers one more time, I'm going to spank you."

Michael looked up at him and then looked back down at the flower bed. Next he raised his foot and smashed the flowers into the ground.

"Okay, come on inside," the minister said. He swatted Michael three times on his bottom, but when he finished, Michael wasn't crying.

"You done?" the little boy asked.

"Yes, but why did you deliberately stomp on those flowers?"

"Because I didn't think you'd spank me."

"Really? Why?"

Michael's answer was in his eyes. They were saying, "No one's loved me enough to discipline me and keep his or her word."

Sometimes parents are afraid to discipline their children because they fear their children won't love them afterward. But children want you to care. Provide your kids with the order and structure they need to succeed in life.[213]

MY THOUGHTS:

___

HOW DO I FEEL ABOUT DISCIPLINING MY CHILDREN?

Good Humor

december 10

Our mouth was filled with laughter, And our tongue with singing. Then they said among the nations, "The Lord has done great things for them."

PSALM 126:2 NKJV

MY THOUGHTS:

_____
_____
_____
_____
_____
_____
_____
_____
_____
_____
_____
_____
_____
_____
_____
_____

SOME WAYS THAT I CAN BE AN EXAMPLE OF GOOD HUMOR TO MY CHILDREN ARE . . .

On a hot June day, Winona and Will had just exchanged their wedding vows and were about to take their triumphant wedding march back down the aisle. Suddenly, Winona's six-foot-tall brother, a groomsman, fainted—and not very delicately at that. In the course of his falling, he toppled another groomsman and lurched against the best man, nearly forcing him down too. Two attendants each grabbed an arm of the fallen man and dragged him out of the church, in full view of the three hundred guests and a horrified young bride.

Winona had no doubt her wedding was ruined and she would be the laughingstock of the town. It was all she could do to keep back the tears as she walked down the aisle with Will. As they neared the back of the church, however, Will burst into laughter—a big, booming, infectious laugh—and Winona had to laugh too. Soon the entire church was guffawing with gusto.

Winona said many years later, "My first reaction to nearly any situation used to be 'Oh, no,' but Will's first reaction has always been to see humor in a situation. I've grown to adopt his point of view. I figure the very least I can glean from a nightmare is a good laugh and a memorable story to tell later."[214]

Keep Trying Till You Get it Right

We are perplexed because we don't know why things happen as they do, but we don't give up and quit.

2 CORINTHIANS 4:8 TLB

Many times Thomas Edison failed the first or second or tenth time in his attempts to discover something new, but he didn't mind. He just kept on trying! It is said that he made thousands upon thousands of attempts before he got his famous electric light to operate.

One day a workman to whom he had given a task came to him and said, "Mr. Edison, it cannot be done."

"How often have you tried?" asked Edison.

"About two thousand times," replied the man.

"Then go back and try it two thousand more times," said Edison. "You have only found out that there are two thousand ways in which it cannot be done."

This story reveals one of the great truths of life. Keep trying until you get it right! Sometimes our pessimism or ego or pride or just plain laziness gets in the way of the things we want to accomplish. Think of it in Edison's terminology—you've only found out how many ways it can't be done.

Set a good example for your children by tackling life's roadblocks with a positive attitude.[215]

MY THOUGHTS:

_____
_____
_____
_____
_____
_____
_____
_____
_____
_____
_____
_____
_____
_____
_____
_____
_____
_____

WHAT IS MY TYPICAL RESPONSE TO ROADBLOCKS? AN EXAMPLE WOULD BE . . .

Courtesy Pays

december 12

The most rewarding things you do in life are often the ones that look like they cannot be done. The fruit of the Spirit is . . . kindness.

GALATIANS 5:22 NIV

MY THOUGHTS:

_____
_____
_____
_____
_____
_____
_____
_____
_____
_____
_____
_____
_____
_____
_____
_____

**HOW CAN I
DEVELOP THE ART
OF BEING
COURTEOUS IN MY
CHILDREN?**

A number of years ago, the Advertising and Sales Executive Club sponsored a Courtesy Campaign in Kansas City. One thousand silver dollars were flown in from Denver. Then, over a period of days, "mystery shoppers" visited all types of stores, banks, and other places of business. They listened to telephone operators and observed bus and street-car drivers. Each day they filed a written report on the persons they found to be the most courteous.

Those chosen as the most courteous people in the city received a silver dollar, along with a "courtesy pays" button and a congratulatory card. The fifteen most courteous people were guests at a banquet, where they were awarded twenty-five dollars each. In all, more than one hundred people were honored.

What resulted was not only a temporary increase in the courtesy of the local residents but also an awareness throughout the city that simple kindness is a nice thing with which to live! The "residual effect" remained long after the campaign, to the point that Kansas City is still regarded as one of the friendliest cities in the nation.

It doesn't cost anything to be kind, but kindness can pay off in big ways quite apart from money.

Children Are a Delight

You are my beloved Son; you are my Delight.
MARK 1:11 TLB

On a recent canoe trip in North Carolina, one man was strengthened and lifted up by the childlike joy of a wonderful moment. The following is how he recorded it in his journal:

Somewhere near the beginning of my river run ... I heard behind me a joyous tumult of laughter from an oncoming raft ... I turned just in time to see a large raft filled to overflowing with madly paddling youngsters, all of them in full-throated laughter. It was a raft full of Down's syndrome kids out for a day on the river. Truly uninhibited joy that is rarely seen except in tiny children was erupting in their voices and on their faces. They were feeding upon the moment with such abandon that all else was swept away. Their whole focus, their whole life was right here. Right now. And the power of it was unconquerable, sweeping up everything within the sound of their voices into an all-encompassing joy.

"Thank you!" I shouted and raised my paddle high in salute to their joy and grace. And wisdom.

Children live in the events of the moment, spontaneously expressing their joy and delight. They don't let thoughts of tomorrow interfere with that joy. Remember to laugh today![216]

MY THOUGHTS:

_____
_____
_____
_____
_____
_____
_____
_____
_____
_____
_____
_____
_____
_____
_____
_____

HOW CAN I LEARN TO BE MORE CHILD-LIKE AND BETTER ABLE TO ENJOY THE PRESENT MOMENT?

Nip It in the Bud

Starting a quarrel is like breaching a dam; so drop the matter before a dispute breaks out.

PROVERBS 17:14 NIV

MY THOUGHTS:

_____

I CAN LOVINGLY COMMUNICATE MY NEEDS BY . . .

Susan was deeply disappointed by the lack of emotional closeness she felt in her marriage, and she began to lash out at her husband. He, of course, reacted with his own defensive anger. Over time their anger grew, threats were exchanged, and eventually divorce became part of their confrontations. Finally, Susan's husband moved out, and she filed for divorce.

The divorce proceedings were bitter, and they fought all the way through them. When they met to sign the final papers, they stopped to look at each other, and Susan saw in his eyes the very feeling she was experiencing—a feeling of longing and yet of resignation. She thought, *I don't want to divorce him, and I don't think he wants to divorce me.*

She voiced her thoughts to her husband, and for a moment it appeared he might also soften and admit he, too, still cared. But then he said in a dull monotone, "We've come this far, I guess we should finish it." Susan left the courtroom realizing she had never really wanted a divorce. She just had wanted her husband to listen.

Don't allow anger to lead you anywhere . . . but especially down a road you truly don't want to travel.

Go Ahead; Lighten Up

When a man is gloomy, everything seems to go wrong; when he is cheerful, everything seems right!

PROVERBS 15:15 TLB

The great evangelist D. L. Moody was a man of wholesome humor and an occasional practical joke. He sometimes told stories with such enthusiasm that he would laugh until he cried. He enjoyed gathering his associates about him at the close of the day to see who could tell the best stories. When someone asked him how he could laugh so fully after preaching so seriously, he answered, "If I didn't laugh, I would have a nervous breakdown at the pace at which I live."

Leslie B. Flynn wrote, "Though people know about the prodigious labors of David Livingstone in opening up Africa for missionary endeavor, few know that in the midst of their lonely life, he and his wife often acted like jolly school kids on an excursion. Mirth saturated their lives so much that Livingstone more than once said to his wife, 'Really, my dear, we ought not to indulge in so many jokes. We are getting too old. It is not becoming. We must be more staid.'"

Appropriate humor is like divine medicine. It cheers the mind, enlightens the message, and relieves the listener.

> Give us, Lord,
>
> A bit of sun,
>
> A bit of work,
>
> And a bit of fun.[217]

MY THOUGHTS:

WHAT STEPS CAN I TAKE TO LIGHTEN THINGS UP A BIT IN OUR HOME?

The Kindness Quotient

When you're kind to others, you help yourself; when you're cruel to others, you hurt yourself!

PROVERBS 11:17 MSG

MY THOUGHTS:

_____
_____
_____
_____
_____
_____
_____
_____
_____
_____
_____
_____
_____
_____
_____
_____
_____
_____

WHAT IS MY FAVORITE SCENT, AND WHAT PLEASANT THOUGHTS OR MEMORIES DOES IT ELICIT?

Can the aroma of coffee and freshly baked cookies make you behave more kindly? Research conducted at a shopping mall in New York indicates that it just may!

Robert Baron, a professor at Rensselaer Polytechnic Institute in Troy, New York, decided to find out if pleasant scents could increase the "kindness quotient" in a typical mall crowd. Choosing a spot near Cinnabon and Mrs. Fields Cookies, he put his students to work gathering data.

In one test, mall patrons were asked to make change for a dollar. In another, the researchers noted how many shoppers retrieved a ball-point pen that had been dropped. In both tests, people were twice as likely to perform an act of kindness in a pleasant-smelling area as they were in another part of the mall that had no pleasant aromas. Baron concluded: nice smells make for nicer people.

Baron is so confident of his research findings that he's built a machine that should be helpful to anyone who is tired of breathing stale air, listening to annoying noises, or living in tight quarters. It is a combination air filter, white-noise generator, and fragrance producer. He suggests that until the machine is on the market, people would be wise to brew more coffee and bake more cookies.[218]

Perhaps better still, increase the kindness by taking that coffee and batch of cookies to someone in need!

A Note From Your Child

Being punished isn't enjoyable while it is happening—it hurts! But afterwards we can see the result, a quiet growth in grace and character.

HEBREWS 12:11 TLB

· Don't spoil me. Teach me to share.

· Don't be afraid to be firm with me. I prefer it . . . it makes me feel more secure.

· Don't correct me in front of people if you can help it. I'll take much more notice if you talk to me in private.

· Don't forget the difference between mistakes and sins.

· Don't protect me from consequences. I need to learn the hard way.

· Don't take too much notice of my small ailments. Sometimes they get me the attention I want.

· Don't nag. Give me instruction and guidance.

· Don't make rash promises. Remember that I feel badly let down when promises are broken.

· Don't forget that I cannot explain myself as well as I would like. This is why I'm not always accurate.

· Don't be inconsistent. That completely confuses me and makes me lose my faith in you.[219]

MY THOUGHTS:

WHAT MEMOS WOULD MY CHILDREN WRITE TO ME?

Honesty is the Best Policy

Provide things honest in the sight of all men.
ROMANS 12:17

MY THOUGHTS:

_____
_____
_____
_____
_____
_____
_____
_____
_____
_____
_____
_____
_____
_____
_____
_____
_____
_____

WHAT STEPS CAN I TAKE TO TEACH MY CHILDREN TO RECOGNIZE AND APPRECIATE HONESTY IN OTHERS?

Bruce Woody, a Dallas County judge, has seen justice served in some unusual ways during his tenure on the bench. One hotly contested case involved a plaintiff who was allegedly injured in an automobile accident. On the day of the trial, the plaintiff entered courtroom using a crutch, limping and groaning in pain. After jury selection, the judge noted that the plaintiff's attorney was absent. The plaintiff graciously offered to go get his lawyer. Then, he sprang from his chair—without his crutch—and strode out of the courtroom past the jury. Moments later, the man's attorney walked into the courtroom alone and stated, "Your Honor, we have decided to drop the lawsuit."

Judge Woody responded, "I thought you might."[221]

Honesty is not only the display of fair and honest behavior but also a motivation of the heart. A man once went to his attorney and said, "I am going into a business deal with a man I do not trust. I want you to frame an airtight contract that he can't break, which will protect me from any sort of mischief he may have on his mind."

His attorney wisely replied, "There is no group of words in the English language that will take the place of plain honesty between men, which will fully protect either of you if one plans to deceive the other."[221]

Remember, if you stay honest in your motivations, you will act accordingly. Therefore, choose to be in association with those who act honestly, for then you will know the motivation of their hearts.

Words Laced with Love

Grandchildren are the crown of the aged, and the glory of children is their parents.

PROVERBS 17:6 NRSV

Janet spent the summer with her grandparents when she was ten. One day their neighbor, Audrey, came over to visit and introduce herself to Janet. Audrey invited her to visit her anytime. She did, and they became fast friends. Audrey's children were grown, but her mothering nature wasn't ready to retire. Or perhaps God let her know how much Janet needed her nurturing, friendship, and wisdom.

As the two of them walked in the flower garden, Audrey explained each type of flower, somehow connecting it with wisdom about people. Then they would go into her house and have punch and cookies. They spent most of the summer together talking, walking, shopping, and becoming dear friends.

Through the time Janet spent with Audrey, she learned how to love herself and others and how to make life full and happy. She learned the value of friendship and loyalty and that people need each other. "There's usually a good side to every bad situation—you just have to look for it," Audrey would tell her.

Janet is now a grandmother herself. To this day, she can still see Audrey's smiling face and hear her wise words laced with love.[222]

MY THOUGHTS:

_____
_____
_____
_____
_____
_____
_____
_____
_____
_____
_____
_____
_____
_____
_____

WHOM COULD I MENTOR AND TO WHOM WOULD I ENJOY LISTENING?

We Are Here for Each Other

december 20

As we have opportunity, let us do good to all people, especially to those who belong to the family of believers.

GALATIANS 6:10 NIV

MY THOUGHTS:

_____
_____
_____
_____
_____
_____
_____
_____
_____
_____
_____
_____
_____
_____
_____
_____
_____

THOSE WHO HAVE
CONTRIBUTED TO
MY LIFE AND WHOM
I'D LIKE TO THANK
INCLUDE . . .

Albert Einstein once reflected on the purpose of man's existence: "Strange is our situation here upon earth. Each of us comes for a short visit, not knowing why, yet sometimes seeming to a divine purpose. From the standpoint of daily life, however, there is one thing we do know: That we are here for the sake of others . . . for the countless unknown souls with whose fate we are connected by a bond of sympathy. Many times a day, I realize how much my own outer and inner life is built upon the labors of people, both living and dead, and how earnestly I must exert myself in order to give in return as much as I have received."

When we truly take stock of our lives, we must admit we have done nothing solely on our own. Our thinking has been fashioned by our many teachers and mentors, including family members. Our ability to function physically is the result, in part, of our genetic code and the productivity of others in providing food, water, and shelter. Our spiritual lives are a gift of God himself. We are what we have received.

Our reaction to these facts drives each of us to give to others the good things we have been fortunate to receive. This is what being a citizen of God's kingdom is all about!

Keep Your Childlike Heart

december 21

"Unless you change and become like children, you will never enter the kingdom of heaven."

MATTHEW 18:3 NRSV

What are children? They are bundles of energy who stop running around and asking questions only when they are totally exhausted and drop off to sleep. They climb trees, dig around in streams, and generally run adults ragged. Some are quieter than others, but they all ask questions. It does not matter to children if this drives adults to distraction or puts big smiles on their faces. They "question" and "do" day in and day out.

Children behave this way because they want to know. They are like enormous dry sponges, soaking up everything around them. It is a priceless moment when they see something special. Their faces light up like Christmas morning. Their eyes bulge open and mouths gape almost in disbelief, and then they smile. We adults have often forgotten how to smile.

Children don't hide a thing. If they are excited or scared, it is obvious. They accept and return love and care with reckless abandon. We may put away childish thinking, but there is a reward in experiencing the joy of a child.[223]

MY THOUGHTS:

WHAT CHARACTERISTICS WOULD I LIKE TO ADOPT FROM MY CHILDREN?

363

Working In and Through You

We are what he has made us, created in Christ Jesus for good works, which God prepared beforehand to be our way of life.

EPHESIANS 2:10 NRSV

MY THOUGHTS:

_____
_____
_____
_____
_____
_____
_____
_____
_____
_____
_____
_____
_____
_____
_____
_____

HOW CAN I ENCOURAGE MY CHILDREN TO ALLOW GOD TO WORK THROUGH THEM?

Millions of people around the world consider Mother Teresa to have been one of the most saintly Christians of this century. Few, however, know the lesson of her life.

She was born in 1910 as Agnes Gonxha Bojaxhiu in Skopje, Macedonia, of Albanian ancestry. At the age of eighteen, she traveled to Ireland to join the Institute of the Blessed Virgin Mary. Barely six weeks later, a novice in the ways of the church and of life, she was sent to India to be a teacher. She studied nursing there and soon moved into the slums of Calcutta, home to some of the most destitute people in the world. She felt especially drawn to the blind, the aged, lepers, the disabled, and the dying. She organized schools and opened centers to treat those whom no one else would touch, much less nurse. Under her guidance, a leper colony called "Town of Peace" (Shanti Naga) was built. In 1950, she founded the Order of the Missionaries of Charity, a congregation of women dedicated to helping the poor.

Trained as a nurse, Mother Teresa lived her life as a nurse, trusting that as she did work, the Great Physician might do His work in her and through her.[224]

In whatever career you are pursuing today, you can trust the Lord to do His work in and through *you*.

Channel That Energy

Whatever turns up, grab it and do it. And heartily!
ECCLESIASTES 9:10 MSG

The best-selling products for Procter and Gamble in 1879 were candles. However, when Thomas Edison invented the light bulb, it looked as if candles might become obsolete and the company would be in trouble. Their fears became reality when the market for candles plummeted. The economic forecast for the company seemed bleak.

However, about this time, a forgetful employee at a small factory in Cincinnati forgot to turn off his machine when he went to lunch. The result was a frothing mass of lather filled with air bubbles. He almost threw the mess away, but instead made it into soap. The soap floated, and thus Ivory soap was born. It became the mainstay of Procter and Gamble. Destiny had played a dramatic part in pulling the struggling company out of bankruptcy.

Why was floating soap so special? During that time, some people bathed in the river. Floating soap would never sink and as a result would not be lost. Ivory soap ultimately became a bestseller across the country.

Teach your children to use their energy and creativity to turn their mistakes into successes![225]

MY THOUGHTS:

HOW CAN I TEACH MY CHILDREN TO TURN THEIR MISTAKES INTO SUCCESSES?

A Costly Experiment

december 24

[Not in your own strength] for it is God Who is all the while effectually at work in you [energizing and creating in you the power and desire], both to will and to work for His good pleasure.

PHILIPPIANS 2:13 AMP

MY THOUGHTS:

_____
_____
_____
_____
_____
_____
_____
_____
_____
_____
_____
_____
_____
_____
_____
_____

I FEEL GOD WANTS ME TO BE PART OF THE ANSWER TO MY OWN PRAYER REGARDING . . .

A pastor once challenged some of the young people in his congregation to spend fifteen minutes every day praying for foreign missions. But he warned them, "Beware how you pray, for I warn you, this is a very costly experiment."

"Costly?" one of the youth asked in surprise.

"Yes, costly," he replied. "When Carey an to pray for the conversion of the world, it cost him himself.

"Brainerd prayed for the dark-skinned savages, and after two years of blessed work, it cost him his life.

"Two students in Mr. Moody's summer school began to pray the Lord of the harvest to send forth more servants into His harvest; and, lo, it is going to cost America five thousand young men and women who have, in answer to this prayer, pledged themselves to missions.

"Be sure it is a dangerous thing to pray in earnest for this work; you will find that you cannot pray and withhold your labour, or pray and withhold your money; indeed, you will find that your very life will no longer be your own when your prayers begin to be answered."[226]

Prayer increases our compassion and can reveal to us God's call on our lives. When we pray for certain things, God's answer may be to tell us what we can do to bring the solution to pass.

The Joyful Christmas Memory

The angel said unto them, "Fear not: for, behold, I bring you good tidings of great joy."

LUKE 2:10

Andrew Wyermann's favorite Christmas memory took place when he was seven years old. He recalls:

Early Christmas Eve, my mother took my brother and me out for a treat. It was her way to get us out of our fifth-floor apartment in the Bronx while my father prepared for the evening festivity. As we climbed the stairs back to the apartment, the shrill sound of a whistle filled the hallway. Our pace quickened and a second burst of the whistle could be heard. We dashed into the apartment. There was my father, playing engineer with the biggest Lionel train ever made. It was so magnificent, so unexpected, so wonderful!

Some fifty years later, I still have the train set and cherish it . . . The train is a warm reminder of the greater gift my parents gave me. Unconditional love was their gift. I never doubted their care for me, and from such grace sprang my own capacity to truth. It was years later that I fully understood the gift my parents gave me had its source in God's gift of the Child to us all. The sound of the whistle and the song of the angels have become one and the same.

Give your children the gift of unconditional love and unexpected laughter. It's an unbeatable combination!

MY THOUGHTS:

_____
_____
_____
_____
_____
_____
_____
_____
_____
_____
_____
_____
_____
_____
_____
_____
_____

WHAT SPECIAL CHRISTMAS MEMORIES DO I WANT TO CREATE FOR MY CHILDREN?

Carrying a Grudge Too Far

december 26

Only by pride cometh contention: but with the well advised is wisdom.
PROVERBS 13:10

MY THOUGHTS:

_____
_____
_____
_____
_____
_____
_____
_____
_____
_____
_____
_____
_____
_____
_____
_____
_____
_____
_____

*HOW DO I HANDLE
INJUSTICES DONE
TO ME? AN EXAMPLE
WOULD BE . . .*

The municipal registrar of births, marriages, and deaths in Hatfield, England, once recorded this name on a death certificate: "Mr. Serious Misconduct of Mill Lane, Welwyn, aged 74." There was no dispute of her entry.

It seems that Mr. Misconduct had actually been christened as Malcolm Mactaggart. In 1939, he had a serious argument with his employer, the London Midland and Scottish Railway Company. The incident arose over his taking two weeks' vacation when the railway company said that he was entitled to only one week. He was fired for "serious misconduct."

Mactaggart never forgave the railway company for firing him. He decided to adopt the slur against his character as his official name. That way, any time someone questioned his name—which was often—he had an opportunity to recall the injustice he felt back been done to him by his former employer. He used the name on all official documents, including his social security payment book, and when he died, his widow registered his death in that name.[227]

In the end, the long-standing grudge you carry may very well become a lasting stain on your own name. Choose to forgive and to stay flexible in your judgment of others.

A Child's Reasoning

Make the most of every opportunity.
COLOSSIANS 4:5 NIV

The following amusing story written by Billy Graham is called "Let Go."

"A little child was playing one day with a very valuable vase. He put his hand into it and could not withdraw it. His father, too, tried his best, but all in vain. They were thinking of breaking the vase when his father said, 'Now, my son, make one more try. Open your hand and hold your fingers out straight as you see me doing, and then pull.'

"To his astonishment the little fellow said, 'Oh no, Father. I couldn't put my fingers out like that, because if I did I would drop my penny.'"

This story has significant meaning for all of us who work with children. Children look at their surroundings with a different perspective from that of adults. The prospect of losing the penny is more important to them than the loss of the expensive vase. They know the penny's value to them in their everyday lives.

Children will continue to surprise all of us by their reasoning processes. However, if we're patient and remember to view the world through their eyes, we'll better understand them.[228]

MY THOUGHTS:

TODAY I'LL VIEW THE WORLD THROUGH MY CHILD'S EYES BY . . .

Loving Gestures

We have kept ourselves pure and have been understanding, patient, and kind. The Holy Spirit has been with us, and our love has been real.

2 CORINTHIANS 6:6 CEV

MY THOUGHTS:

_____

_____

_____

_____

_____

_____

_____

_____

_____

_____

_____

_____

_____

_____

_____

_____

TO WHOM COULD I SHOW MY LOVE TODAY? SOME CREATIVE WAYS TO DO THAT WOULD BE . . .

Never dismiss an act of loving-kindness as being too small or inconsequential. God will magnify even our smallest deeds to reveal His love to others. Consider the following suggestions:

- A warm-from-the-oven casserole taken to the home of a sick friend.
- A bouquet of flowers from your garden given to a neighbor.
- A thank-you note sent to the performers who did such an excellent job during a concert or play you attended.
- A loaf of freshly baked cinnamon bread brought to the office for coffee break.
- A box of cookies taken to the police station on Christmas Day to encourage those who are "on duty" during the holiday.
- A call to ask with genuine care and concern, "How are you doing?"

We may not think of these as acts of Christian witnessing, yet they are. *Every* act of loving-kindness reflects God's loving- kindness for His people. We give because Jesus Christ has so freely given His love to us. He is the example we follow.

Temper Tantrums

It is better to be slow-tempered than famous; it is better to have self-control than to control an army.

PROVERBS 16:32 TLB

There is a legend surrounding Jonathan Edwards, one of America's greatest preachers as well as the third president of Princeton University, and his daughter. His daughter had an uncontrollable temper, although this fault was not known to many people outside of the family. Legend says that a young man fell in love with the preacher's daughter and asked to marry her.

"You can't have her," was Jonathan Edwards' abrupt answer.

"But I love her," replied the young man.

"You can't have her," repeated Edwards.

"But she loves me," the young man replied.

Again Edwards said, "You can't have her."

"Why?" asked the young man.

"Because she is not worthy of you."

"But," he asked, "she is a Christian, isn't she?"

"Yes, she is a Christian. But the grace of God can live with some people with whom no one else could ever live!"

Teach your children that temper tantrums are not acceptable behavior. Anger not only makes everyone else miserable, but it can affect the rest of their lives.[229]

MY THOUGHTS:

WHAT STEPS CAN I TAKE TO REDIRECT MY CHILD'S NEGATIVE EMOTIONAL REACTIONS?

Take a Lesson from the Animals

The heart of the righteous weighs its answers, but the mouth of the wicked gushes evil.

PROVERBS 15:28 NIV

MY THOUGHTS:

_____
_____
_____
_____
_____
_____
_____
_____
_____
_____
_____
_____
_____
_____
_____
_____
_____

TODAY I'LL LET MY WIFE SING BY . . .

The fact is that the members of the animal kingdom are content to be themselves, and they are true in their expression to what they were created to be. Consider the following:

- Birds sing and never have to apologize for their songs.
- Dogs bark and kittens meow . . . and never have to say, "I'm sorry for what I just said."
- Lions roar and hyenas howl . . . but they never have to retract their statements as being untrue.

Many times we human beings find ourselves embarrassed at our own words—feeling apologetic, cringing in an awkward moment, or recognizing we have spoken the wrong words at the wrong time. This happens because we have begun evaluating the performances of others, and we develop a critical attitude.

The blue jay doesn't criticize the robin. The kitten doesn't make snide remarks about the puppy. The lion doesn't ridicule the hyena. In like manner, we should not put down others whom we can never fully understand, never fully appreciate, or never fully emulate.

Stick to singing you own song today, and appreciate the uniqueness of those around you. In doing so, you will easily avoid putting your foot in your mouth!

Just Like You

May the Lord bless you . . . all the days of your life . . . and may you live to see your children's children.

PSALMS 128:5-6 NIV

There are little eyes upon you, and they
are watching night and day;
There are little ears that quickly take in
every word you say;
There are little hands all eager to do
everything you do.
And a little boy who's dreaming of the
day he'll be like you.
You're the little fellow's idol, you're the
wisest of the wise,
In his little mind about you, no
suspicions ever rise;
He believes in you devoutly, holds that all
you say and do,
He will say and do in your way when he's
grown up to be like you.
There's a wide-eyed little fellow who
believes you're always right,
And his ears are always open and he
watches day and night;
You are setting an example every day in
all you do,
For the little boy who's waiting to grow
up to be like you.

UNKNOWN

Children believe in their parents and want to be just like them. Parents are the most important people in their lives. They will remember the example you set for them as long as they live. Savor the time spent with your children and grandchildren. That is one of the greatest gifts you can give them.[230]

MY THOUGHTS:

_____
_____
_____
_____
_____
_____
_____
_____
_____
_____
_____
_____
_____
_____
_____
_____

WHAT STEPS CAN I TAKE TO ENSURE THAT MY CHILDREN HAVE THE TIME WITH ME THAT THEY NEED?

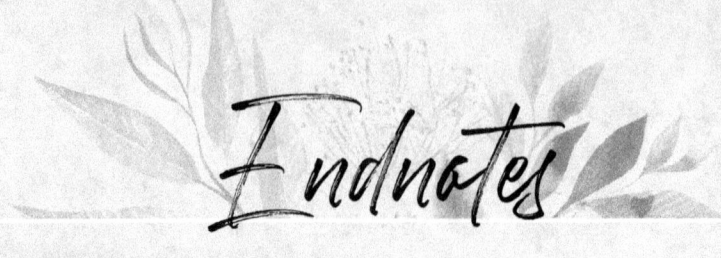

Endnotes

1. *The Guideposts Handbook of Prayer,* Phyllis Hobe, ed. (Carmel, NY: Guideposts, 1982) pp. 49-50.

2. *Encyclopedia of 7700 Illustrations,* Paul Lee Tan, ed. (Rockville, MD: Assurance Publishers, 1979), #4532.

3. *Inspirational Study Bible,* Max Lucado, ed. (Dallas, TX: Word, 1995) p. 1299.

4. Stephen R. Covey, The Seven Habits of Highly Successful People (NY: Simon & Schuster, 1994) pp. 68-69.

5. James S. Hewett, *Illustrations Unlimited* (Wheaton, IL: Tyndale, 1988) pp. 247-248.

6. *Encyclopedia of 7700 Illustrations,* Paul Lee Tan, ed. (Rockville, MD: Assurance Publishers, 1979) p. 2043.

7. Wess Roberts, *Straight A's Never Made Anybody Rich* (NY: HarperCollins Publishers, pp. 111-112.

8. Richard Exley, *Life's Bottom Line* (Tulsa, OK: Honor Books, 1990) pp. 246-247.

9. *Encyclopedia of 7700 Illustrations,* Paul Lee Tan, ed. (Rockville, MD: Assurance Publishers, 1979) p. 678.

11. Jack Canfield and Mark Victor Hansen, A *3rd Serving of Chicken Soup for the Soul* (Deerfield Beach, FL: Health Communications, 1996) pp. 322-325.

12. *Encyclopedia of 7700 Illustrations,* Paul Lee Tan, ed. (Rockville, MD: Assurance Publishers, 1979) pp. 132.

13. Hyrum W Smith, The 10 Natural Laws of Successful Time and Life Management (NY: Warner Books, 1994) pp. 197-198.

14. James S. Hewett, *Illustrations Unlimited* (Wheaton, IL: Tyndale, 1988) p. 486.

15. *Encyclopedia of 7700 Illustrations,* Paul Lee Tan, ed. (Rockville, MD: Assurance Publishers, 1979) pp. 2058-2059.

16. Norman Vincent Peale, *Sin, Sex, and Self-Control* (NY: Doubleday and Co., 1965) p. 200.

17. James S. Hewett, *Illustrations Unlimited* (Wheaton, IL: Tyndale, 1988) p. 460.

18. *Encyclopedia of 7700 Illustrations,* Paul Lee Tan, ed.

(Rockville, MD: Assurance Publishers, 1979) p. 1295.

19. Charles Colson with Ellen Santilli Vaughn, *Against the Night* (Ann Arbor, MI: Servant Publications, 1989) pp. 144-145.

20. Joan Aho Ryan, *Lessons from Mom* (Deerfield Beach, FL: Health Communications, 1996) p. 62.

21. *Encyclopedia of 7700 Illustrations*, Paul Lee Tan, ed. (Rockville, MD: Assurance Publishers, 1979) p. 2069.

22. Ron Hembree, *Fruits of the Spirit* (Grand Rapids, MI: Baker Book House, 1969) p. 55.

23. James S. Hewett, *Illustrations Unlimited* (Wheaton, IL: Tyndale, 1988) p. 182.

24. Ron Hembree, *Fruits of the Spirit* (Grand Rapids, MI: Baker Book House, 1969) p. 55.

25. Ed Young, *From Bad Beginnings to Happy Endings* (Nashville, TN: Thomas Nelson Publishers, 1994) p. 29.

26. Jane Bluestein, *Mentors, Masters and Mrs. MacGregor* (Deerfield Beach, FL: Health Communications, 1995) pp. 14-15.

27. Michael Hodgin, *1001 Humorous Illustrations of Public Speaking* (Grand Rapids, MI: Zondervan Publishing House, 1994) number 301; and from Mikey's Funnies" @ YOUTH SPECIALITIES, title "A Christians Kids," online @ aol; 9/23/98.

28. Walter B. Knight, *Knight's Master Book of 4,000 Illustrations* (Grand Rapids, MI: Wm. B. Eerdmans Publishing Co., 1956, 1994) p. 179.

29. Max Anders, *The Holy Spirit—Knowing Our Comforter* (Nashville, TN: Thomas Nelson Publishers, 1995) pp. 159-160.

30. Top 100 Inspirational Anecdotes and Wisdom (part 4), found online @ www.bizmove.com/inspiration, 1999, pp. 4-5.

31. Bettie Youngs, *Values from the Heartland* (Deerfield Beach, FL: Health Communications, 1995) pp. 109-112.

32. Jane Bluestein, *Mentors, Masters and Mrs. MacGregor* (Deerfield Beach, FL: Health Communications, 1995) pp. 32-33.

33. *Encyclopedia of 7700 Illustrations*, Paul Lee Tan, ed. (Rockville, MD: Assurance Publishers, 1979) p. 1500.

34. *Encyclopedia of 7700 Illustrations*, Paul Lee Tan, ed. (Rockville, MD: Assurance Publishers, 1979) p. 1257.

35. *Norman Vincent Peale's Treasury of Courage and Confidence*, Norman Vincent Peale, ed. (NY: Doubleday and

Co., 1970) pp. 289-290.

36. *Reader's Digest* (April 1996) p. 185.

37. *Encyclopedia of 7700 Illustrations,* Paul Lee Tan, ed. (Rockville, MD: Assurance Publishers, 1979) p. 131.

38. *Guideposts* (July 1995) pp. 20-23.

39. Joan Aho Ryan, *Lessons from Mom* (Deerfield Beach, FL: Health Communications, 1996) pp. 19-21.

40. *Encyclopedia of 7700 Illustrations,* Paul Lee Tan, ed. (Rockville, MD: Assurance Publishers, 1979) p. 2068.

41. *Norman Vincent Peale's Treasury of Courage and Confidence,* Norman Vincent Peale, ed. (Garden City, NY: Doubleday and Co., 1970) pp. 269-271.

42. *Reader's Digest* (July 1996) p. 48.

43. Walter B. Knight, *Knight's Treasury of 4,000 Illustrations* (Grand Rapids, MI: Wm. B. Eerdmans Publishing Co., 1956, 1994) p. 167.

44. San Luis Obispo Telegram-Tribune (September 16, 1996) B3.

45. James S. Hewett, *Illustrations Unlimited* (Wheaton, IL: Tyndale, 1988) p. 226.

46. *Encyclopedia of 1700 Illustrations,* Paul Lee Tan, ed. (Rockville, MD: Assurance Publishers, 1979) p. 759.

47. Dr. Karl Slaikeu and Steve Lawhead, *The Phoenix Factor* (Boston, MA: Houghton Mifflin Co., 1985) pp. 106-107.

48. *Encyclopedia of 7700 Illustrations,* Paul Lee Tan, ed. (Rockville, MD: Assurance Publishers, 1979) p. 2077.

49. Norman Vincent Peale, *Sin, Sex, and Self-Control* (NY: Doubleday and Co., 1965) pp. 160-161.

50. *Reader's Digest* (December 1992) pp. 9-12.

51. *Encyclopedia of 7700 Illustrations,* Paul Lee Tan, ed. (Rockville, MD: Assurance Publishers, 1979) pp. 2041-2042.

52. Ron Hembree, *Fruits of the Spirit* (Grand Rapids, NJ: Baker Book House, 1969) pp. 72-73.

53. Jack Canfield and Mark Victor Hansen, A *3rd Serving of Chicken Soup for the Soul* (Deerfield Beach, FL: Health Communications, 1996) pp. 220-222.

54. *Encyclopedia of 7700 Illustrations,* Paul Lee Tan, ed. (Rockville, MD: Assurance Publishers, 1979) p. 2048.

55. James S. Hewett, *Illustrations Unlimited* (Wheaton, IL: Tyndale, 1988) p. 206.

56. *Encyclopedia of 7700 Illustrations,* Paul Lee Tan, ed. (Rockville, MD: Assurance Publishers, 1979) p. 1230.

57. Catherine Marshall, A *Man Called Peter* (NY: Avon, 1971)

pp. 168-169.

58. Jack Canfield and Mark Victor Hansen, A *3rd Serving of Chicken Soup for the Soul* (Deerfield Beach, FL: Health Communications, 1996) pp. 211-214.

59. *Encyclopedia of 7700 Illustrations,* Paul Lee Tan, ed. (Rockville, MD: Assurance Publishers, 1979) pp. 361,421-422.

60. Hazel Felleman, *The Best Loved Poems of the American People* (NY: Doubleday, 1936) pp. 124-125. Stanzas 1,3, and 6.

61. Richard Exley, *Life's Bottom Line* (Tulsa, OK: Honor Books, 1990) p. 28.

62. Eugenia Price, *Discoveries* (Grand Rapids, MI: Zondervan Publishing House, 1953, 1970) pp. 32-33.

63. Charles R. Swindoll, *Growing Strong in the Seasons of Life* (Portland, OR: Multnomah Press, 1983) p. 133.

64. Jack Canfield and Mark Victor Hansen, A *2nd Helping of Chicken Soup for the Soul* (Deerfield Beach, FL: Health Communications, 1995) pp. 46-48.

65. *Illustrations for Preaching and Teaching,* Craig Brian Larson, ed. (Grand Rapids, MI: Baker Books, 1993) p. 127.

66. Denis Waitley, *The New Dynamics of Winning* (NY: William Morrow & Co., 1993) pp. 171-172.

67. James S. Hewett, *Illustrations Unlimited* (Wheaton, IL: Tyndale, 1988) pp. 361-362.

68. *Encyclopedia of 7700 Illustrations,* Paul Lee Tan, ed. (Rockville, MD: Assurance Publishers, 1979) p. 1506.

69. *Reader's Digest* (May 1995) p. 46.

70. *Inspirational Study Bible,* Max Lucado, ed. (Dallas, TX: Word, 1995) pp. 188-189.

71. Bill Hybels, *Too Busy Not to Pray* (Downers Grove, IL: Inter-Varsity Press, 1988) pp. 9-10.

72. *American Health* (June 1995) pp. 131,133.

73. *Encyclopedia of 7700 Illustrations,* Paul Lee Tan, ed. (Rockville, MD: Assurance Publishers, 1979) #4660.

74. Charles Colson, Born *Again* (NY: Bantam Books, 1977) pp. 390-392.

75. *Encyclopedia of 7700 Illustrations,* Paul Lee Tan, ed. (Rockville, MD: Assurance Publishers, 1979) #4584.

76. Oswald Chambers, *My Utmost for His Highest* (Grand Rapids, MI: Discovery House Publishers, 1992).

77. Catherine Marshal, *Beyond Ourselves* (Carmel, NY: Guide-

posts, 1961) p. 72.

78. Jill Haak Adels, *Wisdom of the Saints* (NY: Oxford University Press, 1987) p. 40.

79. *Encyclopedia of 7700 Illustrations,* Paul Lee Tan, ed. (Rockville, MD: Assurance Publications, 1979) #4639.

80. Bill Hybels, *Too Busy Not to Pray* (Downers Grove, IL: InterVarsity Press, 1988) p. 13.

81. Louis Evely, *Teach Us How To Pray,* Edmond Bonin, trans. (NY: Newman Press, 1967) p. 3.

82. Charles R. Swindoll, *Three Steps Forward, Two Steps Back* (Nashville, TN: Thomas Nelson, 1980) p. 80.

83. *Mother Teresa, Life in the Spirit,* Kathryn Spink, ed. (San Francisco: Harper & Row, 1983) p. 19.

84. Elizabeth Elliot, *Trusting God in a Twisted World* (Old Tappan, NJ: Fleming H Revell Co., 1989) pp. 30-31.

85. John Killinger, Bread for the Wilderness, Wine for the journey (Waco, TX: Word Books, 1976) pp. 128-129.

86. Jill Haak Adels, *Wisdom of the Saints* (NY: Oxford University Press, 1987) p. 39.

87. *Encyclopedia of 7700 Illustrations,* Paul Lee Tan, ed. (Rockville, MD: Assurance Publishers, 1979) #4587.

88. Jerry Bridges, *The Pursuit of Holiness* (Colorado Springs, CO: NavPress, 1978, 1996) p. 128.

89. *Encyclopedia of 7700 Illustrations,* Paul Lee Tan, ed. (Rockville, MD: Assurance Publishers, 1979) #4655.

90. Jeanie Miley, *The Spiritual Art of Creative Silence* (Wheaton, IL: Harold Shaw Publishers, 1989, 1996) pp. 151-152.

91. *Encyclopedia of 7700 Illustrations,* Paul Lee Tan, ed. (Rockville, MD: Assurance Publishers, 1979) #4539 and #4540.

92. Pat Robertson, *The Secret Kingdom* (Dallas, TX: Word Publishing, 1992) pp. 237-239.

93. *Encyclopedia of 7700 Illustrations,* Paul Lee Tan, ed. (Rockville, MD: Assurance Publishers, 1979) #4590 and #4592.

94. Jack Hayford, *The Power and Blessing* (Wheaton, IL: Victor Books (Scripture Press Publications, Inc.), 1994) p.232.

95. Charles R. Swindoll, *Three Steps Forward, Two Steps Back* (Nashville, TN: Thomas Nelson, 1980) p. 75.

96. *Encyclopedia of 7700 Illustrations,* Paul Lee Tan, ed. (Rockville, MD: Assurance Publishers, 1979) #4518, #4519.

97. Larry Dossey, M.D., *Healing Words* [NY: Harper Collins Publishers (Harper San Francisco), 1993] pp. 179-180.

98. James S. Hewett, *Illustrations Unlimited* (Wheaton, IL: Tyndale House, 1988) p. 416.

99. Craig Brian Larson, *Contemporary Illustrations for Preachers, Teachers, and Writers* (Grand Rapids, MI: Baker Books, 1996), number 156. [Information originally appeared in "Epic in the Making," Chicago Tribune (December 1991) Sec 5, Page 1.]

100. Glenn Van Ekeren, *Words for All Occasions* (Paramus, NJ: Prentice Hall, 1988) pp. 35-36, 198-199.

101. *Encyclopedia of Sermon Illustrations,* David E Burgess, ed. (St. Louis, MO: Concordia Publishing House, 1984) #735.

102. Anna B. Mow, *Your Child* (Grand Rapids, MI: Zondervan Publishing House, 1971) p. 34.

103. *Decision* (April 1996) p. 33.

104. Corrie ten Boom, *Not I, But Christ* (NY: Walker and Co., 1986) pp. 22-26.

105. Anna B. Mow, *Your Child* (Grand Rapids, MI: Zondervan Publishing House, 1971) pp. 88-89.

106. Patrick M. Morley, *Walking With Christ in the Details of Life* (Nashville: Thomas Nelson, 1992) pp. 59-60.

107. "In California City, Acts of Kindness Are Becoming Contagious," *Chicago Tribune* (October 29, 1993). Also found in Craig Brian Larson, *Contemporary Illustrations for Preachers, Teachers, and Writers* (Grand Rapids, MI: Baker Books, 1996) number 114.

108. Elizabeth Elliot, *Trusting God in a Twisted World* (Old Tappan, NJ: Fleming H. Revell Co., 1989) pp. 156-157.

109. Glenn Van Ekeren, *Words for All Occasions* (Paramus, NJ: Prentice Hall, 1988) pp. 10-11.

110. Charles Colson, *The Body* (Dallas: Word Publishing, 1992) pp. 212-213.

111. Steven R. Mosley, *God: A Biography* (Phoenix, AZ: Questar Publishers, 1988) pp. 201-202.

112. Elizabeth Elliot, *Keep a Quiet Heart* (Ann Arbor, MI: Servant Publications, 1995) p. 117.

113. Sheila Walsh with Evelyn Bence, *Bring Back the Joy* (Grand Rapids, MI, Zondervan Publishing House, 1998) pp. 150-151.

114. John Killinger, Bread for the Wilderness, Wine for the Journey (Waco, TX: Word Books, 1976) p. 44.

115. Meg Cimino, "My Dad, The Worrier," *Reader's Digest* (June 1997) pp. 137-139. Originally from the *Atlantic Monthly* (March 1997).

116. *Inspirational Study Bible,* Max Lucado, ed. (Dallas, TX: Word, 1995) pp. 196-197.

117. Craig Brian Larson, *Contemporary Illustrations for Preachers, Teachers, and Writers* (Grand Rapids, MI: Baker Books, 1996), number 119. Based upon a Phillip Yancey article that first appeared in *Christianity Today.*

118. *They Walked With God,* James S. Bell Jr., ed. (Chicago: Moody Press, 1993).

119. Glenn Van Ekeren, *Words for All Occasions* (Paramus, NJ: Prentice Hall, 1988) p. 187.

120. Barbara Bailey Reinhold, *Toxic Work* (NY: Penguin Books, 1996) pp. 58-60.

121. Billy Graham, *Unto the Hills* (Waco, TX: Word Books, 1986) p. 158.

122. Dr. Ray Guarendi, *Back to the Family* (NY: Villard Books, Random House, 1990) p. 115.

123. *Encyclopedia of 7700 Illustrations,* Paul Lee Tan, ed. (Rockville, MD: Assurance Publishers, 1979) #4618 and #4558.

124. John. H. Timmerman, Black Gold: Nurturing the Heart, Moody (September 1994) p. 14.

125. Guideposts (July 1995) p. 41.

126. Glenn Van Ekeren, *Words for All Occasions* (Paramus, NJ: Prentice Hall, 1988) p. 290.

127. Elizabeth Elliot, *Keep a Quiet Heart* (Ann Arbor, MI: Servant Publications, 1995) pp. 229-230.

128. *The Complete Book of Christian Prayer* (NY: Continuum Publishing Co., 1995) pp. 84-85.

129. Allan Cox, *Straight Talk for Monday Morning* (NY: John Wiley & Sons, 1990) pp. 235-236.

130. *Mentors, Masters and Mrs. MacGregor,* Jane Bluestlein, ed. (Deerfield Beach, FL: Health Communications, 1995) pp. 12-13.

131. Charles Davis, Parables Etc. (April 1987). Found in Michael Hodgin, *1001 Humorous Illustrations of Public Speaking* (Grand Rapids, MI: Zondervan Publishing House, 1994) number 520.

132. Walter B. Knight, *Knight's Treasury of 4,000 Illustrations* (Grand Rapids, MI: Wm. B. Eerdmans Publishing Co., 1956, 1994) p. 520.

133. Craig Brian Larson, Contemporary Illustrations for Preachers, Teachers, and Writers (Grand Rapids, MI: Baker Books, 1996) number 181.

134. Eleanor Roosevelt, *You Learn by Living* (NY: Harper & Brothers, 1960) pp. 26-27.

135. Craig Brian Larson, *Contemporary Illustrations for Preachers, Teachers, and Writers* (Grand Rapids, MI: Baker Books, 1996) number 221. Quote from "Honest to God," pp. 26-27.

136. *Encyclopedia of 7700 Illustrations,* Paul Lee Tan, ed. (Rockville, MD: Assurance Publishers, 1979) pp. 458-459.

137. Frederic and Mary Ann Brussat, Spiritual Literacy: Reading the Sacred in Everyday Life (NY: Scribner, 1996) pp. 36-37.

138. Tom Riter, *Deep Down* (Wheaton, IL: Tyndale House, 1995) p. 85.

139. Dr. Ray Guarendi, *Back to the Family* (NY: Villard Books, Random House, 1990) pp. 162-163.

140. *Reader's Digest* (November 1996) pp. 19-24.

141. Lou Holtz, *Winning Every Day—The Game Plan for Success* (NY: Harper Collins Publishers, 1998) pp. 112-113.

142. Charles Colson with Ellen Santilli Vaughn, *The Body* (Dallas, TX: Word Publishing, 1992) pp. 325-326.

143. Mark Victor Hansen and Barbara Nichols with Patty Hansen, *Out of the Blue* (NY: Harper Collins, 1996) pp. 100-102.

144. Norman Vincent Peale, *Sin, Sex, and Self-Control* (NY: Doubleday & Co., 1965) pp. 195-197.

145. Craig Brian Larson, *Illustrations for Preaching and Teaching,* (Grand Rapids, MI: Baker Books, 1993) p. 41.

146. *Encyclopedia of 7700 Illustrations,* Paul Lee Tan, ed. (Rockville, MD: Assurance Publishers, 1979) p. 2056.

147. Craig Brian Larson, *Illustrations for Preaching and Teaching,* (Grand Rapids, MI: Baker Books, 1993) #250.

148. Charles Colson with Ellen Santilli Vaughn, *The Body* (Dallas, TX: Word Publishing, pp. 364-365.

149. Charles R. Swindoll, *The Finishing Touch* (Dallas, TX: Word, 1994) pp. 622-624.

150. James S. Hewett, *Illustrations Unlimited* (Wheaton, IL: Tyndale, 1988) p. 220.

151. Martin Yate, *Beat the Odds* (NY: Random House, 1995) p. 157.

152. David E Burgess, *Encyclopedia of Sermon Illustrations* (St. Louis, MO: Concordia Publishing House, 1984) pp. 143-144.

153. Alice Gray, *Stones for the Heart* (Sisters, OR: Questar Pub, 1996) p. 109.

154. *Encyclopedia of 7700 Illustrations,* Paul Lee Tan, ed.

(Rockville, MD: Assurance Publishers, 1979) p. 2038.

155. Donald Grey Barnhouse, *Let Me Illustrate* (Grand Rapids, MI: Baker Book House, 1967) p. 222.

156. Laura Ingalls Wilder, *Little House in the Ozarks,* Stephen W Hines, ed. (Nashville, TN: Thomas Nelson Publishers, 1991) p. 296.

157. Mark Victor Hansen and Barbara Nichols with Patty Hansen, *Out of the Blue* (NY: Harper Collins, 1996) pp. 60-61.

158. *Encyclopedia of 7700 Illustrations,* Paul Lee Tan, ed. (Rockville, MD: Assurance Publishers, 1979) pp. 1499-1500.

159. Janet Bukovinsky, *Women of Words* (Philadelphia, Running Press, 1994) pp. 97-99.

160. Kathleen Norris, *Dakota* (New York, NY: Houghton Mifflin, 1993) p. 114.

161. Mikey's Funnies, by Mike Atkinson@YOUTH SPECIALITIES; on-line @ aol, titled *Another Lesson in Life,* 10/7/98 date of publication.

162. Alice Gray, *Stories for the Heart* (Sisters, OR: Questar Pub, 1996) pp. 91-92.

163. Stephen R. Covey, A. Roger Merrill, and Rebecca R. Merrill, *First Things First* (NY: Simon & Schuster, 1994) pp. 65-67.

164. Michael Hodgin, *1001 Humorous Illustrations of Public Speaking* (Grand Rapids, MI: Zondervan Publishing House, 1994) #385.

165. *Reader's Digest* (March 1995) p. 38.

166. *Encyclopedia of 1100 Illustrations,* Paul Lee Tan, ed. (Rockville, MD, Assurance Publishers, 1979) pp. 678-679.

167. David P Burgess, *Encyclopedia of Sermon Illustrations* (St. Louis, MO: Concordia Publishing House, 1984) p. 78.

168. Roger Connors, Tom Smith, and Craig Hickman, *The Oz Principle* (Englewood Cliffs, NJ: Prentice Hall, 1994) p. 139.

169. Mark Victor Hansen and Barbara Nichols with Patty Hansen, *Out of the Blue* (NY: Harper Collins, 1996) pp. 79-80.

170. Peter Godwin, Mukiwa: A White Boy in Africa (NY: Grove/Atlantic, 1996).

171. *Encyclopedia of 7700 Illustrations,* Paul Lee Tan, ed. (Rockville, MD: Assurance Publishers, 1979) pp. 2047-2048.

172. Craig Brian Larson, Contemporary Illustrations for Preachers, Teachers, and Writers (Grand Rapids, MI: Baker Books) p. 137.

173. Will Oursler, *The Road to Faith* (NY: Rinehart & Co., 1960) pp. 98-99.

174. Sheila Walsh with Evelyn Bence, *Bring Back the Joy* (Grand Rapids, MI: Zondervan Publishing House, 1998) pp. 47-49, 71-72.

175. Ed Young, *From Bad Beginnings to Happy Endings* (Nashville, TN: Thomas Nelson, 1994) pp. 168-169.

176. Frederic and Mary Ann Brussat, Spiritual Literacy: Reading the Sacred in Everyday Life (NY: Scribner, 1996) p. 306.

177. Doris Donnelly, *Learning to Forgive* (New York, NY: Macmillan Publishing, 1979) pp. 24-25.

178. Mikey's Funnies @ YOUTH SPECIALTIES, Forwarded by Mark Rayburn, titled "The Fad," online @ aol, 5/19/98.

179. *Encyclopedia of 7700 Illustrations*, Paul Lee Tan, ed. (Rockville, MD: Assurance Publishers, 1979) pp. 2051-2052.

180. Craig Brian Larson, Contemporary Illustrations for Preacher, Teachers, and Writers (Grand Rapids, MI: Baker Books, 1996), entry 80.

181. John Garvey, "Signs and Wonders," *Commonwealth* (April 22, 1994) p. 10.

182. Glenn Van Ekerens, *Words for All Occasions* (Paramus, NJ: Prentice Hall, 1988) p. 289.

183. Patricia H. Berne and Louis M. Savary, *Building Self-Esteem in Children* (NY: The Continuum Publishing Co., 1981) p. 71.

184. Roy B. Zuck, *The Speaker's Quote Book* (Grand Rapids, Michigan: Kregel Publications, 1997) p. 82.

185. Tom Riter, *Deep Down* (Wheaton, IL: Tyndale House, 1995) pp. 125,130.

186. Kathy Collard Miller and D. Larry Miller, *God's Vitamin C for the Spirit* (Lancaster, Pennsylvania, Starburst Publishers, 1996) p. 64.

187. Michael Hodgin, *1001 Humorous Illustrations for Public Speaking* (Grand Rapids, Michigan: Zondervan Publishing House, 1994) p. 151, #371.

188. *Newsweek* (April 24, 1995) p. 150.

189. Albert P Stauderman, *Let Me Illustrate* (Minneapolis, MN: Augsburg Press, 1983) p. 104.

190. Roy B. Zuck, *The Speaker's Quote Book* (Grand Rapids, Michigan: Kregel Publications, 1997) p. 262.

191. Edward K. Rowell, *Fresh Illustrations for Preaching and Teaching* (Grand Rapids, Michigan: Baker Books, 1997) p. 24.

192. Top 100 Inspirational Anecdotes and Wisdom (part 1),

found online @ www.bizmove.com/inspiration, 1999, p. 6.

193. *Mentors, Masters and Mrs. MacGregor,* Jane Bluestein, ed. (Deerfield Beach, FL: Health Communications, 1995) p. 59.

194. Craig Larson, Choice Contemporary Stories and Illustrations for Preachers, Teachers, and Writers (Grand Rapids, Michigan: Baker Books, 1998) p. 34.

195. Roy B. Zuck, *The Speaker's Quote Book* (Grand Rapids, Michigan: Kregel Publications, 1997) p. 137.

196. *Illustrations for Preaching and Teaching,* Craig Brian Larson, ed. (Grand Rapids, MI: Baker Books, 1993) p. 200.

197. Dean Merrill, *Focus on the Family* magazine, 1996, found online @ *www.focusonthefamily,* 1999, p. 2.

198. *Encyclopedia of 7700 Illustrations,* Paul Lee Tan, ed. (Rockville, MD: Assurance Publishers, 1979) p. 2044.

199. Found online by Philippe, Just for Parents, @ http://members.xoom.com/XMCM/BouBou/pr/parents8.htm, 1999, p. 8.

200. Roy B. Zuck, *The Speaker's Quote Book* (Grand Rapids, Michigan: Kregel Publications, 1997) pp. 234, 236.

201. Top 100 Inspirational Anecdotes and Wisdom (part 4), @ www.bizmove.com/inspiration, 1999, p. 2.

202. Norman Vincent Peak, Norman Vincent Peale's Treasury of Courage and Confidence (Garden City, NY: Doubleday & Co., 1970) pp. 6-7.

203. Jacob Braude, *Braudes Treasury of Wit & Humor for All Occasions* (Paramus, New Jersey: Prentice Hall, 1991) p. 139.

204. James S. Hewett, *Illustrations Unlimited* (Wheaton, Illinois, Tyndale House Publishers, 1988) p. 235.

205. Kimberly Southall, *Grandpa's Legacy,* 1997, found online @ *www.nytimes/Christian,* 1999.

206. Kathy Collard Miller and D. Larry Miller, *God's Vitamin C for the Spirit* (Lancaster, Pennsylvania, Starburst Publishers, 1996) p. 29.

207. James S. Hewett, *Illustrations Unlimited* (Wheaton, IL: Tyndale, 1988) pp. 446-447.

208. Ruth A. Morgan, "By Faith Not Sight," *Encyclopedia of 7700 Illustrations,* Paul Lee Tan, ed. Rockville, MD: Assurance Publishers, 1979) p. 404.

209. Herbert Prochnow, *Treasury of Inspiration* (Grand Rapids, Michigan: Baker Book House, 1958) pp. 66-67.

210. *Encyclopedia of 7700 Illustrations,* Paul Lee Tan, ed. (Rockville, MD: Assurance Publishers, 1979) p. 2044.

211. Herbert Prochnow, *Treasury of Inspiration* (Grand Rapids, Michigan: Baker Book House, 1958) pp. 79-80.

212. Walter B. Knight , "I Know Something Good About You," *Knight's Master Book of New Illustrations* (Grand Rapids, MI: Eerdmans Publishing Co., 1956) pp. 174-175.

213. Found online @ focusonthefamily/parentsplace, 1999, p. 3.

214. Barbara Rachel Pollack, "Disaster Weddings and How Couples Coped," *Redbook* (August 1995) p. 102.

215. Herbert Prochnow, *Treasury of Inspiration* (Grand Rapids, Michigan: Baker Book House, 1958) p. 21.

216. Claire Cloninger, *A Childlike Heart, Women's Devotional Bible #2,* NIV (Grand Rapids, Michigan: Zondervan Publishing House, 1995) p. 519.

217. George Sweeting, *Who Said That* (Chicago, Illinois: Moody Press, 1995) pp. 247-248.

218. San Luis Obispo Telegram-Tribune (October 14, 1996) p. A7.

219. Top 100 Inspirational Anecdotes and Wisdom (part 2), found online @ www.bizmove.com/inspiration, 1999, pp. 8-10.

220. *Reader's Digest* (April 1996) p. 42.

221. James S. Hewett, *Illustrations Unlimited* (Wheaton, IL: Tyndale, 1988) p. 288.

222. Found online @ *www.christianity.net/tcw/8w5/8w5066.html,* Sherrie Lathrop, *Today's Christian Woman,* (Jackson, Washington), September/October 1998.

223. *Like a Child,* Christian Fellowship Devotionals, found online @ *www.cfdevotionals.org,* August 5, 1999.

224. Compton's Encyclopedia/America Online.

225. *Top 100 Inspirational Anecdotes and Wisdom* (part 5), online @ www.bizmove.com/ inspiration, 1999, p. 7.

226. *Encyclopedia of 7700 Illustrations,* Paul Lee Tan, ed. (Rockville, MD: Assurance Publishers, 1979) #4586.

227. *Encyclopedia of 7700 Illustrations,* Paul Lee Tan, ed. (Rockville, MD: Assurance Publishers, 1979) p. 1360.

228. *Top 100 Inspirational Anecdotes and Wisdom* (part 4), found online @ www.bizmove.com/inspiration, 1999, p. 5.

229. George Sweeting, *Who Said That* (Chicago, Illinois: Moody Press, 1995) p. 45.

230. Roy B. Zuck, *The Speakers Quote Book* (Grand Rapids, Michigan: Kregel Publications, 1997) p. 148.

Additional copies of this book and other titles in the *God's Little Devotional* series are available at your local bookstore.

God's Little Devotional Book for the Workplace
God's Little Devotional Book for Moms
God's Little Devotional Book for Dads
God's Little Devotional Book for Couples
God's Little Devotional Book for Men
God's Little Devotional Book for Women
God's Little Devotional Book for Parents
God's Little Devotional Book for Leaders
God's Little Devotional Book for Students
God's Little Devotional Book on Success
God's Little Devotional Book on Prayer
God's Little Devotional Journal
God's Little Devotional Journal for Women
God's Little Devotional Journal for Teens